LECTURES ON ETHICS

IMMANUEL KANT

LECTURES

ON ETHICS

Translated by LOUIS INFIELD

Foreword by LEWIS WHITE BECK

HACKETT PUBLISHING COMPANY
Indianapolis • Cambridge

IMMANUEL KANT: 1724–1804

Lectures on Ethics was originally published in 1930

Foreword copyright © 1963 by Lewis White Beck
Printed in the United States of America

Cover design by Richard L. Listenberger

For further information, please address
  Hackett Publishing Company, Inc.
  P.O. Box 55573, Indianapolis, IN   46205

Library of Congress Cataloging in Publication Data

Kant, Immanuel, 1724–1804.
  Lectures on ethics.

  Translation of Eine Vorlesung Kant's über
Ethik im Auftrage der Kantgesellschaft.
  Reprint of the 1979 ed. published by Methuen,
London.
  1. Ethics. I. Infield, Louis, 1888–
II. Title.
B2794.V63E54 1980   170   80–22092
ISBN 0–915145–09–X
ISBN 0–915145–08–1 (pbk.)

CONTENTS

CONTENTS

FOREWORD by LEWIS WHITE BECK

THOSE who know their Kant only from reading the great and imposing *Critiques,* and those who do not know him at all because frightening stories of page-long sentences have kept them from attempting those formidable masterpieces, have a surprise in store for them when they turn to his lectures and occasional essays. Here they meet a writer who would not, it seems, have written such a thorny book as the *Critique of Pure Reason;* here they meet a writer whose sentences are short and pithy and whose earnestness is spiced with dry humor. Only here will they find the Kant of whom they may believe that he was a great conversationalist in an age when conversation was a fine art. It will no longer be hard to believe the words of one of his friends: "How often he moved us to tears, how often he agitated our hearts, how often he lifted our minds and feelings from the fetters of selfish eudaemonism to the high consciousness of freedom, to unconditional obedience to the law of reason, to the exhaltation of unselfish duty! The immortal philosopher seemed to us to be inspired with a heavenly power, and he inspired us, who listened to him in wonder. His hearers certainly never left a single lecture in his ethics without having become better men." Herder's recollections will be confirmed: "Speech, the richest in thought, flowed from his lips. Playfulness, wit, and humor were at his command. His lectures were the most entertaining talks. His mind, which examined Leibniz, Wolff, Baumgarten, Crusius, and Hume, and investigated the laws of nature of Newton, Kepler, and the physicists, comprehended equally the newest works of Rousseau and the latest discoveries of science. He weighed them all, and always came back to the unbiased knowledge of nature and the moral worth of man. The history of men and peoples, natural history and science were the sources from which he enlivened his lectures and conversation."

Perhaps even the words another student addressed to him may seem less incredible: "If Jesus could have heard your lectures on ethics, I think He would have said, 'That is what I meant by the love of God.' "

Nowadays we accept as a matter of course that a philosopher will be a professor of philosophy. But it was not always so; indeed, it was not even usual before the time of Kant. No great figure in the history of modern philosophy before Kant made his living by fulfilling academic duties. In the modern sense of the word, Immanuel Kant was the first great professor of philosophy. His entire professional life was spent as a lecturer and professor in the University of Königsberg. Students came from all Germany to attend his lectures. Several series of his lectures were taken down stenographically or almost stenographically by his students, and we have his own copious notes for others. We can, therefore, read what Kant said to his own students as well as what he wrote for the learned world in general, on physical geography, philosophy of religion, logic, ethics, and pedagogy. Though they do not contain his most subtle and profound and original thoughts, being adjusted to the experience and interest of his hearers, they do contain much that we cannot find elsewhere.

The lectures included in this volume were transcribed by (or perhaps for) three students whose manuscripts have come down to us: Theodor Friedrich Brauer, Gottlieb Kutzner, and Chr. Mrongovius. It is likely that the Braeur manuscript is the most authentic and that the others are at least in part drawn from it. It may well be that they are all variant copies of an original now lost. It is, at any rate, clear that we have in these manuscripts a substantially accurate transcription of Kant's lectures on ethics as he gave them in the years 1775 to 1780, and probably in the form they took in the later part of this period. Paul Menzer edited the first published edition of these lectures in 1924, on the occasion of the bicentenary of Kant's birth, using the Brauer manuscript as fundamental but checking it against the others. Louis Infield, in turn, translated the Menzer edition in 1931, and his translation is reprinted in this volume.

Translating Kant is difficult, for many of the terms he uses were originated by him and did not have a fixed meaning even in his own writings; after all, German philosophical vocabulary is almost wholly Kant's own invention, the textbooks he used and the lectures of his predecessors having been almost exclusively in Latin. Different translators will render Kant's

German in different ways; there are no standards which can be mechanically applied so that Mr. Infield's translation could be brought strictly in line with others' translations of Kant's other works, even if that should be considered desirable. I have made no effort, therefore, to modify Mr. Infield's version. But I should call attention to a few of his practices, as John MacMurray did in his preface to the original edition. *Gesinning* he translated as "disposition," not as "intention." *Triebfeder* becomes "motive," *Motiv* becomes "Motive" (upper case), and *Bewegungsgrund* becomes "impulsive ground" or "ground of impulse." *Verbindlichkeit* is rendered as "obligation," while *Obligation* is "Obligation" (upper case). Similarly *Gegenstand* becomes "object," and *Objekt*, "Object;" *Vorstellung* becomes "idea" and *Idee*, "Idea." *Recht* is usually translated as "Law," *Gesetz* as "law." With this as a key to the equivalences adopted by Mr. Infield, the careful student who wishes to compare these lectures with Kant's other writings as translated by other scholars can do so with ease.

The regulations of the German university of Kant's time required the use of an approved textbook. For these lectures, Kant chose two volumes by Alexander Baumgarten, *Initia philosophiae practicae primae* (1760) and *Ethica philosophica* (1740; third ed., 1763). The order of topics in the lectures was, in general, fixed by the order of sections in these textbooks; when he departed from this order, Kant called his students' attention to the divergence. Fortunately the reader, unlike the student of 1780, need not be expected to have his Baumgarten at hand in order to follow the lectures. Kant, like any good teacher, sometimes "fought the textbook;" but more often he ignored it, having chosen it simply to comply with regulations. Unlike his students, we need bother no more about Baumgarten; we are interested in Kant and in his subject matter, not in having Baumgarten explained to us.

The lectures interest us for three reasons. First, they let us see Kant in the role his students and colleagues saw—not as the author of almost unreadable books but as the *galanter Magister*, with a style as polished and sharp as the dagger he wore on the podium. Even in the transcription of hurried and perhaps ill-informed students (their ignorance evidenced by errors they made when Kant referred to someone or something they did not quite get, so that they made stabs at proper names and perpetrated the first set of "boners" we have in the history of philosophy), the lectures have often the spirit and style of the English essay of characters, and show his emula-

tion of Swift, Dr. Johnson, and, most of all, Addison. Kant's
sharp etching of the miser and the man of greed, his descrip-
tion of the uses and abuses of wealth, and his discussion of
our regard for animals are superior examples of the familiar
but earnest essay. In particular, the long portrayal of friendship is probably the best it has received in philosophical literature since the *Nicomacheaen Ethics* of Aristotle.

If our first interest is belletristic, our second is ethical.
Kant's writings on ethics in the *Foundations of the Metaphysics of Morals* and in the *Critique of Practical Reason* are
rigorous in their treatment and rigoristic in their teachings.
Everything anthropological and narrative or anecdotal, everything that would make perspicuous the relation of philosophical morals to the conduct of life, is there apparently sacrificed
for an abstract intellectual articulation. It is no wonder, then,
that Kantian ethics has since appeared to be forbidding in its
intellectualism; to be rationalistic at the expense of emotion,
habit, and institutions in the make-up of the good life; to
have sacrificed all the graces for a few of the virtues. Only in
his last work on ethics, the *Metaphysics of Morals* (which has
only just now been translated into English)[1], and in these
Lectures do we see what Kant never forgot, but what he expected his readers to remember even when he was talking of
other things—viz., that the good life is more than mechanical
obedience to the categorical imperative, that right action requires more than right thinking, and that man is more than a
thinking machine. But since most readers of Kant have not
known that in his lectures and in the *Metaphysics of Morals*
he did deal with these other things as conditions and compo-
nents of the life of the good man, they have erroneously taken
the part (albeit the most characteristic and important part)
as if it were the whole, and have criticized Kant in the way
made popular by Schiller's famous satiric verses. The Kant of
the *Lectures* and of the *Metaphysics of Morals* must be taken
in full seriousness to correct this caricature, to put flesh on the
bones of the critical ethics. Indeed, once made cognizant of
these things in the *Lectures* and in the *Metaphysics*, one can
then see that even the *Critique of Practical Reason* is not the
unearthly and inhuman thing it has often been said to be.

Finally, these *Lectures* are our most valuable source of information about the development of Kant's ethical views.[2]

[1] Harper Torchbook, 1963.
[2] The only study in English of the place of these *Lectures* in the
evolution of Kant's thought is by Paul A. Schilpp, *Kant's Pre-critical
Ethics* (Evanston, second ed., 1960).

The 'seventies were the silent decade in Kant's life; he was writing the *Critique of Pure Reason* and publishing almost nothing. The lectures during that period, if we had them all, would undoubtedly show the stages in Kant's maturing thought and would resolve many an intricate issue in the interpretation of the *Critique*. These *Lectures* do give us a very complete picture of his ethical views toward the end of that decade. They prepare us for the chapters on ethics in the *Critique of Pure Reason* and in the great ethical treatises of the 'eighties. We see Kant still using, but already going far beyond, the British and French moralists (Shaftesbury, Hutcheson, Hume, Adam Smith, Montaigne, Rousseau, and others) who had strongly influenced him in the early years; we see his slow and tentative efforts to formulate some of the most characteristic doctrines of the later years, such as the theory of the three kinds of imperatives and the teaching concerning the relations of duty to happiness and of ethics to religion. How much of his definitive theory of the freedom of the will he had at this time we do not know. His silence on this question may come from his not yet having formulated the theory, for which he is now remembered, to take the place of the one he had used ten years earlier. Or it may be due to the fact that (as he said) while he did not teach what he did not believe, he did not teach all that he did believe, out of consideration for his hearers. This is a fascinating question for the student of Kant, but even though the *Lectures* do not answer it, they remain the richest document we have for understanding the history of the most important ethical theory of modern times.

As I have said, the order of topics generally follows that given in Baumgarten; and in one respect we need to know why Baumgarten divided the material as he did. The eighteenth century divided "universal practical philosophy" into several parts, only one of which is ethics. It studies the principles of all conduct of any free agent, and therefore concerns itself with the logic of technical, prudential, and legal thought and behavior as well as with ethical thinking and conduct. Hence it is a propaedeutic to the study of both jurisprudence and morals. Ethics is the division of universal practical philosophy which deals with the intrinsic goodness found in some but not in all actions, dispositions, and maxims. The source of the moral law is internal; legal prescriptions require an external lawgiver. Ethics, then, concerns our actions only insofar as they evince a certain motive which no external lawgiver can require us to have, but which we may freely assume; the law, on the other hand, requires certain actions, and it does not take thought of the motives from which they are done. Naturally a ready obedience to law is a moral virtue; but the external lawgiver requires obedience and does not require what he cannot enforce, a certain virtuous disposition. While this distinction between statute and moral law and, per corollary, that between universal practical philosophy and ethics were established in philosophy before Kant, it is absolutely basic to an understanding of his theory of law, morals, and religion. Though Kant does not slavishly adhere to this distinction in these lectures as he does in the *Metaphysics of Morals,* if the reader keeps it in mind the major division in Kant's discussions will become clear, and some of the apparent but not real repititiousness will disappear.

The explanatory footnotes in this edition are selected from those in the Menzer edition; in some of them Infield is followed, but in others we have gone back to the Menzer source. Otherwise the present translation is entirely Infield's.

University of Rochester
October 1962

LECTURES ON ETHICS

LECTURES ON ETHICS

UNIVERSAL PRACTICAL PHILOSOPHY

PROEM

PHILOSOPHY is either theoretical or practical. The one concerns itself with knowledge, the other with the conduct of beings possessed of a free will. The one has Theory, the other Practice for its object—and it is the object that differentiates them. There is another distinction of philosophy into speculative and practical. In general, we call sciences theoretical and practical, without reference to their objects. They are theoretical if they are the ground of the conception of the object; practical, if they are the ground of the exercise of our knowledge of the object. We have, for instance, theoretical geometry and practical geometry, theoretical mechanics and practical mechanics, and so with medicine, and also with jurisprudence. In all these cases the object is the same; it is the form of the science which is different. The theoretical form judges the object; the practical produces it. If, without regard to the object, we draw the distinction between theoretical knowledge and practical knowledge, the differentiation is one of form only; the theoretical form studies, the practical produces the object. But in our present distinction between practical philosophy and theoretical philosophy the difference is not one of form, but of the object. Practical philosophy is such not by its form, but by reference to its object, namely, the voluntary conduct of a free being. The object of practical philosophy is conduct; that of theoretical philosophy

1

cognition. Practical philosophy, being the philosophy of action, is thus the philosophy which provides rules for the proper use of our freedom, irrespective of particular applications of it. Just as logic deals with the use of the understanding in general and not in particular conditions, so does practical philosophy deal with the use of the free will not in specific circumstances but independently of the particular. Logic provides rules concerning the use of the understanding, practical philosophy concerning the use of the will. Understanding and will are the two powers from which springs the whole content of our mental disposition. The understanding is the supreme faculty of knowledge, the free will of desire. We have two disciplines for these two powers: logic for the understanding and practical philosophy for the will; but the lower powers cannot be disciplined, for they are blind.

We thus postulate a being—not only man, but any rational being—which has freedom of will, and we are concerned here with the principles or rules for the use of that freedom. This is general practical philosophy. Its rules are objective. The subjective practical rules are the concern of anthropology. An objective rule lays down what ought to occur, even though it never actually occurs. But the subjective rule deals with actual happenings. Even the wicked have rules of conduct. Thus anthropology observes the actual behaviour of human beings and formulates the practical and subjective rules which that behaviour obeys, whereas moral philosophy alone seeks to formulate rules of right conduct, that is, of what ought to happen, just as logic comprises the rules for the right use of the mind. When we say that something ought to be, we mean that a possible action is capable of being good, it comprises rules for the proper use of the will.

Practical philosophy (that is, the science of how man ought to behave) and anthropology (that is, the science of man's actual behaviour) are closely connected, and the former cannot subsist without the latter: for we cannot tell whether the subject to which our consideration applies is capable of what is demanded of him unless we have knowledge of that subject. It is true that we can pursue the study of practical philosophy without anthropology, that is, without the knowledge of the subject. But our philosophy is then merely speculative, and an Idea. We therefore have to make at least some study of man.

We are for ever hearing sermons about what ought to be done from people who do not stop to consider whether what they preach can be done. As a result, the exhortations, which are tautological reiterations of the rule which everyone knows already, prove terribly boring. They express nothing that we are not already familiar with, and sermons consisting of such exhortations are very empty, unless the preacher has an eye to practical wisdom at the same time. Spalding[1] is in this the best of them all. Consequently we must know whether mankind is capable of performing what is demanded of him.

Consideration of the rule is useless, unless people can be made willing to follow the rule, and this is the reason for the connection of these two sciences. The case is comparable to the combination of theoretical physics with experiment, because we experiment with human beings also, as when, for instance, we test a servant to see if he is honest. There should therefore be an examination for preachers, not only to test their knowledge of dogmatics, but equally to test their character and heart.

We have thus established that practical philosophy is practical not in respect of its form, but of its object. It is a theory of practice. Just as logic is a science of reason, not in respect of its form but because its object is the mind, so ethics must have a practical object, i.e. practice. And just as anthropology is a science of the subjective laws of the free will, so practical philosophy is a science of its objective laws. It is a philosophy of the objective necessity of free action, of the Ought—that is, of all possible good actions. Moreover, like logic, practical philosophy does not concern itself with a particular sort of cases of practical activity but deals with the practice of free actions in general without reference to any case whatever.

The objective laws of the free will, the laws which tell us what ought to be, are divisible into three classes: technical, prudential and moral. All of them are expressed

[1] Spalding, Johann Joachim S. (1714–1804): *Über die Nutz bar Keit des Predigtamts und deren Beförderung* (1772).

by an imperative, unlike subjective practical laws, which are not so expressed. Thus the old are fond of saying that things don't happen as they ought to. For instance, a man ought to be less saving in his old age than he was in his youth because he has fewer years of life to look forward to and will consequently need less.

There are then three kinds of Imperative : the technical, the prudential and the moral. Every imperative expresses an Ought, and thus an objective necessity, and indeed a necessity of the free and good will, for it is a property of the imperative that it necessitates objectively. All imperatives involve an objective necessitation, even on the assumption of a good and free will. The technical imperatives are problematical, the prudential imperatives are pragmatic and the moral imperatives are ethical.

Problematic imperatives imply a necessitation of the will in accordance with a rule to an arbitrarily chosen end. The means are stated assertorically, but the end is problematical. If, for instance, we set ourselves the task of constructing a triangle, a square, or a hexagon, we must proceed in accordance with the rules implied : the problem is at our choice, but having chosen it our means to it are defined. Geometry, mechanics, and, in general, the practical sciences contain technical imperatives. These imperatives are of the greatest utility and must take precedence over all others ; for only if we are in a position, and have the means, to fulfil ends of our own choosing can we be sure of fulfilling ends set for us. Technical imperatives are merely hypothetical ; for the necessity of using the means arises only on a condition, namely of the end being given.

Practical philosophy contains no technical rules : it contains only rules of prudence and of morality, and it is, therefore, pragmatic and ethical. It is pragmatic in respect of the laws of prudence, and ethical in respect of those of morality.

Prudence is the ability to use the means towards the universal end of man, that is, happiness. We, therefore, have here (as is not the case with technical rules) a determined end. Rules of prudence require us both to define the end and the means to be used to attain it. We need, therefore, a rule for judging what constitutes happiness and the rule for using the means to this happiness. Prudence is thus the ability to determine both the end and the means to the end. First we must establish what happiness is. This is still a matter of controversy: some say it is found in abstinence, others in acquisition. He who has no means, but needs nothing which can be acquired by those means, appears to be happier than he who has means in plenty but needs them in plenty. It follows, therefore, that the first object of prudence is to determine the end of happiness and in what it consists, and the second, to determine the means. No problematic condition attaches to the dictates of the prudential imperatives: their condition is assertorical, universal and necessary, inherent in human nature. We do not say to a man: 'In so far as you would be happy you must do so and so'; but since every one wishes to be happy, all must observe what is presupposed of all. It is a subjective and not an objective necessary condition. It would be objective if we were to say: 'You ought to be happy'; but what we do say is: 'Because you want to be happy, you must do this and that.'

But we can conceive an imperative where the end is governed by a condition which commands not subjectively but objectively. Moral imperatives are such. Take, for example: 'Thou shalt not lie.' This is no problematic imperative, for in that case it would mean, 'If it harm thee to lie, then do not lie.' But the imperative commands simply and categorically: 'Thou shalt not lie'; and it does so unconditionally, or under an objective and necessary condition. It is characteristic of the moral imperative that it does not determine an end, and the action is not governed by an end, but flows from the free will and has no regard to ends. The dictates of moral imperatives are absolute and regardless of the end. Our free doing and refraining has an inner goodness, irrespective of its end. Thus moral goodness endues man with an immediate, inner, absolute moral worth. For example, the man who keeps his word has always an immediate inner worth of the free will, apart altogether from the end in view. No such intrinsic worth accrues from any pragmatic goodness.

THE ETHICAL SYSTEMS OF THE ANCIENTS

The ethical systems of the ancients are all based on the question of what constitutes the *summum bonum*—the Supreme Good—and it is in their answers to this question that is to be found the difference between their various systems. We may call this *summum bonum* an ideal, that is, the highest conceivable standard by which everything is to be judged and weighed. To form a judgment of anything we must first sketch a pattern by which to judge it. The *summum bonum* is scarcely possible of attainment and is only an ideal—that is, the pattern, the idea, the archetype for all our concepts of the Good.

What constitutes the Supreme Good? The supreme created good is the most perfect world, that is, a world in which all rational beings are happy and are worthy of happiness.

The ancients realized that mere happiness could not be the one highest good. For if all men were to obtain this happiness without distinction of just and unjust, the highest good would not be realized, because though happiness would indeed exist, worthiness of it would not.

In mankind therefore we have to look both for happiness and for merit. The combination of the two will be the highest good. Man can hope to be happy only in so far as he makes himself worthy of being happy, for this is the condition of happiness which reason itself proposes.

They further realized that happiness sprang from man's freedom of will, from his intention to make use of everything with which nature so richly endows him. Of the wealthy man we ask to what use he intends to put all those treasures which he has in plenty. Thus the nature and perfectness of the free will, in which dwells the ground of the worthiness to be happy, constitutes ethical perfection. The physical good or well-being, for which health and wealth are requisite, is not by itself the greatest good; the ethical good, right conduct, worthiness of being happy, must be added to the former, and we then have the Supreme Good. Let us imagine a world inhabited by intelligent beings, all of whom behaved well, and so deserved to be happy, but were destitute and lived in the most wretched circumstances. Such beings would have no happiness, and there would, therefore, be no Supreme Good in these conditions. If, on the other hand, all beings were happy but not well-behaved and not worthy of being happy, we should again have no Supreme Good in such circumstances.

The ancients recognized three forms of the ideal of the *summum bonum* :

1. The Cynic ideal of the school of Diogenes.
2. The Epicurean ideal.
3. The Stoic ideal of the school of Zeno.

The Cynic is the ideal of innocence, or rather of simplicity. Diogenes taught that the highest good is to be found in simplicity, in the sober enjoyment of happiness.

The Epicureans set up the ideal of prudence. Epicurus' doctrine was that the highest good was happiness and that well-doing was but a means to happiness.

The ideal of the Stoics was that of wisdom and is in contrast with the ideal of Epicurus. Zeno taught that the highest good is to be found only in morality, in merit (and thus in well-doing), and that happiness is a consequence of morality. Whoever conducts himself well is happy.

The Cynics argued that the Supreme Good springs from nature and not from art. Diogenes sought it by negative means. He argued that man is by nature satisfied with little ; he has no wants by nature and therefore does not feel privation (that is, the lack of means), and so it is in conditions of privation that he finds happiness. There is much in this argument ; for the more plentiful nature's gifts and the greater our store of the world's goods the greater are our wants. With growing wealth we acquire fresh wants, and the more we satisfy them the keener becomes our appetite for more. So our hearts are restless for ever. That refined Diogenes, Rousseau, holds that our will is by nature good, but that we ourselves became more and more corrupt ; that nature provides us with all necessaries, but that we create wants for ourselves, and he would have children educated on negative lines. Hume disagrees with these views, and argues that the Supreme Good is a thing of art, and not of nature.

Diogenes teaches that we can be happy without abundance, and moral without virtue. His philosophy is the shortest cut to happiness, for if we are content with little it is no hardship to do without things, and we can live happily; and it is likewise the shortest cut to morality, because if we have no wants we have no desires and in that case our actions conform to morality. To be honest involves no sacrifice; so virtue would be merely an idea. Simplicity is thus the shortest cut to morality.

The Epicureans taught that the Supreme Good was a matter of art, and not of nature, and they thus placed themselves in exact opposition to the Cynics. It is true, said Epicurus, that we have by nature no vices, but we nevertheless have an inclination to vice, and innocence and simplicity cannot, therefore, be secured without the assistance of art. Zeno was in agreement with Epicurus in thus regarding virtue as a matter of art. If, for instance, a simple country girl is free of the usual vices, she is so merely because she has no opportunity of going astray; and if a peasant makes do and is quite content with poor fare, he does not do so because it is all the same to him whether his food is simple or sumptuous, but because it is his lot, and if he had an opportunity of living on a higher scale he would take it. Simplicity, therefore, is only a negative thing. For this reason Epicurus and Zeno accepted art, although in different senses.

The Supreme Good consists of the physical good and the moral good—of well-being and well-doing. Inasmuch as all philosophy strives to bring unity into knowledge and to reduce its first principles to a minimum, attempts have been made to combine into one these two principles of well-being and well-doing. Now it is the end and not the means which determines what we call anything. So according to the notion of Epicurus happiness was the end and merit only a means, which would make morality a consequence of happiness. Zeno also sought to unite the two principles, and according to his notion it was morality which was the end, virtue and merit were in themselves the Supreme Good, and happiness was merely a consequence of morality.

For their ideal, their pattern, Diogenes took the natural

man, and Epicurus the man of the world. Zeno's pattern or *Idea archetypon* is the sage. The sage is happy in himself, he possesses all things, he has within himself the source of cheerfulness and righteousness, he is a king because he is lord of himself and, being his own master, he cannot be mastered. Such perfection could be attained only by strength in overcoming obstacles, and so a sage was regarded as even greater than the gods themselves, because a god had no temptations to withstand and no obstacles to overcome.

We can also conceive a mystical ideal, in which the Supreme Good consists in this; that man sees himself in communion with the highest being. This is the Platonic ideal, a visionary ideal.

The Christian ideal is that of holiness and its pattern is Christ. Christ is also merely an ideal, a standard of moral perfection which is holy by divine aid. This ideal ought not to be confused with those who call themselves Christians. These only seek to come nearer to their ideal pattern.

Epicurus taught that virtue had a motive, namely happiness; Zeno took away the motive. Epicurus saw value in merit, but none in virtue, while Zeno exalted the intrinsic value of virtue. Epicurus placed the Supreme Good in happiness, Zeno in virtue. Both were at fault.

Happiness, in the case of Epicurus, was synonymous with pleasure, by which he meant a contented disposition and a cheerful heart; but his philosophy was not, as it has been wrongly taken to be, one of sensual pleasure. He taught that we must so act as to be safe from reproaches from ourselves and from others, and a letter [1] has come down to us in which he invites a guest to dinner with the intimation that he has nothing better to offer than a cheerful heart and a meal of polenta, poor fare indeed for an 'epicure'. His was the pleasure of a sage, and while he denied worth to virtue, he made morality the means to happiness.

Zeno inverted the position. To him happiness had value, but virtue no motive. Motives are springs of the will which are drawn from the senses. If a man is con-

---

[1] Presumably his letter to Menoeceus, given by Diogenes Laertius, *Lives and Opinions of the Eminent Philosophers*.

scious of deserving happiness that is not sufficient to appease his desires, and if his desires are unsatisfied he is not happy, even though he feels himself worthy. Virtue pleases uniquely but it does not satisfy; if it did, all men would be virtuous. His very virtue intensifies a man's yearning for happiness. The more virtuous and the less happy a man is, the more painful is the feeling that he is not happy, though deserving happiness. Such a man is satisfied with his conduct, but not with his condition.

Epicurus taught that man would be satisfied with himself if he saw to it that his condition was happy; Zeno that man would be satisfied with his condition if he so conducted himself that he was satisfied with himself.

A man can be satisfied or dissatisfied with himself either pragmatically or ethically, but he very often mistakes the one type of satisfaction or dissatisfaction for the other. He often mistakes for remorse what is in fact a fear of the tribunal of prudence. If, for instance, we slight some one in public we may reproach ourselves in the privacy of our home, but these are the reproaches of the Judge of Prudence within us, since we must suppose that we have made an enemy. The reproach for an action through which damage arises is always a reproach of prudence. If we knew that the other did not notice the offence given we should be satisfied. It follows, therefore, that what we feel is a reproof of prudence which we take for a reproof of morality. Epicurus, however, taught that if we so conduct ourselves as to deserve no reproaches, either from ourselves or from others, we are happy.

The ideal of holiness is, philosophically, the most perfect in that it is the ideal of the highest pure and moral perfection; but as it is humanly unattainable it bases itself on the belief in divine aid. Not only does the notion of deserving happiness acquire in this ideal its highest moral perfection, but the ideal itself contains the most potent motive, that of happiness beyond this world. Thus the ideal of the Gospels contains the purest morality as well as the strongest motive—that of happiness or blessedness.

The ancients had no conception of any higher moral perfection than such as could emanate from human nature. But as human nature is very imperfect, their ethical principles were imperfect. Thus their system of ethics was not pure ; it accommodated virtue to man's weakness, and was, therefore, incomplete. But the ideal of the Gospels is complete in every respect. Here we have the greatest purity and the greatest happiness. It sets out the principles of morality in all their holiness. It commands man to be holy, but as he is imperfect it gives him a prop, namely divine aid.

THE GENERAL PRINCIPLE OF MORALITY

Having considered the ideal of the highest moral perfection, we must now see wherein the general principle of morality consists. So far we have said no more than that it rests upon the goodness of the free will. We must now investigate what it essentially is. To establish the general principle of science is by no means easy, particularly if the sciences have already reached a certain stage of development. Thus, for instance, it is difficult to establish the general principle of law or of mechanics. But as we all need a basis for our moral judgments, a principle by which to judge with unanimity what is morally good and what bad, we apprehend that there must exist a single principle having its source in our will. We must therefore set ourselves to discover this principle, upon which we establish morality, and through which we are able to discriminate between what is moral and what immoral. However capable and talented a man may be, we still ask about his character. However great his qualities, we still ask about his moral quality. What then is the one principle of morality, the criterion by which to judge everything and in which lies the distinction between moral goodness and all other goodness ? Before we decide these questions we must cite and classify the various points of view which lead to the definition of this principle in various ways.

The theoretical concept (not yet a theory, but merely a concept from which a theory can be constructed) is that morality has either an empirical or an intellectual basis, and that it must be derived either from empirical or from intellectual principles. Empirical grounds are derived from the senses, in so far as the senses find satisfaction in them. Intellectual grounds are those in which all morality is derived from the conformity of our actions to the laws of reason. Accordingly, *systema morale est vel empiricum vel intellectuale.*

If an ethical system is based upon empirical grounds, those may be either inner or outer grounds, as they are drawn from the objects of the inner or of the outer sense. The ethics derived from inner grounds gives us the first part of the empirical system; ethics derived from outer grounds, the second part. Those who derive ethics from the inner grounds of the empirical principle, presuppose a feeling, either physical or ethical.

The physical feeling which they take is self-love, which has two constituents, vanity and self-interest. Its aim is advantage to self; it is selfish and aims at satisfying our senses. It is a principle of prudence. Writers who follow the principle of self-love are, among the ancients, Epicurus (who grounds his philosophy in general upon an intuitional principle), and, among the moderns, Helvetius and Mandeville.

The second principle of the inner ground of the empirical system appears when the ground is placed in the ethical feeling whereby we discriminate between good and evil. Among those who build on this basis the foremost are Shaftesbury and Hutcheson.

To the empirical system of the theoretical concept of ethics belong, in the second place, outer grounds. Philosophers who base ethics on these argue that all morality rests upon two things, education and government, which in turn are a matter of custom; we judge all actions in a customary way by what we have been taught or by what the law tells us. Example or legal precept are thus the sources of the moral judgment. While Hobbes takes precept as his thesis and argues that the sovereign power may permit or prohibit any act, Montaigne bases himself on example and points out that in matters of morality men differ with environment, and that the morality of one locality is not that of another. He quotes as instances the permission of theft in Africa, that in China parents may desert their children with impunity, that the Eskimos strangle them, and that in Brazil children are buried alive.

On these grounds it is not permissible for reason to pass ethical judgments on actions. Instead, we act by reference to customary example and the commands of authority, from which it follows that there is no ethical principle, unless it be one borrowed from experience.

But now, in the empirical system, the first principle of ethics is based upon contingent grounds. In the case of self-love, contingent circumstances decide the nature of the action which will advantage or harm us. Where ethical feeling is the basis, and we judge actions by liking or disliking, by repugnance, or in general by taste, the grounds of judgment are again contingent, for what may please one individual may disgust another. (Thus a savage will turn from wine with abhorrence, while we drink it with pleasure.)   It is the same with the outer grounds of education and government.

In the second *Systema morale*, which is the intellectual, the philosopher judges that the ethical principle has its ground in the understanding and can be completely apprehended à priori. We say, for instance: ' Thou shalt not lie.'   On the principle of self-love this would mean : ' Thou shalt not lie if it harm thee ; if it advantage thee then thou mayest lie.'   If ethical feeling were the basis, then a person so devoid of a refined ethical feeling, that in him lying evoked no disgust, would be at liberty to lie.   If it depended on up-bringing and government, then, if we were brought up to telling lies and if the Government so ordained, it would be open to us to tell lies.   But if the principle lies in the understanding we say simply : ' Thou shalt not lie, be the circumstances what they may.'   This, if I look into my free will, expresses the consistency of my free will with itself and with that of others ; it is a necessary law of the free will.   Such principles, which are universal, constant and necessary, have their source in pure reason ; they cannot be derived from experience.   Every ethical law expresses a categorical necessity, not one drawn from experience, and as every necessary rule must be established à priori, the principles of morality must be intellectual. The moral judgment never occurs at all in virtue of sensuous or empirical principles, for the ethical is never an object of the senses, but purely of the understanding.

The intellectual principle may be of two kinds :

1. Internal—if it depends on the inner nature of the action as apprehended by the understanding.

2. External—where our actions bear some relation to an external being.

But just as we have an ethical theology, so we have theological ethics, and the external intellectual principle is of that kind ; but it is false, because discrimination between moral good and evil does not depend on any relation to another being. It follows, therefore, that the basic moral principle is of the first (i.e. the internal) of the above two kinds of intellectual principle. *Principium morale est intellectuale internum.* Our aim in what follows will be to discern and determine its constitution ; but this can only be done gradually.

All imperatives are formulæ of a practical necessitation. Practical necessitation is the necessitating of a free action. But all our free actions may be necessitated in two ways. They may be necessary in accordance with laws of the free will, when their necessity is practical ; or of our sensuous inclination, when their necessity is pathological. Accordingly, our actions are determined either practically, i.e. in accordance with laws of freedom, or pathologically, in accordance with laws of our sensuous nature. Practical determination is an objective determination of the free act, while pathological determination is subjective. Accordingly, all objective laws of action are practically and not pathologically necessary.

Every imperative is a formula of practical necessitation, and only that. It expresses a determination of our actions, assuming their goodness. The formula of practical necessitation is that of the *causa impulsiva* of a free act, and because it necessitates objectively it is called a *motivum*. The formula of pathological necessitation is that of the *causa impulsiva per stimulos* because it necessitates subjectively. Thus all subjective *necessitationes* are *necessitationes per stimulos.*

To each of the three types of imperative there is a corresponding type of good, the objective determination of which is in each case expressed in the corresponding imperative :

1. *Bonitas problematica.* This follows from the *Imperativus problematicus* which says that a thing is good as a means to some optional end.

2. *Bonitas pragmatica.* This corresponds to the pragmatic imperative, the imperative of the judgment of prudence, which expresses the necessity of an action as a means to our happiness. Here the end is determinate, and therefore, although the determination of action is conditional, the condition is of absolute and of universal validity.

3. *Bonitas moralis.* This is expressed in the ethical imperative, which asserts the goodness of an action in and for itself. Ethical necessitation is therefore categorical and not hypothetical, constituted as it is by the absolute goodness of the free act.

The three types of imperative lead to the following deductions.

Moral necessitation constitutes an Obligation ; but pragmatic necessitation, the consequence of an action from rules of prudence, does not. The obligation, being moral, is practical. Every obligation is either one of duty or one of compulsion, of which much more anon.

An obligation implies not that an action is necessary merely, but that it is made necessary ; it is not a question of *necessitas*, but of *necessitatio*. Thus, while the divine will is, as regards morality, a necessary will, the human will is not necessary, but necessitated. It follows that, in the case of the Highest Being, practical necessity does not constitute an Obligation. God's acts are necessarily moral, but not from obligation. We do not say that God is obliged to be true and holy. Further, moral necessity is objective ; if it happens to be also subjective it ceases to imply necessitation. Moral necessity, then, makes an action necessary objectively, and constitutes an Obligation if the subjective necessity is contingent. Every imperative expresses the objective necessitation of actions which are subjectively contingent. Suppose, for example, that I say, ' You must eat when you are hungry and you have something to eat.' Here we have both an objective and a subjective necessity; consequently necessitation falls away and there is no Obligation. In the case, therefore, of a perfect will, for which the moral necessity is not only objective but is also subjective, there is no room for necessitation or Obligation ; but in the case of an imperfect will, for which the ethical good is objectively necessary, we have a place for necessitation and so also for obligation. Moral actions must therefore be contingent if they are to be determined, and human beings, whose wills are ethical, but imperfect, are subject to obligation.

Every obligation is a *necessitatio practica*, not *pathologica*—an objective, not a subjective determination. We have pathological necessitation where the impulse comes from the senses, or from the feeling of what is pleasant or unpleasant. The man who does a thing because it is pleasant is pathologically determined ; he who does it because it is good, and because it is good in and for itself, acts on Motives and is practically determined. In so far, therefore, as *causae impulsivae* proceed from what is good, they are of the understanding ; in so far as they proceed from what is pleasant, they are of the senses. He who is impelled to action by the former acts *per motiva* ; he who is impelled by the latter acts *per stimulos*.

It follows from this argument that all Obligation is not pathological or pragmatic, but moral necessitation. As for the Motives, these have either a pragmatic basis, or else the moral basis of intrinsic goodness.

Pragmatic Motives are conditioned solely by the consideration that actions must be a means to happiness. Actions, being thus a means, do not contain their ground in themselves, and it follows that all *imperativi pragmatici hypothetice necessitant et non absolute*.

Imperativi morales, however, *necessitant absolute* and express a *bonitas absoluta*, just as *imperativi pragmatici* express a *bonitas hypothetica*. Thus honesty may possess a mediated goodness on grounds of prudence, as in commerce, where it is as good as ready money. But from an absolute point of view, to be honest is good in itself, good whatever the end in view, and dishonesty is in itself pernicious. Thus moral necessitation is absolute and the *motivum morale* expresses *bonitas absoluta*. We cannot at this stage explain how it is possible that an action should have *bonitas absoluta*; we must first interpolate the following remarks. If the will is subordinated to the dictate of ends universally valid, it will be in harmony with all human purposes, and herein is to be found its inherent goodness and absolute perfection. To exemplify this is not easy, but truthfulness, for instance, conforms to all my rules; it is in accord with every purpose; it is in harmony with the will of others, and every one can guide his conduct by it; one truth is consistent with another. On the other hand, lies contradict each other and are inconsistent with my purposes and with those of others. Moral goodness consists, therefore, in the submission of our will to rules whereby all our voluntary actions are brought into a harmony which is universally valid. Such a rule, which forms the first principle of the possibility of the harmony of all free wills, is the moral rule. Neither nature nor the laws determine a free action ; and freedom, leaving our actions, as it does, quite undetermined, is a terrible thing. Our actions must be regulated if they are to harmonize, and their regulation is effected by the moral law. A pragmatic rule cannot do this. Pragmatic rules may make our actions' consistent with our own will, but they will not bring them into harmony with the wills of others : in point of fact they may not even make them consistent with our own will; for the source of such rules is our well-being, and this cannot be determined à priori ; rules of prudence can thus be laid down only à posteriori, and they cannot, therefore, apply to all actions, for in order to do that they would have to be à priori rules. Pragmatic rules are not, therefore, consistent with the wills of others and may not be consistent even with our own. But we must have rules to give our actions universal validity and to mould them into a general harmony. These rules are derived from the universal ends of mankind, and they are the moral rules.

The morality of an action is a quite peculiar thing : there is a distinct difference between a moral act and any pragmatic or pathological action ; morality is subtle and pure and calls for special consideration on its own. There are actions for which moral Motives are not sufficient to produce moral goodness and for which pragmatic, or even pathological, *causae impulsivae* are wanted in addition ; but when considering the goodness of an action we are not concerned with that which moves us to that goodness, but merely with what constitutes the goodness in and for itself.

The *motivum morale* must, therefore, be considered purely in and for itself, as something apart and distinct from other Motives, whether of prudence or of the senses. Nature has implanted in us the faculty of drawing a subtle but very definite distinction between moral goodness and problematic and pragmatic goodness, and action which has a moral goodness is as pure as if it came from heaven itself. A pure moral ground is a more potent impulse than one intermingled with pathological and pragmatic Motives. These latter have a greater effect on our sensuous nature, but the motive power to which the understanding looks is one of universal validity. It is true that morality is not very impressive : it is not particularly pleasing, but it refers to a pleasure of universal validity : as such it must please the Supreme Being, and this constitutes the strongest motive force.

Prudence requires a good understanding, morality a good will. If our conduct as free agents is to have moral goodness, it must proceed solely from a good will. The will can, therefore, be good in itself. In the case of prudence everything depends, not on the end, since the end is always the same, namely happiness, but on the understanding which apprehends the end and the means to attain it ; one individual may be a greater adept at this than another. But while a sound understanding is requisite to prudence, to morality what is requisite is a will which is simply good in itself. Thus, for instance, the will to be rich is good in reference to its end, but not in itself.

We now proceed to examine what exactly constitutes that will, simply good in itself, on which moral goodness depends.

There is not only a clear distinction between a moral

and a pragmatic Motive, but the one is not in the least comparable to the other.   This statement requires some explanation.

All ethical Motives are either merely *obligandi* or *obligantia*.   *Motiva obligandi* constitute grounds for an Obligation: if the grounds are adequate they become *obligantia*, binding.   Not all grounds of obligation are also binding grounds.   *Motiva moralia non sufficientia non obligant, sed motiva sufficientia obligant.*   There are, therefore, ethical rules which impose a plain obligation and render the action obligatory—as, for instance, ' Thou shalt not lie '.   But if we combine *motiva pragmatica* with *motiva moralia* are they *homogenia* ?   No more than lack of candour in a person can be compensated by his possession of money ; no more than a deficiency of good looks can be made good by wealth, which cannot turn ugliness into beauty. No more can we suppose that *motiva pragmatica* are of the same order as *motiva moralia,* or comparable to them. But their determining force can be compared.   We get the illusion that it is advisable, on the judgment of the understanding, to prefer advantage to virtue.   Nevertheless, moral perfection and advantage cannot be compared, for they are essentially different.   How, then, is it that we actually fall into this confusion ?   We may say, for instance, when we meet a person in distress, that we should relieve his want and affliction, but only in so far as we can do it without detriment to ourselves.   Judged by the understanding, though there is a difference here between moral and pragmatic action, there is no distinction between moral and pragmatic Motive, because both prudence and morality tell me to study my interest.   I ought not to give to the poor wretch more than I can spare, for if I were to give away what I cannot spare I should myself be in want, I should myself have to seek the charity of others, and I should cease to be in a position to act morally.   Objectively, therefore, moral and pragmatic motives cannot be set in opposition, for they are unlike.

DE OBLIGATIONE ACTIVA ET PASSIVA

Obligatio activa is an *obligatio obligantis, obligatio passiva* is an *obligatio obligati*, but the distinction is of no great substance.

All obligations to high-minded action are *obligationes activae*. There are actions which we are bound in duty to do and by performing which we can place others under an obligation towards us. Such actions are services. We may have an obligation to act in a certain way towards a man without being under an obligation to *him*. *Obligati sumus ad actionem ita, ut illi non obligati simus.* Our obligation is to the action, not to the person. We are, for example, under an obligation to help the afflicted. The obligation here is one to the action and not to the afflicted person. This is *obligatio activa*. But if we have contracted a debt, we are under an obligation not only to the action of repayment but also to the creditor. This constitutes *obligatio passiva*.

But it may be contended that all *obligatio* is *passiva*, because if we are under an obligation we are under necessity. *Obligatio activa*, however, is a necessity of reason. My obligation arises from my own reflection and there is nothing passive about it, and when it is only my reason that dictates to me I remain my own master. On the other hand, *obligatio passiva* owes its existence to some one else.

Obligatio passiva est obligatio obligati erga obligantem. Obligatio activa est obligatio erga non obligantem. (Aliter: Obligatio activa est obligatio obligantis erga obligatum.)

Baumgarten sets up the proposition that Obligations can be large or small, but cannot be conflicting. No two Obligations can clash, because what is rendered morally necessary by one cannot be made otherwise by another. Take, for instance, our duty to pay our creditors, and our duty to be grateful to our parents. If the one duty is an Obligation, the other cannot properly be termed so. Towards our parents we are under a conditional, towards our creditors under a categorical Obligation. The one is an

Obligation, the other is not ; the one implies necessitation, the other does not.   When speaking of conflict, we mean a clash of Motive, but not of duty.

Many Obligations arise, grow, and cease.   When a child is born an Obligation is created ; as it grows the obligations grow ; when it reaches man's estate it ceases to be under the obligation which rested upon it as a child.   The man is, to be sure, still under an Obligation, but this arises from the benefits he has received from his parents and is not the Obligation of his childhood.   Again, the more a labourer works, the greater the Obligation, but when he is paid for his work the Obligation ceases.   But there are some Obligations which can never be extinguished.   Such, for instance, is the Obligation towards a benefactor.   However much I repay a benefit or favour, I can never alter the fact that my benefactor was first in the field, and I remain constantly under Obligation to him, unless indeed he subsequently plays me false, in which case my Obligation ceases ; but this does not often happen so long as one remains grateful towards one's benefactor.

The action which gives rise to an Obligation is called an *actus obligatorius*.   Every contract is such an act.   An *actus obligatorius* can give rise to an obligation towards me, but it can also give rise to an Obligation towards another.   Thus, for instance, the production of children is an *actus obligatorius* : by it the parents take on an Obligation towards their children, but the author doubts whether this act itself imposes any Obligation upon the children.   The children are, of course, under an Obligation towards their parents because the latter protect and maintain them, but the author doubts whether the fact of existence in itself imposes any Obligation ; the mere fact of existence does not spell happiness.   On the contrary, in order to be unhappy one must have existence.

Actions which are not free and do not involve one's personality do not give rise to obligations.   Thus no man can be placed under an obligation to give up swallowing, for the very reason that it would not be within his powers.   Obligation, therefore, presupposes the use of freedom.

We can divide Obligation into *positiva* and *naturalis*. The former is a positive product of the will ; the latter

flows from the nature of actions. Every law is either
natural or arbitrary. An Obligation which arises *e lege
naturali*, and the ground of which is to be found in the
action itself, is an *obligatio naturalis* ; but one which
arises *e lege arbitraria*, and the ground of which is to be
sought in the will of some one else, is an *obligatio positiva*.

Crusius [1] maintains that every obligation is related to
the will of another person. In his view, therefore, Obligation is a necessitation *per arbitrium alterius*. It would
certainly seem as though in the case of an Obligation we
were necessitated *per arbitrium alterius*, but in point of
fact we are necessitated *per arbitrium internum*, not *externum*, and therefore through the necessary condition of
will in general. It is this which gives rise to the existence
of an obligation in general.

No *obligatio positiva* is directed immediately upon the
action. It obliges us to do an action which is in itself
indifferent. Therefore *obligatio positiva est indirecta* and
not *directa*. If, for instance, the reason why I ought not
to lie were that God had forbidden it, because it pleased
Him so to do, then it would follow that He might have
refrained from forbidding it, had He so willed. *Obligatio
naturalis*, on the other hand, is *directa*. I ought not to
lie, not because God has forbidden it, but because lying
is evil in itself. All morality rests on this, that we do
what we do on account of the inner character of the act
itself. Consequently what gives rise to morality is not
the act, but the disposition from which its performance springs. If I do a thing because it is commanded
or because it brings advantage, and if I avoid doing a
thing because it is forbidden or because I would be a loser
by it, there is no question of any moral disposition ; but if
I do a thing because it is absolutely good in itself, my
disposition is a moral one. We ought, therefore, to do a
thing not because God wills it, but because it is righteous
and good in itself—and it is because it is good in itself
that God wills it and demands it of us.

---

[1] *De appetitibus insitis voluntatis humanae*, 1742. In para. 49
we read : ' Est igitur obligatio illa inter superiorem et inferiorem
relatio, qua hic ad voluntati illius parendum ob suam ab illo depen-
dentiam impellitur.'

Obligatio can be either *affirmativa* or *negativa*. The former bind us *ad committendum*, the latter *ad omittendum* ; and (just as in law) the opposite of *negativa* is not *positiva* but *affirmativa*.

The *consectaria* of an action are either good or bad ; they can be *naturalia* or *arbitraria, physica* or *moralia.* The consequences of the character of an action are *consectaria physica.* Baumgarten differentiates simply between *consectaria naturalia* and *arbitraria* : the former flow from the action itself, the latter from the will of another being, for example, punishment. Actions are good or bad either directly, that is in themselves, or else indirectly, that is contingently. The goodness of an action is, therefore, *vel interna vel externa.*

Moral perfection is *vel subjectiva vel objectiva.* Objective perfection is in the action itself ; subjective goodness lies in the conformity of the action to the will of another. *Moralitas objectiva*, therefore, is in the action itself, and the supreme will which contains the ground of all morality is the divine will. In all our actions, therefore, we may have in view either objective or subjective morality. There are objective laws of action which are called *praecepta,* and subjective laws which are maxims. The latter are not often in agreement with the objective laws.

We may regard all objective morality as the subjective morality of the divine will, but never as the subjective morality of the human will. All dispositions of the divine mind are morally good, which is not true of the human mind. The dispositions of the divine mind, i.e. the divine subjective morality, is in accordance with objective morality, and action which is objectively moral is thus in conformity with the divine will. All moral laws are, therefore, *praecepta* in that they are rules of the divine will.

In so far as the moral judgment is concerned, all its grounds are objective : none of them should be subjective ; but subjective grounds exist for the moral impulse. Grounds for decision are, therefore, objective, but grounds for execution can be also subjective. The distinguishing between what is morally good and what bad must be done by the understanding, and therefore objectively ; but for executing an action there may also be subjective grounds.

The question whether an action is moral relates to the action itself. Moral goodness is, therefore, objective in character because it does not depend on any harmony with our inclinations, but on itself as such. Every subjective law is derived from the character of this or that Subject and is valid only in respect of this or that Subject, but moral laws ought to be of general validity and ought to apply to all free actions irrespective of the diversity of Subjects. In the case of God the subjective laws of His divine will are one with the objective laws of the good will in general, but God's subjective law is no ground of morality. God is Himself good and holy because His will conforms to this objective law. It follows, therefore, that subjective grounds have no bearing on the question of morality, which can be established only upon objective grounds.

To differentiate between objective and subjective morality is absurd. Morality cannot be other than objective, though the conditions of its application may be subjective.

Baumgarten's [1] first moral law is:

FAC BONUM ET OMITTE MALUM

And in summary form:

FAC BONUM

We must distinguish between the good and the pleasant. The latter is of the senses, the former of the understanding. The concept of the good is the idea of something which satisfies all, and it can thus be judged by the understanding, what is pleasant is a matter of individual appreciation. Baumgarten's proposition could, therefore, be construed to mean that we should do what our understanding sets before us as good and not what is pleasant to our senses. But we know that all imperatives call upon us to do what is good and not what is pleasant. The 'ought' always designates the quality of goodness and not of pleasantness. On this construction, therefore,

[1] On p. 39 this law is ascribed to Wolff. (*Trans.*)

the rule is tautological. But what if we qualified goodness and made the proposition mean, ' do what is morally good ' ? We should then need a rule to tell us what constitutes moral goodness. We see, therefore, that Baumgarten's rule can in no way be a principle of morality.

What Baumgarten means is that not all *imperativi* are *obligationes*. Thus *imperativi problematici et pragmatici* are not *obligationes*, as was said above.

But according to him the good contains in itself impulsive grounds of action, and that which is a superior good contains superior impulsive grounds. This must mean that Obligation is the coupling of actions to their highest grounds. The statement ' *fac bonum et omitte malum* ' cannot, however, be a basic principle of moral obligation, because the good can be good in diverse ways according to the end chosen, the statement being thus an axiom of skill or of prudence, whereas for it to embody a moral principle it would have to imply that which is good for moral action. It is, therefore, a *principium vagum* ; and not only so, it is also a *principium tautologicum*. A rule is tautological if it resolves a question by an empty answer. If we ask what it is that we ought to do, what, in fact, is the obligation which devolves upon us, and we are told to do good and to avoid doing evil, the answer tells us nothing, because ' *fac* ' implies ' it is good that the action should happen '. The meaning of the proposition is simply, ' it is good that you should do what is good,' which is tautological. It tells us nothing about what is good, but merely that we ought to do what we ought to do. There is no branch of knowledge which so abounds in tautological propositions as ethics, offering as the answer what was in fact the question. The problem and its resolution are then tautologous, because what is explicitly expressed in the resolution was already implicit in the problem. Ethics is full of such propositions, and teachers are prone to believe that they have done everything required of them when their explanations and indications to their pupils are as if a medical man told a patient suffering from constipation that he ought to loosen his bowels and to perspire freely and digest his food well. This is just telling him to do what he wants to know how to do. Such propositions are tautological rules of decision.

The real question then is, 'What are the conditions under which our actions are good ? ' Baumgarten says : *Bonorum sibi oppositorum fac melius.* This is a deduction from the tautological proposition just examined. It implies abnegation, which in this connexion means sacrifice and self-denial—that is, putting up with an evil in order to avoid a greater and renouncing a small good for the sake of a greater. Abnegation can be either pragmatic or moral. It is *abnegatio pragmatica* if I sacrifice an advantage in order to gain a greater ; it is *abnegatio moralis* if on moral grounds I leave an action undone in order to do a better action.

Quaere perfectionem, quantum potes is another proposition offered by Baumgarten as a ground of Obligation. This one is a little more definite, and is not wholly tautologous. It is, therefore, of some use. But what is perfection ? Perfection of a thing is not the same as perfection in man. The former implies the presence in sufficiency of all factors requisite for constituting the thing and so, speaking generally, connotes completeness, whilst the latter is the possession by man of the powers, capacities and skill requisite for the achievement of whatever ends he sets before himself and is not synonymous with moral goodness; it does not imply morality. There are degrees of perfection : one man can be more perfect than another ; but goodness is the quality which enables us to make proper use of all our faculties. Moral goodness thus lies in the perfection, not of the faculties, but of the will. But the functional completeness of all our powers is required in order that the dictates of the will should be made operative. Perfection, therefore, appertains to morality indirectly, and this proposition of Baumgarten's is thus indirectly moral.

Another of Baumgarten's first principles of ethics is : *Vive convenienter naturae.* This is a Stoic principle. Now when a system of ethics contains several first principles, it in fact contains none ; because there can only be one true first principle. But even if we amplify the proposition to read, ' Live in accordance with the laws which nature provides for you through your reason,' it is still tautological, because to live in accordance with nature would mean that we ought to direct our actions so that they accord with the physical order of natural things, and this would mean that the rule was one of prudence, and not a principle of morality.   It would not even be a good rule of prudence, because when told that we should so order our actions that they conform to nature we do not know whether this conformity with nature is a good thing.   Still less is it a principle of morality.

The last of Baumgarten's principles is : *Ama optimum quantum potes*. This rule is of as little use as the others we have just dealt with.   All that pertains to our perfection, all that is instrumental thereto, that each one of us has and loves ; but there are two ways of loving, from inclination and from principle.   A rogue loves what is good from principle, but what is evil from inclination.

None of these propositions, then, are principles of morality.

MORAL COMPULSION

In discussing compulsion we must first observe that there are two types of necessitation, objective and subjective.   Subjective necessitation is the representation of the necessity of an action *per stimulos*, or *per causas impulsivas* in the Subject ; objective necessitation is the necessity of an action on objective grounds. Subjective compulsion is the determination of a person by that in himself as Subject which has the greatest determining and moving force.   It is not a question of the necessity of an action, but of being determined to it.   But the creature which is determined must be such that, if not subject to such determination he would not only not do the action, but would indeed have reasons against it.   God cannot, therefore, be determined.   Compulsion is thus a determination to the unwilling performance of an action.   This determination can be either objective or subjective, as in the case of a conflict between two inclinations.   An example is that of a miser who will forgo a small advantage in order to gain a greater, but will do so with reluctance because he would rather gain both advantages.

Compulsion is either pathological or practical. In the former an action which we do unwillingly is rendered necessary *per stimulos* ; in the latter *per motiva*. Because his will is free no man can be pathologically compelled. The human will is an *arbitrium liberum* in that it is not determined by stimuli, but the animal will is an *arbitrium brutum* and not *liberum* because it can be determined *per stimulos*. However much, for instance, we may try by torture to force a man to action we cannot compel him to do it if he does not will it ; if he so will he can withstand every torment and not yield. In a relative sense he can be compelled, but not in an absolute sense. In spite of every instigation of the senses, a man can still leave an action undone. This is the characteristic of *liberum arbitrium*. Animals are determined *per stimulos*. Thus when a dog is hungry and there is food before him he must eat ; man, however, in a similar situation, can restrain himself. It follows, therefore, that pathologically man can be compelled only in a relative sense, as, for instance, by torture. An action is necessary if we cannot resist doing it ; and if its impulsive grounds are such that human powers are not adequate to resist them, they have a determining force.

But man can be compelled practically, *per motiva*. He is not in effect compelled but impelled, and the compulsion is not subjective but objective, for otherwise it would not be practical. The action occurs *per motiva* and not *per stimulos*, for *stimuli* are *motiva subjecte moventia*.

In the case of a free being an action can be necessary—and necessary in the highest possible degree—and yet it need not conflict with freedom. Thus God must necessarily reward men whose conduct conforms to the moral laws, and in so doing He acts according to the rules of His own good pleasure because the conduct in question, by conforming to the moral laws, accords with the divine will. Again, an honest man cannot tell a lie, but he refrains of his own free will from telling lies. Actions can, therefore, be necessary and yet not be contrary to freedom. Practical necessitation can, however, take place only in the case of man and not in that of God. No man, for example, would willingly give away all his possessions ; but he will do so if this be the only way whereby he can save his children : he is then practically necessitated. Consequently, he who is determined by impulsive grounds of reason is determined without this being contrary to freedom. We act reluctantly in such cases, to be sure, but do the actions because they are good.

PRACTICAL NECESSITATION

Necessitation is practical, never pathological. Practical necessitation is objective, never subjective. If it were subjective it would be *necessitatio pathologica*. There is no necessitation which accords with freedom save practical necessitation *per motiva*. These *motiva* can be *pragmatica* or *moralia*. The former are derived from *bonitas mediata* ; the latter from the *bonitas absoluta* of the free will. The more he can be morally compelled, the freer a man is ; the more he is compelled pathologically (and this, as we have seen, can only be relative compulsion) the less free he is. It is remarkable that the more one is subject to compulsion—moral compulsion—the more free one should be. We compel a person morally by means of *motiva objective moventia*, by means of impelling grounds of reason without any inducements and without depriving him of any fraction of his freedom. That being so, a high degree of freedom is requisite for moral compulsion, for then the *arbitrium liberum* is more powerful, and in its freedom from *stimuli* it can submit to the compulsion of rational grounds of action. The freer a man is from *stimuli*, the more he can be compelled morally, and the degree of his freedom grows with the degree of his morality.

There is no such thing as *necessitatio practica* for God, since in His case subjective and objective laws are the same. In the case of man, however, *necessitatio practica* arises because he acts reluctantly, and therefore he must be compelled ; but the more he gives way to moral grounds of impulsion, the freer he is. The less he is obliged, the freer a man is.   So far as a man is placed under Obligation, so far he is not free.   When Obligation ceases, he is free. Our human freedom is therefore circumscribed by Obligation ; but in the case of God moral necessity does not diminish freedom ; God is not obliged ; a perfect good will is not obliged because such a will in itself wills only what is good and so cannot be obliged.   But men can be placed under obligation because their will is evil.   Thus a man who has accepted favours is not free.   We can be relatively freer in one situation than in another.   A man who is under *obligatio passiva* is less free than one who is under *obligatio activa.*   We cannot be compelled to a magnanimous action, but we are nevertheless under an obligation to perform such actions and we are consequently under an *obligatio activa.*   We can be compelled to discharge our debts, and in such a case we are under *obligatio passiva.* If, then, I am under *obligatio passiva* to a person, I am less free than that person who can oblige me.

We have also *obligationes internae erga nosmet ipsos.*   In so far as these are concerned we are externally completely free.   Each of us can do with his body what he will ; it concerns no one else.   But internally we are not free : each of us is bound by the necessary and essential ends of humanity.   Every obligation is a kind of compulsion. If this compulsion is moral we are either compelled externally or else we compel ourselves.   The latter is *coactio interna.*   I can be compelled morally and externally by another person if the latter forces me by moral motives to do an action which I do reluctantly. Assume, for example, that I am in debt to a man and he says to me : If you would be an honest man you must pay me ; I will not sue you, but I cannot relieve you of the debt because I need the money.   This is a case of external moral compulsion by the will of another.

The more a man can compel himself the freer he is. The less he need be compelled by others, the greater is his inner freedom.   In this connexion we must discriminate between capacity for freedom and the state of freedom. The former can be great, though the latter be small.   The greater the capacity for freedom, the freer from *stimuli* a man's freedom is, the freer is he.   If man did not need self-compulsion he would be completely free. His will would then be completely good and he would willingly do all that is good, because he would stand in no need of compelling himself. This, however, is not the case with any man, though one man may come nearer to it than another, that is if impulses of sense, the *stimuli*, exercise less influence upon him. The more a man practises self-compulsion the freer he becomes. Some men are by nature more disposed to magnanimity, forgiveness, righteousness. It is easier for these to compel themselves and they are to that extent the freer. But no man is above self-compulsion.

All obligation is either external or internal. *Obligatio externa est necessitatio moralis per arbitrium alterius. Obligatio interna est necessitatio moralis per arbitrium proprium.* To will is to have a desire which is within our own control ; to wish is to have a desire which is not within our control. Necessitation by some one else's will is *necessitatio moralis externa,* because the other man has it in his power to compel me. The obligation which arises in that event is an *obligatio externa.* But *necessitatio moralis,* which occurs not through the will of another but by one's own will, is a *necessitatio moralis interna,* and the obligation to which it gives rise is an *obligatio interna.* Take, as an instance, the obligation which rests upon each of us to help our neighbour. This is an inner Obligation. But to make restitution for an insult is morally necessary by reason of the will of another. This is a case of *obligatio externa.*

The outer are wider than the inner *obligationes,* because an outer is at the same time an inner *obligatio,* but an inner is not also an outer. *Obligatio externa* assumes that actions in general fall under moral rules, and it is accordingly also *interna.* For the *obligatio externa* is an *obligatio* precisely because the action is already an Obligation *interne.* Because the action is a duty, there is an inner obligation to perform it ; but because I can exercise compulsion upon the agent, by my will, to do this duty, it is also an *obligatio externa.* In the case of *obligatio externa* a man's action must accord with the will of another and he can be compelled to it by the other ; and if he does not allow himself to be compelled morally the other may compel him pathologically. He has authority to do this. Speaking generally, every legal rule contains authority for pathological compulsion.

Inner *obligationes* are imperfect because we cannot be compelled to fulfil them: but *obligationes externae* are *perfectae*, because here, in addition to the inner obligation, there is also a determination from without. If the ground which moves us to comply with an Obligation is from within we call it a duty; if it is from without we call it compulsion. If the cause of my fulfilling an obligation is the will of another, it is external. I am coerced and I act under compulsion. *Stimulus pro arbitrio alterius necessitans est coactio.* But if I fulfil an obligation of my own free will, the impulsive ground is within me and my act is done from duty. Whether I act from duty or by compulsion, in either case I discharge my obligation, but in the one case impulsive ground is within me—it is inner—and in the other without me—it is outer. A ruler does not care whether his subjects' obligations towards him are discharged from duty or compulsion: it is all the same to him; but parents demand that children should fulfil their obligations towards them from duty.

Baumgarten errs in dividing obligations into those from duty and those from compulsion.[1] Obligations cannot be classified under these two headings. Compulsion does not make an obligation. Obligations, as has been shown above, are divisible in themselves into *internae* and *externae* according as they arise *ex arbitrio proprio* or *ex arbitrio alterius*; but whether the obligations are *internae* or whether they are *externae*, their *motiva satisfaciendi* are divisible into those of duty and those of compulsion according as they are from within us or from without us, that is, according as they flow from our own or from some one else's will. A Motive can be of duty or of compulsion whatever the *obligatio*. Objective grounds of impulsion come from without: they are taken from the object and are the reasons why a thing should be done; subjective grounds are grounds of the disposition and

---

[1] Baumgarten, para. 50. Kant's remark is not quite just to Baumgarten.

direction of our wills to comply with a rule. On objective grounds, then, obligations are either inner or outer ; on subjective grounds they are either duties or compulsions.

Ethical obligations are those with subjective or inner impulsive grounds ; obligations with objective or external impulsive grounds are, strictly speaking, juridical. The first are obligations of duty, the second obligations of compulsion. It is not in the nature of the obligations they contain that jurisprudence and ethics differ, but in the grounds which each supplies for discharging obligations. Ethics discusses all obligations—those of charity and generosity, as well as those of indebtedness—and considers them all together, but from the standpoint of the inner grounds of impulsion it reflects on their origins in duty and in the nature of things themselves, not in compulsion. Jurisprudence, however, is not concerned with the discharge of obligations from duty, but from compulsion ; it considers them in their relation to compulsion, and stresses the sanctions of compulsion. Take, for instance, our obligations towards God. We have such obligations, and God demands not only that we should discharge them, but that we should do it willingly and from inner grounds of impulse.   If we do what an *obligatio* towards God demands of us, but do it from compulsion and not from duty, we do not discharge the Obligation. If I do something with pleasure and from a good disposition, I do it from duty, and my action is right in the ethical sense ; but if I do it under compulsion my action is right in the legal sense.

It is more correct, therefore, to divide Obligations into *internae et externae*. This division does not, however, indicate the difference between ethics and jurisprudence. That difference is to be found in the grounds which move to the fulfilment of the obligations. *Obligationes externae* can be fulfilled from duty or from compulsion : we can be forced to fulfil them by the will of another ; if he does not force us and we yet fulfil them, we do so from duty ; if he does, we do it from compulsion. An *obligatio* is not *externa* because we can be compelled by means of it. The authority to compel flows from the Obligation and is a consequence of that.

LAWS

Every formula which expresses the necessity of an action is called a law. Thus we can have natural laws which are those universal rules under which actions fall, and also practical laws. Every law is therefore either physical or practical. The practical laws express the necessity of free actions, and they are either subjective or objective. They are subjective in so far as they are actually complied with by men; they are objective in so far as they ought to be complied with. Objective laws are either pragmatic or moral. We are concerned here with the moral laws.

Justice (Recht), in the sense of legal competence, is the conformity of actions to the rule of Law, in so far as these actions are not in opposition to the rule of the will; it is the moral practicability of an action, provided that the action is not in opposition to the laws of morality. As a department of knowledge, on the other hand, Justice is the aggregate of all the ordinances of Law. *Jus in sensu proprio est complexus legum obligationum externarum, quatenus simul sumuntur. Jus in sensu proprio est vel jus late dictum, vel jus stricte dictum. Jus late dictum* is the Law of equity; *jus stricte dictum* is the strict Law with authority to compel others; it is stringent and coercive. When we contrast ethics and the law, the contrast is not between ethics and *jus* in general, but between it and *jus strictum.* Ethics concerns itself with the laws of free action in so far as we cannot be coerced to it, but the strict law concerns itself with free action in so far as we can be compelled to it. *Jus stricte* is either *positivum seu statuarium* or else *jus naturale. Jus positivum* has its origin in the human will, but *jus naturale* comes from that insight which the understanding obtains into the nature of actions. *Jus positivum* is *vel divinum vel humanum.* The content of *jus positivum* is commandments, of *jus naturale* laws; but divine laws are at the same time commandments, so that *jus naturale* is equally the *jus positivum* of the divine will, though not in virtue of being the precepts of the divine will merely, but as they are implied in the nature of man. The converse of this, however, does not hold good. All divine laws are natural laws, because God also can lay down positive laws. *Jus positivum,* as well as *jus naturale,* can be either a free or else a coercive Law. Many laws are merely rules of equity. But the *jus æquitatis* is not as widely cultivated as we could wish ; it cannot operate in the ordinary courts of justice, where judgment must be pronounced *valide.* It is not an external law : its validity is only *coram foro conscientiae.* In *jus positivum* and *jus naturale* we are concerned always with *jus strictum* and not with *jus æquitatis,* which belongs only to ethics. Duties, whether they are compulsory or not, appertain to the sphere of ethics as soon as the impulsive ground of their performance is derived from their own nature. According to its content a law can belong either to ethics or to Law ; but not only so ; it can belong either to Law or to ethics in accordance with its impulsive ground. Thus an overlord demands the payment of taxes : he does not demand that they should be paid willingly ; ethics, however, demands that they should be so paid. Some of his subjects will pay because they are forced to pay, others will do so willingly : they all pay as his subjects, but the overlord cannot dictate in what spirit his subjects should pay ; whether they pay in a willing or an unwilling spirit is beyond his control, for it is internal, within themselves ; but ethics demands that the spirit should be good. It is only in the observance of the divine laws that ethics and Law coincide. In so far as God is concerned both are compulsory ; for God can compel us to ethical as well as to legal action, but He demands that we should act not from compulsion but from duty. If it is in accordance with the compulsory law an action possesses *rectitudo juridica,* but it is moral only if it complies with the laws from duty and from conviction. It is thus the willing disposition which constitutes morality. We must discriminate, therefore, between the moral goodness of an action and its *rectitudo juridica.* *Rectitudo* is the genus. It is juridical only, and therefore does not imply moral goodness. Thus if we act in accordance with the divine commands because we must and not from a good

disposition, our religion possesses only *rectitudo juridica.*
God, however, does not look upon the action, but upon
the heart. The heart is the principle of moral disposition,
and it is moral goodness which God demands. It is this
which is worthy of reward. We ought, therefore, to
cultivate a right disposition in performing our duties, and
this is what the teacher of the Gospel means when he
says that we should do all from the love of God. To love
God is to do as He commands with a willing heart.

Leges can also be *praeceptivae,* or *prohibitivae,* or *per-
missivae.* The first command, the second forbid, and the
third allow an action. *Complexus legum praeceptivarum* is
jus mandati, complexus legum prohibitivarum is *jus vetiti* ;
and a system of *jus permissi* is also conceivable.

THE SUPREME PRINCIPLE OF MORALITY

In this connexion we must first notice that there are
two points to consider ; the principle of the discrimination
of our obligation and the principle of its performance or
execution. We must distinguish between measuring-rod
and mainspring. The measuring-rod is the principle of
discrimination ; the mainspring is the principle of the performance of our obligation. Confusion between these has
led to complete falsity in the sphere of ethics. If we ask,
' What is morally good and what is not ? ' it is the principle
of discrimination which is in question, in terms of which
I decide the goodness of the action. But if we ask, ' What
is it that moves me to act in accordance with the laws
of morality ? ' we have a question which concerns the
principle of the motive. The equity of the action is
the objective ground, but is still not the subjective
ground. The *motiva subjective moventia* are what moves
me to do that which the understanding tells me I ought
to do.

The supreme principle of all moral judgment lies in the
understanding : that of the moral incentive to action lies
in the heart. This motive is moral feeling. We must
guard against confusing the principle of the judgment

with the principle of the motive. The first is the norm; the second the incentive. The motive cannot take the place of the rule. Where the motive is wanting, the error is practical; but when the judgment fails the error is theoretical.

We shall now proceed to indicate shortly and negatively what does not constitute the principle of morality. Firstly, there is nothing pathological about it. It would be pathological if it were derived from subjective grounds, from our inclination and feeling. There is no pathological principle in ethics because its laws are objective, and deal with what we ought to do, not with what we desire to do. Ethics is no analysis of inclination but a prescription which is contrary to all inclination. A pathological principle of morality would consist in an instruction to satisfy all our desires, and this would constitute a bestial, not the real, Epicureanism.

We can conceive two *principia pathologica* of morality, the one aiming at the satisfaction of all our inclinations, the other at the satisfaction of one particular inclination, the inclination to morality. The aim of the first would be merely physical feeling; the second would be based on an intellectual inclination. But an intellectual inclination is a contradiction in terms; for a feeling for objects of the understanding is in itself an absurdity, so that a moral feeling resulting from an intellectual inclination is also an absurdity and is, therefore, impossible. A feeling cannot be regarded as something ideal; it cannot belong both to our intellectual and to our sensuous nature; and even if it were possible for us to feel morality, it would still not be possible to establish a system of rules on this principle. For a moral law states categorically what ought to be done, whether it pleases us or not. It is, therefore, not a case of satisfying an inclination. If it were, there would be no moral law, but every one might act according to his own feeling. Even if we assumed that all men had a like degree of feeling, there would still be no Obligation to act according to feeling, for we could not then say that we *ought* to do what pleases us, but only that so-and-so might do such-and-such *because* it pleased him. The moral law, however, commands categorically.

Morality cannot, therefore, be based on any pathological principle, neither on a physical nor yet on a moral feeling. Moreover, to have recourse to feeling in the case of a practical rule is quite contrary to philosophy. Every feeling has only a private validity, and no man's feeling can be apprehended by another. If a man argues that ' he feels in himself that it is so ', his argument is a tautology. His feeling can have no value for others, and the man who once appeals to his feelings forswears all rational grounds. There is, therefore, no such thing as a pathological principle of morality, and there must accordingly be an intellectual principle in the sense that it must be derived from the understanding. This principle will consist in a rule of the understanding, either because the understanding provides us with the means so to direct our actions that they conform to our inclinations or because the ground of morality is immediately apprehended by the understanding. If the former, the principle is no doubt intellectual, inasmuch as the understanding provides the means ; it is nevertheless evidently rooted in inclination. Such a pseudo-intellectual principle is pragmatic, and depends on the capacity of the rule to satisfy our inclinations. This principle of prudence is the true Epicurean principle. To be told that we ought to promote our happiness is in effect to be told that we ought to employ our understanding to discover the means for satisfying our inclinations and our desire for pleasure. This principle is intellectual in so far as it requires the understanding to provide the rules for the employment of the means to promote our happiness. But as this happiness consists in the satisfaction of all our inclinations, the pragmatic principle is dependent on the inclinations. Morality is, however, independent of all inclination, and it is not, therefore, grounded in any pragmatic principle. Were it so grounded, there could be no agreement amongst men in regard to morality, as every individual would seek to satisfy his own inclinations. Morality cannot, however, be based on the subjective laws of men's inclinations, and so it follows that the principle of morality cannot be pragmatic. It must, to be sure, be intellectual, but not, as in the case of the pragmatic principle, mediately so ;

it must be an unmediated principle of morality in the sense that the ground of morality is apprehended immediately by the mind. The ethical principle is, therefore, a sheerly intellectual principle of the pure reason. But this pure intellectual principle must not be tautologous. It must not consist in the tautology of pure reason as does, for example, Wolff's rule, ' do good and eschew evil ',[1] which, as we have already shown, is empty and unphilosophic.

Another tautological principle is that enunciated by Cumberland. It is the principle of truth. Cumberland asserts that we all seek perfection, that we are misled by appearance, but that ethics shows us the truth.

A third is that of Aristotle, the principle of the mean, which is consequently tautologous.

The pure intellectual principle cannot, however, be a *principium externum*, in terms of the relation of our actions to a foreign being. It does not, therefore, depend on the divine will. It cannot, for instance, take the form : ' Thou shalt not lie, because lying is forbidden.' Accordingly, as it cannot be external, it cannot be tautological. There are those who argue that we must first have God and then morality—a very convenient principle; but ethics and theology are neither of them a principle of the other. It is true that theology cannot subsist without ethics and vice versa. We are not, however, discussing here the fact that theology is a motive for ethics—which it is, but we are investigating whether the principle of ethical discrimination is theological—and it cannot be that. Were it so, then before a nation could have any concept of duties it would first have to know God. Consequently, nations which had no right concept of God would have no duties, and this is not the case. Nations had a right idea of their duties, and were aware that lies were detestable, without having the proper concept of God. Other peoples,

---

[1] On p. 24 this rule was described as Baumgarten's ' first moral law '. Kant is presumably summarizing Wolff's formula which, in para. 205 of his *Philosophia practica universalis*, 1744 edition, is given as : ' Lex naturae praescribit facienda, quae bona, honesta, licita, recta et decora sunt; atque non facienda, quae mala, inhonesta, illicita, minus recta et indecora sunt.'

besides, have constructed for themselves concepts of God
which were merely sacred, and erroneous, who yet had
proper concepts of the duties. Duties must, therefore, be
derived from another source. Men have derived morality
from the divine will because the moral laws are expressed
in the form ' thou shalt ', and this has led to the belief
that a third being must have promulgated the command.
But whilst it is true that the moral laws are commands,
and whilst they may be commandments of the divine will,
they do not originate in the commandment. God has commanded this or that because it is a moral law, and because
His will coincides with the moral law. Moreover, it
would seem as though there were no obligations but such
as had reference to an obligator ; that Obligation itself
implied a reference to a being *universaliter obligans*, and
that God, therefore, was the obligator of the moral laws.
It is true that in the matter of performance we must have
a third being to make it necessary for us to do that which
is morally good, but for the judging of morality no third
being is needed. Moral laws can be right without a third
being, but in the absence of such a being to make their
performance necessary they would be empty. Men were
right, therefore, in recognising that the absence of a
supreme judge would make all moral laws ineffectual.
There would be no incentive, no reward and no punishment. Knowledge of God is, therefore, necessary to make
the moral laws effective, but it is not necessary for the
mere apprehension of those laws. For this latter purpose
it is not necessary to presuppose the existence of a third
being. How do we know the divine will ? None of us
feels it in his heart ; we cannot know the moral law from
any revelation ; for if we did so know it, then would those
who had no revelation be wholly ignorant of it, and Paul
himself asserts that the latter are guided by their reason.
It is by our reason that we apprehend the divine will.
We imagine God as possessing the most holy and the most
perfect will. But what then is the most perfect will ?
The moral law shows us what it is, and herein we find the
whole of ethics. We say that the divine will accords with
the moral law and is, therefore, the holiest and the most
perfect. Thus we recognize the perfection of the divine

will from the moral law. God wills all that is morally good and proper and His will is, therefore, the most holy and the most perfect. But what is it that is morally good ? Ethics supplies the answer to this question.

The more corrupt the moral concepts, the more corrupt are the theological concepts. If the ethical concepts in theology and religion were pure and holy, no man would strive to please God in a human and improper manner. Every one imagines God in terms of that concept which is most familiar to himself. We may, for instance, imagine Him as a great and mighty lord, something beyond the mightiest of the lords of this earth. Each man, therefore, forms for himself a concept of morality which corresponds to his concept of God. As a consequence, men endeavour to find favour with God, by testifying in His favour and by singing His praises ; they extol Him as a great lord, than whom there can be no greater ; they recognize their faults, and think that all men have such faults that none is able to do anything good ; they take all their sins and lay them at God's feet, and sigh, and think thereby they honour God ; they fail to see that such mean and petty eulogy from worms such as we are is but a reproach to God. They do not see that man cannot praise and eulogize God. To honour God is to obey His commandments with a willing heart, not to sing songs of praise to Him. An upright man who strives from an inner impulse to give expression to the moral law on account of the inner goodness of such action, who keeps God's commandments with a willing heart,—such a one honours God. If, however, we do as God has commanded because He has commanded it and because He is so mighty that He can force us to it, we act under orders, from fear and fright, not appreciating the propriety of our actions and not knowing *why* we should do as God has commanded nor *why* we should obey Him. Might cannot constitute a *vis obligandi*. Threats do not impose an obligation, they extort. If then we comply with the moral law from fear of punishment and of the power of God, and for no other reason than that God has so commanded, we act not from duty and obliga- tion, but from fear and fright. Such conduct does not make the heart better. But if we act from inner principles, if we do a thing simply because it is good in itself and do it with a liking, such conduct is truly pleasing in the sight of God. God looks to our dispositions, and these derive only from a principle within us. If we do a thing with a liking, we do it from a good disposition. We cannot even give a proper exposition of divine revelation except on the inner principle of morality. Theology may regard willingness as piety, but it is not so : virtue consists in moral conduct ; and moral conduct in accordance with the divine, beneficent will becomes piety.

Having examined what the principle of morality is not, we must now examine what it is. Now the principle of morality is *intellectuale internum*, and must, therefore, be sought in the action itself by the pure reason. Wherein then does it consist ? Morality is the harmony of actions with the universally valid law of the free will : it is always the relation in which actions stand to the general rule. In all our actions that which is called moral is regular. It conforms to a rule. The essence of morality is that our actions are motivated by a general rule, that is, that the reasons for the actions are to be found in such a rule. If we make it the foundation of our conduct that our actions shall be consistent with the universal rule, which is valid at all times and for every one, then our actions have their source in the principle of morality. Take, for example, the keeping of a promise. To break a promise as it please our sensibility is not moral, for if no man were willing to keep his promise simply in terms of the original proposal promises would in the long run become useless. But I may judge the matter in terms of the understanding, to discover whether it is a universal rule that promises should be kept. I then find that as I wish that all others should keep their promises to me, I must keep my promises to others. My action then conforms to the universal rule of will in general. Take again the practice of benevolence. Assume that I meet a man who is in the most distressed circumstances, and though I have the wherewithal to assist him, I am indifferent to his sufferings and prefer to spend my money on my own pleasures. Let me test this by my understanding ; let me see whether my conduct can be a universal rule ; let me see whether such indifference on the part of another, if I were in distress, would accord with my will; and what do I find? I find that it would not. Such conduct, therefore, is not moral.

Every immoral man has his maxims. While a precept is an objective law in accordance with which we ought to act, a maxim is a subjective law in accordance with which we actually do act. Every one regards the moral law as something which he can publicly profess, but his maxims as something which must be concealed because they are contrary to morality and cannot serve as a universal rule. Take, for example, a man whose maxim is to become rich. He cannot and will not declare it, or else he would fail in his purpose. If it came to be used as a general rule, every one would want to grow rich, and then it would be impossible to become rich, because everyone would know about it and everyone would want to be so. Examples from the sphere of duties towards oneself are the least well known and are, therefore, somewhat more difficult to understand. They are often confused with the pragmatic rules (of which more anon) for promoting one's well-being. May a man, for instance, mutilate his body for profit? May he sell a tooth? May he surrender himself at a price to the highest bidder? What is the moral aspect of such questions as these? I apply my understanding to investigate whether the intent of the action is of such a nature that it could be a universal rule. What is that intent in these cases? It is to gain material advantage. It is obvious, therefore, that in so acting man reduces himself to a thing, to an instrument of animal amusements. We are, however, as human beings, not things but persons, and by turning ourselves into things we dishonour human nature in our own persons. The same applies to suicide. By the rules of prudence there might be cases in which, in order to have done with misery, one might commit suicide, but not so by rules of morality. Suicide is immoral; for the intention is to rid oneself of all pains and discomforts attendant upon one's state by sacrificing that state, and this subordinates human nature to animal nature and brings the understanding under the control of animal impulses. In doing this I contradict myself, if I still desire to possess the rights of man.

In all moral judgments the idea which we frame is this, 'What is the character of the action taken by itself.' If the intent of the action can without self-contradiction be universalized, it is morally possible; if it cannot be so universalized without contradicting itself, it is morally impossible. Consider, for instance, the case of telling a lie in order to gain a large fortune. If this were made a universal principle, it would be impossible to maintain it, because the end would be known to every one. That action is immoral whose intent cancels and destroys itself when it is made a universal rule. It is moral, if the intent of the action is in harmony with itself when it is made a universal rule. Understanding is the faculty of the rule of our actions, and actions which are in harmony with the universal rule are in harmony with the understanding, and thus their impulsive grounds are in the understanding. If then an action is done because it harmonizes with the universal rule of the understanding, it has its source in the *principium moralitatis purum intellectuale internum*. As, therefore, the understanding is the faculty of the rule and of judgment, morality is the subordination of actions in general to the principle of the understanding. How the understanding can contain a principle of action is somewhat difficult to apprehend. In no sense does the understanding contain the *end* of action; rather, morality is constituted by the universal *form* of the understanding (which is purely intellectual), the action being taken, in fact, universally, so as to constitute a rule. And it is here that the distinction we have drawn above between the objective principle of discrimination and the subjective principle of performance comes in. Of these two principles it is the objective principle of judgment that we are here concerned with. We have already, in another connexion, rejected the subjective principle, moral feeling, which is the motive of action. Moral feeling is the capacity to be affected by a moral judgment. My understanding may judge that an action is morally good, but it need not follow that I shall do that action which I judge morally good: from under-

standing to performance is still a far cry.   If this judgment were to move me to do the deed, it would be moral
feeling; but it is quite incomprehensible that the mind
should have a motive force to judge.   The understanding,
obviously, can judge, but to give to this judgment of the
understanding a compelling force, to make it an incentive
that can move the will to perform the action—this is the
philosopher's stone !

The understanding takes account of everything which
has a bearing on its rule.   It accepts all those things
which conform to the rule and opposes those which conflict with it.   But immoral actions conflict with the rule;
they cannot be made a universal rule;   the understanding
is, therefore, hostile to them, as they are hostile to its
principle.   Thus in a sense a motive force is embedded
in the understanding in virtue of its own nature.   All
action ought, therefore, to be so constituted that it agrees
with the universal form of the understanding; it must be
such that it can at all times become a universal rule;   if
it is so constituted, it is moral.   Does it then depend on
the mind that any particular action is immoral, or does it
depend on the will ?   If it is the understanding that is
at fault in the discrimination of the action, that is, when
it is badly instructed, the action is morally imperfect;
but the depravity or wickedness of an action is not constituted by discrimination, and so does not lie in the understanding; it consists in the motive of the will.   Having
learnt to discriminate actions, man still lacks the incentive
to perform the actions.   An action is, therefore, immoral
not because the understanding is at fault, but because the
will or the heart is depraved.   The will is depraved if
the sensibility overpowers the motive force of the understanding.   The understanding has no *elateres animi*, though
it possesses impulsive force and *motiva*, but these are not
capable of overpowering the *elateres* of the sensibility.   A
sensibility in harmony with the impulsive force of the
understanding would be moral feeling.   It is true that
we cannot feel the goodness of an action ; but the understanding sets itself against an evil action because it runs
contrary to the rule.   This opposition of the understanding
is the impulsive ground.   If this impulsive ground of

understanding could move the sensibility to conformity and induce motives in it, this would constitute moral feeling. On what then does man's possession of such a moral feeling depend ? Anyone can see that an action is disgusting, but only the man who feels disgust at it has moral feeling. The understanding sees that a thing is disgusting and is hostile to it, but it cannot be disgusted : it is only the sensibility which is disgusted. If then the sensibility is disgusted with that which the mind sees to be disgusting, we have moral feeling. It is quite impossible to make any man feel disgust at vice. We can only tell him what our understanding apprehends and bring him to the point of apprehending it also, but if his sensibility is dull we cannot make him feel disgust. He recognizes that the action is abhorrent ; he wishes that all actions were so, if only he could make profit from them thereby ; he feels it better to have something in his purse. So nothing is achieved in general by such methods. Man is not so delicately made that he can be moved by objective grounds ; he is not endowed by nature with a spring which could be wound up to produce the desired result. But we can produce a *habitus*, which is not natural, but takes the place of nature, and is produced by imitation and oft-repeated practice. The various methods, however, for making us regard vice with abhorrence are falsely conceived. From its earliest infancy we ought to instil in the child an immediate hate and disgust of hateful and disgusting actions ; an immediate, not a mediated abhorrence, which has only a pragmatic usefulness ; an action should, therefore, be represented to the child not as forbidden or harmful but as in itself detestable. For instance, a child which tells lies should not be punished, but shamed : it should feel ashamed, contemptible, nauseated as though it had been bespattered with dirt. By repeated doses of such treatment we can inspire the child with such an abhorrence of vice as will become in him a *habitus*. If, however, he is punished instead—say, at school—he thinks to himself that once out of school he runs no risk of being punished and he will also try by jesuitical tricks to escape punishment. Again, some old people conceive the notion of becoming converted towards the end of their lives and think that they can thereby make amends for all past misdeeds and place themselves in the same position as if they had lived morally all their lives. Such people consider sudden death as the greatest misfortune. Education and religion ought, therefore, to aim at instilling an immediate aversion from evil conduct and an immediate predilection for moral conduct.

DE LITTERA LEGIS [1]

Littera legis is the connection of the law with the causes and grounds on which it rests. The best way to apprehend the sense of the law is to apprehend the principle from which the law is derived; but it is possible for us to determine the sense even without apprehending the principle. *Anima legis* is the true sense which the words bear in the law. The words have, of course, a sense of their own; but they may also have another sense, one that goes beyond the ordinary meaning of the words, and this is the *anima legis*. Thus, for instance, in the divine positive law regarding the Sabbath, the true sense of ' Sabbath ' is not rest in general, but solemn rest. *Anima legis*, however, when it bears the full meaning of 'the spirit of the law', means not the sense, but the impulsive ground. In every law, the action which it commands is conformable to the letter of the law, but the disposition from which the action proceeds is the spirit of the law; the action itself is the *littera legis pragmaticae*, the intention is the *anima legis moralis*. Pragmatic laws have no spirit; they demand no disposition, only actions. Moral laws, however, have a spirit; they demand disposition, and the action as such ought merely to be an expression of the disposition. To perform an action, therefore, without a good disposition is to comply with the letter of the law but not with its spirit. Divine and moral laws, regarded pragmatically, can be fulfilled only *quoad litteram*. Take, for example, a man who, nearing

[1] In the German edition this heading reads: ' Baumgarten speaks here *de Littera Legis.*' (*Trans.*)

the end of his days, thinks to himself that if God exists, He must reward all good actions and that he cannot, therefore, in his own interests employ his wealth to better advantage than by doing good with it, and he does so, but only with a view to earning God's reward. This is what the Bible refers to as the unrighteous Mammon, saying that the children of darkness are wiser than the children of light. Such a one complies with the moral law, but without the proper disposition; he thus fulfils the law *quoad litteram*. But the *anima legis moralis*, which demands a truly moral disposition, remains unfulfilled. The grounds of impulse to action are far from being immaterial. Only laws, therefore, which have a spirit are moral laws. Now that which has a spirit is, in general, an object of reason; but my own advantage is no object of reason, and therefore an action which is performed with this end in view, has no spirit.

In his discussion of law Baumgarten enters into much detail and explanation of mere expressions, but does not differentiate between the ethical and the legal. An obligation is ethical if the ground of Obligation lies in the nature of the action itself; it is legal if the ground of Obligation lies in the will of another person. We may say, therefore, that ethics differs from law in that :—

1. Its laws do not relate to other people, but only to God and to oneself.

2. Where it touches laws other than its own, the obligation to action does not arise from the *arbitrium* of some one else, but from the action itself.

3. The ground of impulse to satisfy our obligation is not compulsion, but free disposition or duty.

Compulsion is the external impulsive ground and, when it applies, the action belongs to the legal sphere; duty is the internal ground, and in this case the action is ethical. Legal Obligation does not concern itself with disposition, which does not matter to it so long as the action is performed. But in the case of ethical Obligation, the impulsive ground must be an inner one; the action must be done because it is proper that it should be done. We must, for instance, pay our debts not because we can be compelled but because it is right that we should.

Baumgarten discusses in this connexion transgression and observance of laws and injury to persons affected by our actions. We can injure a person, but not a law; a law can be transgressed. But injury is not a question for ethics, for we injure no man by failing to perform an ethical duty towards him. Injury consists in *oppositio juris alterius.*

Antinomy or opposition can arise in laws if they enunciate only the basis of Obligation; there can be no contrariety where the laws themselves express the obligation.

Baumgarten lays down three propositions which he regards as ethical axioms:

1. *Honeste vive.*
2. *Neminem laede.*
3. *Suum cuique tribue.*

We shall proceed to indicate the meaning of these statements, so far as they can rightfully be regarded as valid ethical axioms.

The first proposition—*vive honeste*—we may regard as an ordinary principle of ethics, for here the ground of impulse to fulfil one's obligation is derived, not from compulsion, but from the inner impulsive ground. *Honestas* is that quality and that conduct which makes a man honourable. The rule might, therefore, be construed to mean that we should do that which will make us Objects of respect and esteem. All our duties towards ourselves have such a reference to self-respect in our own eyes and favour in the eyes of others. The less inner worth a man has, the less esteem does he deserve. If we abuse others we excite hatred, but if we are worthless we earn contempt. The rule tells us that we should so conduct ourselves as to be worthy of honour—that our conduct if it were generally known should earn for us universal respect and esteem. Thus, for instance, to be guilty of unnatural sins is to dishonour humanity in one's own person; a man who commits such sins is not honourable, and if his conduct becomes generally known he is despised. For a man to be worthy of positive honour his actions must be meritorious, they must involve more than is strictly required of him; but so long as a man avoids doing what is shameful, he is not unworthy of honour;

he is honest, but honesty is not merit; it is the minimum of morality, because as soon as it is lacking in the least degree the man becomes a rogue.   Hence a country where honesty is held in high regard is in a bad state; were honesty not rare but a normal thing it would not be so highly regarded.   But only those actions are ethical which involve more than is strictly required.   If we so behave that we do no more than is required of us, we merely live honestly, but we do not on that account deserve honour; but if we do more than is strictly demanded, our action is worthy of honour, and we are then truly honourable men.   This particular proposition is, therefore, a possible principle of ethics.

The other two can be regarded as principles of legal obligation, for they relate to compulsory duties.   To say that we ought to give to each his own is as much as to say that we must give to a man that which he can forcibly claim from us.   The two propositions—*neminem laede*; *suum cuique tribue*—can be combined, because if I deprive a man of what is his own I injure him.   We can injure a man by omission or by commission, by not giving to him what is his own or by taking from him what belongs to him.   We can thus deprive a man of what is his either negatively or positively.   The first of these is the more important, for there is more in not taking what is another's than in not giving it him.   Injury consists in the action which violates another's law; if we injure a person, that person has a right to demand from me what is requisite in accordance with the universal laws of the will.

In ethics laws have a relation to the happiness of others; in the case of legal obligation they have a relation to the will of others.   *Ethice obligans respectu aliorum est felicitas aliorum, juridice obligans respectu aliorum est arbitrium aliorum.*   Ethical duties, however, presuppose as a prior condition the fulfilment of legal obligations. That obligation which flows from another's right must first be fulfilled, for so long as it remains unfulfilled we are, in being under legal Obligation, subject to another's will and are not free.   But to perform an ethical duty is to perform a free duty, and a man who is under legal Obligation must first free himself from it by discharging

it before he can go on to discharge the ethical duty
Many people leave undone their bounden duties and yet
think that they can perform those which will be accounted
to them for merit.   Such are the men who are guilty
of much injustice in the world, who rob their fellows
and then proceed to make testamentary bequests to
hospitals.   But a penetrating, iron voice cries out
against them that they have failed in their bounden
duties, and try as they may they cannot silence it by
would-be meritorious acts.   Such acts, indeed, aggravate
their guilt, for they are like bribes offered to the Supreme
Being to make good their offences.

It is not happiness, therefore, which is the chief ground
of impulse to all duties ; and, accordingly, to try to make
another happy against his will is to do him wrong.   It is
an act of violence to force another to be happy in one's
own way, though that is a pretext used, for example, by
the upper classes in their dealings with their dependents.

THE LAWGIVER

The distinction between moral and pragmatic laws is
that in the former it is the disposition and in the latter the
action which is required.   Governments, therefore, ordain
not dispositions, but only actions.   We can make pragmatic laws—that is obvious ; but can any man make
moral laws and so lay an injunction upon our dispositions,
which it is not in his power to control ?   Let us examine
this question.

A man who propounds that a law which is in accordance
with his will shall be binding on others, promulgates a
law, and is a lawgiver.   Except in the case of contingent
laws, the lawgiver is not their author ; he merely declares
that they are in accordance with his will.   It follows that
no one, not even God, can be the author of the laws of
morality, since they have no origin in will, but instead a
practical necessity.   If they were not necessary, it is conceivable that lying might be a virtue.   But the moral
laws can nevertheless be subject to a lawgiver.   There

can exist a being which has the power and authority to execute these laws, to declare that they are in accordance with his will, and to impose upon every one the obligation of acting in accordance with them. This being is therefore the lawgiver, though not the author of the laws. In the same way, God is in no sense the author of the fact that the triangle has three angles.

The spirit of moral laws is in the disposition. As these laws are in accordance with the divine will, they can at the same time be regarded as divine commandments. Further, having regard only to the actions which the laws require, we can look upon these laws as pragmatic laws of God also. Thus, for instance, the moral law demands that we should promote the happiness of all men ; God commands the same. If we act in accordance with the divine will and do good in order to receive God's rewards, our conduct does not spring from a moral disposition ; we comply with the divine will for the sake of reward ; we satisfy the divine law pragmatically, but we do fulfil the law, and though our disposition is not pure, inasmuch as we do what God wills us to do, we may hope for good results. But it is the disposition that God requires ; it is morality which is in conformity with His will, and His laws, being moral laws, impose a perfect Obligation. Conduct which accords with morality is in the highest measure in accordance with the divine will. We must, therefore, look upon God not as a pragmatic but as a moral lawgiver.

REWARD AND PUNISHMENT

We must draw a distinction between *praemium* and *merces*.

There are two kinds of *praemia, auctorantia* and *remuner-antia*. The former apply where the actions are done solely for the sake of a promised reward, where the action is motivated by the reward. The latter apply where the action proceeds solely from a good disposition, from pure morality, where it is not motivated by the reward. The former are inducements, the latter recompenses. It follows that *praemia auctorantia* are not, while *praemia remunerantia* are *moralia*, and that *praemia auctorantia* are *pragmatica*. If we are moved to do something for reasons of physical welfare, purely for the sake of the promised reward, the action has no morality; and the agent cannot expect *praemia remunerantia*, though he can expect *praemia auctorantia*. Actions, however, which result solely from good disposition and pure morality are qualified for *praemia remunerantia*.

Praemia auctorantia are often merely natural consequences or the promise of them. Thus, for instance, good health is a *praemium auctorans* of temperance, though we can also be of temperate habits on moral grounds. Again, when a man is honest because he gains advantage and earns approval by his honesty, his is also a *praemium auctorans*; if he is honest for moral reasons, he is qualified for a *praemium remunerans*. This latter type of *praemium* is greater than the other, for it implies harmony between action and morality, and it is this which is the most worthy of happiness. Similarly, *praemia moralia* must be greater than the *pragmatica*. The former have an eternal, the latter a determinate value. The morally minded man is qualified for an eternal reward and happiness because he is ever ready to do good deeds. It is not right for religion to represent its *praemia* as *auctorantia*, to tell us to be moral for the sake of future reward. No man can demand that God should reward and make him happy. He may hope for reward from the Supreme Being, he may expect that God will see to it that he does not suffer for his good deeds, but reward must not be the impulsive ground of his action. Man may hope for happiness, but this hope ought not to be his incentive, merely his consolation. The man who lives morally can hope to be rewarded with a cheerful spirit because of his morality, but reward ought not to be his impulsive ground, for no man can properly imagine his future happiness, no man knows in what it will consist, for this Providence has carefully hidden from us. If man were acquainted with happiness he would wish to attain it soon; instead, he desires to linger ever longer here

below; and though we paint ever so alluring a picture
of eternity and compare it with the miseries of this life, no
man wishes to reach it quickly; he thinks rather that he
will get there all in good time. And it is quite natural
that every one of us should have a greater appreciation
of our present life, which we can know and feel more
clearly. It is thus a useless proceeding to represent the
praemia as *auctorantia*; but to depict them as *remunerantia*
is not so; every man hopes for the latter. In fact, the
natural moral law implies such promises to every man who
is of good moral disposition, and such a man stands in no
need of having these *praemia remunerantia* recommended
to him or hearing their praises sung. Every righteous
man believes in them. No man can possibly be righteous
without having the hope, from the analogy of the physical
world, that righteousness must have its reward. He
believes in reward on the same ground that he believes
in virtue.

Merces is remuneration which we can rightfully claim
from some one. It is not the same thing as reward. My
expectation of remuneration is a demand for the payment
of a debt. We can have no claim for payment against
God. Whatsoever we do is done not for God's benefit,
but for our own: we do what we ought. But whilst we
cannot look for payment from God for services, we can
look forward to *praemia gratuita*. These rewards can
nevertheless be regarded as payment, particularly in so
far as they relate to our good deeds towards other people;
for God requites services to others to which those others
have no claim upon us, and He may be regarded as one
who pays men's debts. For services to others (there can
be no services to God, but only to other men) place those
others under a debt to us which they can in no way discharge and which God discharges for them. To quote
the Gospels: 'Inasmuch as ye have done it unto one
of the least of these my brethren, ye have done it unto
me.'

Thus we earn payment from others, but it is God who
recompenses us. We ought not, however, in this connexion to embrace a fanciful purity of ethical theory by
discarding all services; for God wants mankind to be

happy. He wants men to be made happy by men, and if only all men united to promote their own happiness we could make a paradise of Novaya Zemlya. God has set us on the stage where we can make each other happy. It rests with us, and us alone, to do so. Wretchedness and misery are our own fault. If a man be in distress, as so many of us are, it is not because God wills it so. God does not wish any one of us to be wretched; His purpose is that we should all unite in helping each other, and if a man is in distress, God leaves him in that state as a sign to his fellows who allow him to suffer though they could combine to help him. Accordingly, when Baumgarten tells us to do that which promises the greatest reward, he promulgates a rule which is obviously contrary to morality. To set up as an incentive that which offers the greatest reward is wrong; but it would be correct to say that we ought to do that which is *worthy* of the greatest reward.

Punishment in general is physical evil accruing from moral evil. It is either deterrent or else retributive. Punishments are deterrent if their sole purpose is to prevent an evil from arising; they are retributive when they are imposed because an evil has been done. Punishments are, therefore, a means of preventing an evil or of punishing it. Those imposed by governments are always deterrent. They are meant to deter the sinner himself or to deter others by making an example of him. But the punishments imposed by a being who is guided by moral standards are retributive.

Punishments appertain either to the lawgiver's justice or to his prudence. In the first case they are moral, in the second pragmatic. Moral punishments are imposed because a sin has been committed; they are *consectaria* of moral transgression. Those which are pragmatic are imposed in order that there should be no sin; they are a means of obviating transgression. Baumgarten calls these latter *poenae medicinales*; he calls the former either *correctivae* or *exemplares*. *Correctivae* are meant to improve the culprit: they are *animadversiones*. *Exemplares* are imposed as an example to others. All punishments imposed by sovereigns and governments are pragmatic; they are designed either to correct or to make an example.

Ruling authorities do not punish because a crime has been committed, but in order that crimes should not be committed. But apart from this actual punishment, every transgression has a penal desert for the reason that it has been committed. Punishment which must follow from the action by such a necessity is moral and therefore a *poena vindicativa*. Just so reward follows a good deed not in order to encourage to further good deeds, but because of the deed itself. If we compare rewards and punishments we notice that neither should be regarded as incentives to action. Just as rewards ought not to be the grounds for doing good deeds, so punishments ought not to be the grounds for avoiding evil deeds. If they are, a mean condition of mind tends to be set up, an *indoles abjecta*. This means, in the case of the man who is moved to the performance of good acts by the hope of reward, *indoles mercennaria*, and in the case of the man who is restrained from evil acts by fear of punishment, *indoles servilis*. The two together constitute the *indoles abjecta*. The impulsive ground ought to be moral. The ground for doing a good action should not lie in the reward but the action should be rewarded because it is good ; the ground for not doing an evil action should not lie in the punishment but the action should not be done, because it is evil. Reward and punishment are merely subjective incentives, to be used only when the objective ones are no longer effective, and they serve merely to make up for the lack of morality.

The Subject must first be habituated to morality. Before we speak to people of reward and punishment we must first try to develop the *indoles erecta*. The moral feeling must be enlivened so that the Subject can be swayed by moral Motives. If this fails, we must then have recourse to the subjective incentives of reward and punishment. A man who is rewarded for good conduct will repeat that conduct not because it is good, but because it is rewarded ; one who is punished for evil conduct will hate not the conduct but the punishment ; he will repeat the evil deed and try with jesuitical craftiness to escape punishment. It is wrong, therefore, for religion to preach that men should avoid doing evil in order to escape eternal punishment; such preaching will lead to wicked conduct, for men will think that they can escape punishment in the long run by a sudden conversion. Nevertheless, reward and punishment can serve indirectly as a means of moral training. If a man does good for the sake of reward, he will gradually acquire the habit of good deeds and will ultimately do them regardless of reward and merely because they are good. Similarly, a man who refrains from doing evil because of fear of punishment will in the long run get accustomed to it and will feel that it is better to leave such things undone. A drunkard who gives up drink because of the harm it does to him will ultimately acquire the habit of sobriety and will come to see that it is better to be temperate than to be a drunkard. Rewards are an even better means for inculcating good conduct than are punishments for inculcating the avoidance of evil. Reward is pleasant, and we can take pleasure in the law which promises a pleasant result provided we act in a certain way; but we cannot love a law which merely threatens punishment. Rewards are thus more in harmony with morality than are punishments. Love is a stronger ground of impulse to performance. It is, therefore, better in religion to begin with reward rather than with punishment.

Punishments must be in keeping with nobility of mind, with *indoles erecta*. They must not be insulting or contemptuous; otherwise they induce an ignoble type of character.

DE IMPUTATIONE

To impute responsibility is to judge, in accordance with certain practical laws, how far an action is due to the free agency of a person. Responsibility presupposes free agency and a law. We can attribute an action to a person without holding that person accountable for it. We can, for instance, attribute certain actions to a lunatic or to a drunken man, but we cannot hold them accountable for them, for they are not free agents. The drunkard can, to be sure, be held responsible for his drunkenness when he is sober, but not for his actions when in drink.

A deed is a free action which falls under the law. Now if I have respect to the deed my imputation of responsibility will be *imputatio facti* ; if to the law, it will be *imputatio legis.*

In the case of *imputatio facti* we have to notice the *momenta facti,* that is to say, the manifold in the deed, which is the ground of imputation. These *momenta* are *elementa* of the ground, parts of the sufficient reason ; so that we say that *in facto* are the *momenta* of imputation. These *momenta* are divisible into *essentialia* and *extra essentialia.* The *momenta essentialia* must first be collected ; when all the *momenta essentialia in facto* are determined, we have the *species facti,* all that expressly appertains to the *factum.* The *extra essentialia facti* are not *momenta facti,* and therefore are not included in the *species facti.*

Imputatio facti does not necessarily imply also *imputatio legis.* Thus, for instance, when a man has killed another it does not necessarily follow that he has murdered him. The first question which arises is whether he has in fact done the deed. If he is also to be held responsible for the *factum* before the law, then he has a double responsibility. The question of legal responsibility is whether the action falls under this or that practical law. But can we hold a man responsible for something which he does on the authority of the law ? Can, for instance, a general be adjudged accountable for the death of enemy soldiers on the field of battle ? Possibly for their death, but not for murder. In so far as he is not a free agent, but is coerced by the law, he is not responsible : responsibility for the action, regarded as a legal action, lies with the lawgiver ; but in so far as the general acts as a free agent he is accountable.

Generally speaking, responsibility is either imputed as merit (*in meritum*) or as offence (*in demeritum*). A person can be held responsible or otherwise for the effects and consequences of an action.

RESPONSIBILITY FOR CONSEQUENCES OF ACTIONS

If we do either more or less than is required of us we can be held accountable for the consequences, but not otherwise—not if we do only what is required, neither more nor less. If all the good that we do is just what is required and no more, the consequences of our actions cannot be adjudged to our credit. If, for instance, I discharge a money debt and the lender employs the money which I pay him so that it brings him a large fortune, I can· claim no credit for the consequences : I did only what was required of me, and there is no surplus in my action which could be accounted to me for merit. At the same time, if we do just what we ought and no less, any untoward consequences are in no way our fault and cannot be debited to us ; we cannot be held responsible for them. On the other hand, if we do either more or less than we need, the consequences can be imputed to us, either as merit or as demerit. Assume, for instance, that I lend a friend money and it brings him a fortune : I have done more than could be required of me, and I can claim credit for the results of my action. On the other hand, if I owe money and I do not pay my debt when I ought, then if my creditor goes bankrupt in consequence, it is my fault : I did less than I ought to have done, and blame can be laid at my door. But if I do just exactly what is required of me, the consequences are neither my fault, nor are they to my credit. If a man says to me that had I at such and such a time advanced him a certain sum of money it would have prevented misfortune befalling him, he is wrong in imputing to me any responsibility for his misfortune, for I was under no obligation to lend him the money. So far as a man is fulfilling an obligation, he is not free. What he does the law obliges him to do. If, however, he acts against his obligation, if he does less than he ought, he must bear the responsibility ; for in that case again he acts freely, in defiance, indeed, of the law which lays the obligation upon him. He then abuses his freedom, and can be held legally responsible for all the consequences; for to act in contravention of one's indebtedness is once again to exercise freedom.

Juridice, I do not impute *in demeritum* the consequences of an action which a person is obliged to perform, because in such circumstances he has ceased to be free. He is responsible for the *factum* in itself, but not for the illegitimacy of the *factum*. In his moral actions, however, man is a free agent and is, therefore, liable for consequences of actions done, but not for consequences of actions left undone, for in the latter case he is leaving undone something which he is not required to do, and this cannot be reckoned as an action. Another's misfortune, for instance, resulting from a refusal by me to lend him money, cannot be laid to my account, because I was under no obligation to lend to him. But leaving undone what we are required to do is an action for which I can be held responsible. We ought, for example, to pay our debts: if we omit to do so, our omission is an action for which we are accountable. Thus moral omissions are completely inadequate; but legal omissions are actions and can give rise to responsibility, for they are failures to do what I can be compelled by law to do. But in the moral sphere compulsion has no place; no one can compel us to acts of kindness or charity. Thus moral omissions and their consequences can never be imputed, but legal omissions can. Conversely, moral acts of commission with their consequences can be imputed, but legal acts of commission cannot, since they are obligatory acts.

In a word, the key to the imputation of responsibility for consequences is freedom.

GROUNDS OF *IMPUTATIO MORALIS*

State law as well as ethical law involves *imputatio moralis*, which may be either *in meritum* or *in demeritum*. The observance of the law of the State and the transgression of the ethical law can be imputed neither *in meritum* nor *in demeritum* respectively. If, for instance,

I pay a legal debt, I do only what I can be compelled by law to do, and I have done no more than is required of me. It follows that my observance of the law *cum omnibus consectariis* cannot be imputed to me *in meritum.* If I transgress an ethical law, I have left undone something that I cannot be compelled to do, and to leave undone something which no law can compel us to do is no action, and therefore no wrongdoing. The transgression of an ethical law, therefore, cannot be imputed *in demeritum.* Still less can it be imputed *in meritum.* Thus if I refuse to lend a man money and the result is that he is encouraged to industry, the satisfactory consequences of my refusal cannot be imputed to me *in meritum.* Conversely, the transgression of the laws of the State and the observance of the ethical laws must in every case be imputed *in demeritum* and *in meritum* respectively. To transgress a law of the state is to omit to do that which we can be compelled to do and so to do less than is required of us. Consequently it will be assigned to me *in demeritum.* It follows that in State law there can be no question of *meritum* either by way of reward or, much less, of punishment, for actions done in accordance with it ; in ethical laws, however, as these are not coercive, there can. To comply with an ethical law is at all times meritorious ; to omit to do so is never a demerit. Any *meritum* invariably involves positive consequences—reward or punishment. No such consequences accrue either from observance of State laws or from transgression of ethical laws. There is no *meritum,* and so no reward, in the one case, and no *demeritum,* and so no punishment, in the other. If I comply with a law of the State by discharging a debt, for example, the consequences are purely negative ; in the instance quoted I avoid being summoned before a judge. But if I transgress such a law, the consequences are positive : I incur punishment. Similarly, if I comply with an ethical law the consequence is positive, namely, reward. Thus the observance of laws of the State carries with it no positive consequence of reward, and the transgression of ethical laws carries with it no positive consequence of punishment.

The above remarks regarding imputation are only valid in respect of other men and not in respect of God.

IMPUTATIO FACTI

Facta juridice necessaria are not free and cannot therefore be imputed. But *facta* which contravene the law can be imputed. Such actions are free; they are, in fact, an abuse of our freedom to act against the law. Ethically it is the other way about. We cannot be held responsible for *facta* which are not in accordance with the ethical law because omission to do something which we are not bound to do is no action. Ethical laws are not coercive; State laws are. Actions for which we can be held to account are, therefore, legally only those which are evil and ethically only those which are good.

DEGREES OF RESPONSIBILITY

The degree of responsibility depends on the degree of freedom. Freedom involves capacity to act, and in addition, cognizance of the impulsive ground and objective character of the action. These are the subjective conditions of freedom, and in their absence responsibility cannot be imputed. If a child destroys something useful, we cannot hold it to account because it does not recognize the objective character of the action. There are, however, various degrees in which responsibility can be imputed. Whatever appertains to freedom can be imputed to us, whether it arises directly through our freedom, or is derived indirectly from it. A drunken man cannot be held responsible for his drunken acts; he can, however, for his drunkenness. The causes which make it impossible to impute responsibility to a person for his actions, may themselves be imputable to him in a lower degree. In imputing responsibility we must consider impediments and conditions. The greater the obstacles to action which we

must overcome, the more accountable we are for the
action ; the less an action results from our freedom, the
less responsible we are for it. The degree of morality of
an action ought not to be confused with the degree of
responsibility for the *factum*. If a man kills another in a
fit of jealous temper his deed is not as evil as (though as
factum it may be more heinous than) that of a man who
in cold blood and of malice prepense encompasses the
death of another. The more I have to force myself to
do an action, the more obstacles I have to overcome in
doing it, and the more wilfully I do it, the more it is to
be accounted to me ; and for that reason it is all the less
accounted to me if I leave it undone. If, for instance,
a starving man steals something from the dining-room,
the degree of his responsibility is diminished by the fact
that it would have required great self-restraint for him
not to do it. But seeing that we ought to restrain our
appetites, is this to be pleaded in diminution of our degree
of responsibility ? Would not this lead to extraordinary
results ? We must for this purpose draw a distinction
between natural and lustful appetites. We may be gentler
in attributing responsibility in the case of the former
than in that of the latter. Sensuality is a thing which
can be eradicated ; we can prevent it taking deep root.
If, therefore, a man does a thing because sensuality drives
him to it he must be held more responsible than when he
is driven by hunger. At the same time the greater the
fight a man puts up against his natural inclinations the
more it is to be imputed to him for merit. Hence it is
that virtue is more meritorious in us than it is in angels
who have fewer obstacles to overcome. The more a man
is driven to action by external forces, the less is his
responsibility ; but if he overcome the external pressure
and does not act in accordance with it, his merit is the
greater. There are *merita* and *demerita conatus*, along with
which we may reckon *merita* and *demerita propositi*. Many
people propose to do something and reckon the intention
as a merit in themselves. But no action can be imputed
as *propositum*, since it is not yet an action. As *conatus*
it can, for that is already an action. The conditions in the
Subject are complete, his forces are expended, although

through *their* insufficiency, there is a failure in the event.
Since it is only from the result that we can infer the
sufficiency of the agent's forces, and so cannot know
whether there actually was a *conatus*, but an insufficiency
of power to execute the attempted action, courts of justice
do not impute the *conatus* in the way that ethical laws
do.   Take, for example, the case of a man who enters a
room with the intention to kill and is caught with a dagger
in his hand but before carrying his plan into execution.
The *conatus* is there and yet in the eyes of the law he is
not a murderer.   The reason is that it is often not possible
to regard the *conatus* as an *actus*.   It may happen that a
man conceives such a wicked purpose in his heart, that
the *conatus* is there, but that when it comes to the point
of carrying it out, he is appalled at his own dastardly
intention, shrinks from it and changes his mind.   Since
proof of this is impossible, the judge chooses the course
which will most certainly ensure that innocence shall not
be punished.   Morally, however, a complete *propositum* is as
good as the executed deed.   Only the *propositum* must be
such that it could be carried out in practice unaltered,
because it often happens that the *propositum* is changed
before its execution.   It may happen, for instance, that
I make up my mind to be annoyed with a friend and to
be rude to him when we next meet, but when in fact we
do meet I change my mind.

The man for whom a certain action has become a
necessity through habit is called a *consuetudinarius*.
Habit makes an action easy until at last it becomes a
necessity.   Such necessity as a result of habit, because it
fetters our will, diminishes our responsibility ; yet the
actus through which the habit was acquired, must be
imputed to us.   If, however, those actions were not of
his volition his responsibility is less.   A man, for instance,
who is brought up by gipsies until the habit of evil conduct
has become a necessity, is responsible in a lesser degree.
Nevertheless, habit is proof of frequent repetition of the
action and so increases the responsibility to be imputed.
A man who by frequent good deeds acquires the habit
of doing good increases his merit.   The same applies to
wicked deeds and the increase of demerit.   Accordingly,

we should be held less responsible for habits which are innate than for those which we acquire. Habits which by repeated excitements have become a necessity are a proof of misdemeanours and imply so much the more demerit.

We now come to the last two considerations which limit imputability, namely, the weakness and the infirmity of human nature. When we talk of the weakness of human nature we mean its lack of the degree of moral goodness required to make its actions adequate to the moral law. Its infirmity is not merely a deficiency in moral goodness, but rather the presence in it of strong principles and motives to evil action. Morality consists in this, that an action should arise from the impulsive ground of its own inner goodness, and this is a matter of moral purity (*rectitudo moralis*). The supreme ground of impulse to action is therefore *rectitudo moralis*. That it is so is well appreciated by the understanding. Nevertheless this impulsive ground has no driving force. Moral perfection has indeed the approbation of our judgment, but because this impulsive ground is the creation of the understanding, it has not the strong driving force of the motives of sensibility. It is in this deficiency of moral goodness and *rectitudo* that the weakness of human nature consists. But we should be on our guard against becoming hypercritical about it, against probing too deeply into its incapacity to attain moral purity. Those who are for ever on the look-out for moral impurities in their actions tend to lose confidence in their ability to do good and moral actions. They convince themselves that they are too weak and that morality is beyond them. We must rather believe that *rectitudo moralis* can be a strong impulsive ground of our actions. The human soul is not altogether devoid of all impulsive grounds of pure morality. Let, for instance, some poor wretch come to us with his tale of sorrow and we are moved to pity and help him, though a written request from him would not have achieved the same result. Again, a traveller who sees people starving by the roadside and gives them alms is not actuated by any self-interest or considerations of honour : he is a stranger to them and to the place and will soon be miles away ; he does it from the inner goodness of the action. There is, therefore, that in our heart which is morally pure though it has not a complete sufficiency of driving force to contend against the impulses of our sensibility. But the judgment upon the moral purity of actions attracts to and connects with itself, through association, many grounds of impulse to purity, so becoming a stronger spur to our activity, until this becomes a habit with us. We ought not, therefore, to be on the look-out for blemishes and weaknesses in the lives, for instance, of men such as Socrates. The practice is not only useless but harmful. It provides us with examples of moral imperfection and enables us to flatter ourselves whatever our own moral imperfection. Eagerness to discover faults in others betrays malice and envy of the morality we see shining in others when we are conscious of its absence in ourselves.

The rule which applies in our consideration of the weakness of human nature is this. Moral laws must never take human weakness into account, but must be enunciated in their perfect holiness, purity and morality, without any regard to man's actual constitution. This is an important point to notice. The moral laws of the ancient philosophers were not pure because they made no demands on man beyond those which human nature could perform. They thus accommodated their laws to the capacity of human nature. Where they went beyond these limitations and enjoined abnormal courage or munificence, the incentive was not the pure moral judgment, but pride or honour. Only since the time of the Gospel has the full purity and holiness of the moral law been recognized, although indeed it dwells in our own reason. The moral law must not be indulgent, but must be the expression of supreme purity and holiness, and in so far as man is weak and unable to comply unaided with the holy law he must look for divine aid to make up for the deficiency and to render him capable of compliance with the law. The law in itself must be pure and holy; for the reason that it must be a model, a pattern, a standard, and as such it must be exact and precise or it could not be a basis of judgment. It is, therefore, our highest duty to present the moral law in all its purity and holiness, as it is the height of transgression to detract a whit from its purity.

As regards the infirmity of human nature we notice that the fault lies not merely in the absence of positive good, but in the presence of positive evil. Now all moral evil springs from freedom; otherwise it would not be *moral* evil. However prone by nature we may be to evil actions, the latter have their source in our freedom. For that reason they are attributed to us as vices. The first principle in regard to the infirmity of human nature is this. In judging actions I must pay no heed to the infirmity of human nature. The law in us must be holy, and the sentence of this law must be just, which means that the penalties of the law must be applied to the actions of men with all exactness. *Fragilitas humana* cannot be a ground for lessening our responsibility *coram foro humano interno*. The judge within us is just. He takes the action for what it is and makes no allowance for human defectiveness, if only we have the will to listen for his voice and do not stifle it. Assume, for instance, that on the spur of the moment I give offence to some one by a hasty word: I cannot dismiss it from my mind and I long for an opportunity to make amends; try as I may I cannot rid myself of reproaches; I may find all manner of excuses which would satisfy an earthly judge, I may urge that I am only human and that it is the easiest thing in the world to let a word slip, but the judge within us will not be satisfied; it is nothing to him that human nature is frail, his concern is only with the action as it is. This makes it clear that there are in human nature purely moral grounds of impulse, and that it is not necessary to decry human nature so sorely for its weakness. *Fragilitas* and *infirmitas humana* ought to be taken into account in judging of the actions of others, but not by way of excuses for our own misdeeds. As a pragmatic lawgiver and judge man must give due consideration to the *infirmitas* and *fragilitas* of his fellows and remember that they are only human, but as far as his own actions are concerned he must leave *fragilitas* and *infirmitas* out of account.

Imputatio valida is an imputation of responsibility with legal force whereby the *effectus a lege determinata* is brought into operation through the *judicium imputans*. We can judge all men : each of us can judge ; but we cannot enforce our judgments, for our *imputatio* is not *valida* ; it has no authority to bring into effect any consequences *a lege determinata*. A judgment which has the authority to bring into operation the *consectarium* determined by the law is legally valid : it has legal sanction and is enforceable ; but to make it effective, that is to enforce the consequences, it requires force. Since therefore no judgment has legal validity apart from force, there must exist a force to put into execution the consequences determined by law. He who has the authority to pass legally valid judgments and also the power to enforce them is a judge. The office of judge requires, therefore, two things : authority to pass judgments according to law which have judicial validity, and the power to enforce those judgments. A judge has the authority to decide whether a *factum certum casus datae legis* is before him, but he must also be able to apply the law to the *factum valide*. He must therefore have the power to see that the law is satisfied.

A person with the authority and the power to make valid judgments and to enforce them constitutes a *forum*. This person may be *vel physica vel moralis*, that is to say, either a single individual or a number of individuals considered as one.

A *forum* is *competens* in respect of the relation of its authority and power to specific persons and specific types of *facta*. Different persons, as well as different actions, fall to be dealt with by different *fora*.

A judge is not competent (*non competens*) either if his understanding is inadequate or if he lacks the authority to judge because it has been taken from him, that is to say, abrogated, or if the *factum* does not fall under the law with which his authority deals, even though he is a properly constituted judge, or if he is unable to procure justice for any one.

There are two kinds of *forum* : the *forum externum*, which is the *forum humanum*, and the *forum internum*, which is the *forum conscientiae*. This *forum internum* we couple with the *forum divinum*, because it is only *per conscientiam* that our actions can be assessed before the *forum* of God. The *forum internum* is therefore, in this life, the *forum divinum*. A *forum* ought to exercise compulsion : its judgment ought to have the force of law : it ought to be able to bring about compulsorily the *consectaria* of the law. We are possessed of the faculty of judging between right and wrong in our own actions as well as in those of others ; this faculty lies in our understanding. We also have a faculty of desire and aversion, of judging what pleases or displeases in ourselves and in others : this is the faculty of moral feeling. Given the moral judgment and the moral law, we find in ourselves yet a third thing, an instinct, an involuntary and irresistible impulse in our nature, which compels us to pass a judgment with the force of law upon our actions, visiting us with an inner pain when we do evil and an inner pleasure when we do good, in accordance with the relation our actions bear to the law. This is the conscience, the instinct to judge and pass sentence upon our actions. It is an instinct, not a faculty. Were it a voluntary faculty it could not force us and could not be a tribunal. If it is to be an inner tribunal it must have the power to compel us to bring our actions involuntarily to judgment and to pass sentence in our hearts, condemning or acquitting ourselves. We all have the faculty of speculative judgment at our will's discretion, but there is something else within us which compels us to judge our actions, which points us to the law, which forces us to appear before the judge, which passes sentence upon us whether we will or no, and which is therefore a true judge.' This *forum internum* is a *forum divinum*. It judges us by our very dispositions ; and we can form no conception of the *forum divinum* other than this, that we are bound to be our own judges in terms of our dispositions. Actions and dispositions which can have no outward manifestation, fall to be judged by the *forum internum*. The *forum externum humanum* can have no jurisdiction over dispositions. Conscience is, therefore, the representative of the *forum divinum*. Ethical actions are not within the competence of the *forum externum humanum*, because external compulsion, which is all that an external judge possesses, is not their sanction. His sanctions and proofs of fact must be externally valid. External grounds of account-ability are those which derive their validity from external universal laws. Such *imputationes* as have no externally valid grounds, appertain not to the *forum externum* but to the *internum*. Attempts are made to use the *forum internum* in the *forum externum* in cases where externally valid grounds are wanting. A man is compelled to take an oath. He is thus haled before the *forum divinum*, before which in his heart he has already appeared ; forced to recognize himself as liable to its penalties, if he is guilty, and to declare the same publicly. The *forum internum*, his liability before it, are already facts ; yet the declaration makes a greater impression upon him. Man may believe that if he makes no declaration upon oath he is not punishable *in foro divino*, but he will in fact be punished whether or not he says openly that he under-takes to be punished if he is in the wrong. Thus for a man to swear, calling down upon himself some dire calamity if what he swears to is not true is quite pre-posterous. It is absurd, for instance, to say, ' May I be struck with a palsy if it isn't true.' It depends in no way upon our will whether we are struck with a palsy. The Gospel therefore well says, ' Swear not by Heaven, for it is not thine, neither by thy head, for thou canst not dispose of one hair thereof.' [1]

But however this may be, the procedure is adapted to human nature in that it presents to man's mind a picture of the danger of divine condemnation.

Baumgarten goes on to speak of several matters, such as legal process and sentence, which need only be referred to.

Legal process is a methodical *imputatio legis*, whereby, *per actionem civilem* I seek to secure my rights *in foro externo*. Legal deeds are totalities of imputation. The sentence is the judgment.

---

[1] St. Matthew 5, vv. 34 and 36. Kant misquotes the passage.

ETHICS

INTRODUCTORY OBSERVATIONS

FOR every action discrimination supplies the necessity, but it is an impulsive ground which leads to performance. We may act from grounds of compulsion or from those of the intrinsic goodness of the action. In the first case the necessity is legal, in the second ethical.

Ethics studies the intrinsic quality of actions; jurisprudence whether they are lawful. Ethics concerns itself solely with disposition, but jurisprudence pays no regard to this, treating only of authority and compulsion. Ethics is not, however, excluded from the legal field, but expects that even those actions to which we are bound by law should be performed by us not because we have to but because they are in themselves right and we are so disposed. Even legal actions have, therefore, their ethical aspect (in so far as the ground of impulse is ethical) and in this respect ethics covers the field of jurisprudence; but there is a distinct difference between the legal and ethical aspects of an action. Ethics is not a science which excludes coercive laws and coerced actions: it includes them, but examines them from the point of view not of compulsion but of inner quality. Ethics is philosophy of disposition; and as dispositions are the cardinal principles of action and correlate actions and their grounds of impulse, ethics is a practical philosophy.

It is not easy to give an explanation of the exact meaning of disposition. Take, for instance, a man who pays his debts. He may be swayed by the fear of being punished if he defaults, or he may pay because it is right and proper that he should. In the first case his conduct has *rectitudo juridica* and marks him as a good citizen, but it is only in the latter case that it has the *rectitudo ethica* which constitutes him a good man; for then he acts from or on account of the inner goodness of the action, and his disposition is moral.   This is an important consideration in matters of religion.   There are those who regard God as the supreme lawgiver and lord who demands strict compliance with His laws and does not look to the ground of impulse.   To them the only difference between God and a worldly judge is that God has a better insight into our actions and is less easily deceived.   They comply with God's laws for fear of punishment, and their conduct is of course good, but its goodness is a *rectitudo juridica* only. To be ethical our conduct must involve a belief that God is holy and that He demands good dispositions from us, so that we abstain from wrongdoing not from any fear of incurring punishment but because the action is inherently abhorrent.   The Teacher of the Gospel lays stress upon this.   He calls upon man to conduct himself ethically by telling him that in all that he does he should act from love of God.   But to love God is to do his bidding willingly and from a good disposition.   The topic of loving God will be discussed more fully in a subsequent part of this book. From what has been said, however, it follows that ethics is not merely a philosophy of the good act but of the good disposition.

Ethics is sometimes described as the theory of virtue. Virtue consists in *rectitudo actionum ex principiis internis*. A man who complies with coercive laws is not necessarily virtuous.   To be virtuous man must, to be sure, respect the law and be punctilious in his observance of human rights ; but virtue goes beyond this, to the disposition from which the action, which possesses *rectitudo juridica*, arises.   Virtue, therefore, consists not in *rectitudo juridica*, but in dispositions.   A man whose actions have *rectitudo juridica* may be a good citizen without necessarily being a virtuous man.   Consequently we must beware of arguing from the *rectitudo juridica* of external acts to the goodness of the disposition.   Take, for instance, the man whose word is his bond.   It may so be that he is scrupulously honest for fear of punishment or because it pays him best.

He may argue that honesty is the best policy, because to
have a name for reliability and trustworthiness is all-
important to his credit as a business-man: people will
trust him and his word will then be as good as his bond.
Such a man keeps his word. His action is in itself good.
But if we ask whether he has fulfilled the law, the answer
is a double one. He has, but not morally. If we consider
the moral necessity of an action which is legally binding,
we see that the action may be performed either in a legal
or in an ethical sense. In the former case, the action is
conformable to the law, but not to the disposition. Thus
we say that the law of the State falls short of morality.
It is only for ethical laws that morality is an absolute
requisite, since even if the laws of the State are morally
necessary, their ground of impulse is still compulsion, and
not disposition.

The idea of virtue hardly suffices to express the nature
of moral goodness. Virtue signifies strength in self-control and self-mastery in respect of the moral disposition.
I am here concerned with the first source of disposition,
leaving out of consideration a point which will become
clear only in the sequel. The words *Sitten* and *Sittlichkeit*
have been used to express the idea of morality. *Sitten*,
however, is a comprehensive term for the proprieties.
Virtue implies a certain degree of this social goodness
(*sittliche Bonität*), a certain self-control and self-mastery.
Nations like the French may have *Sitten*, a code of social
propriety, without having virtue ; others may have virtue
without such a code. (*Conduite* means good form in
social behaviour.) A science of social ethics (*Sitten*) is
not yet a theory of virtue : and virtue in turn is not yet
morality. But because we have no other word to express
the nature of morality, we confuse morality and social
propriety (*Sittlichkeit*) ; virtue we cannot so substitute
for morality.

The spirit of the moral law commands the disposition, its
letter commands action. In ethics, therefore, we enquire
how the spirit of the moral law is fulfilled, and pay no heed
at all to actions. Ethics may lay down laws of social propriety, lenient laws which are framed to meet the weakness
of human nature, and so accommodate itself to humanity

that it requires of men no more than they can perform. On the other hand, Ethics may also be rigorous in its demand for the highest perfection of social morality. The moral law must likewise be vigorous, and must clearly express its own condition of lawfulness. It must not indulge man and make allowance for his limited capacity, since it contains the standard of moral perfection, and the standard must be exact, invariable and absolute. A rule of ethics must, like a rule in mathematics, be defined with theoretical accuracy and irrespective of how far man can observe it. The centre of a circle, or any mathematical point, is defined, but it cannot actually be made small enough to comply with the definition. So it is with rules of ethics. These are measuring-rules of action and ought to set before us the standard of moral necessity. They ought not to be trimmed in consideration of man's capacity. Any system of ethics which accommodates itself to what man can do corrupts the moral perfection of humanity. The moral law must be pure. But its purity must not be that of the fantastic theologian or moralist who puzzles his mind over things that do not matter and with sophistry and needless subtlety tries to extract some moral essence from them. Ethics has no room for such purism. Its purity lies in its principles. It is the moral law that must be pure. The moral law of the Gospel, unlike that of any of the ancient philosophers, has this purity; and although the Gospels many times and oft repeat that external observance (*cultus externus*) is of no importance and that moral purity is all that matters, there were at the time of Christ many brilliant Pharisees to whom strict observance was everything. The Gospels do not suffer even the least imperfection : they are stringent and pure and demand unrelentingly compliance with the law. A law such as this is holy. It does not ask too much of us in order to be satisfied if we observe one-half of its demands, and it is apparent to each and all of us that its ground lies in the understanding, so that each of us can find proof of its truth in himself. This punctiliousness, subtlety, strictness and purity of the moral law we call *rectitudo*, and we find constant tokens of it in our own experience. Assume, for instance, that we happen to find ourselves among strangers, and that we unwittingly offend some one : then though we shall soon be leaving and so have nothing to fear, we nevertheless reproach ourselves for what we have done, and we can neither avoid these reproaches nor alter the law which prompts them. The man who conceives the moral law in such a way that it allows his feeble conduct to pass muster, who fashions lenient precepts for himself, we call a *latitudinarius*. Our ethics must be precise and holy. The moral law is holy not because it has been revealed to us. Its holiness is original and our own reason is capable of revealing it to us. This fact makes us ourselves judges of the revelation, since holiness is the highest, most perfect good which we can derive from ourselves, from our understanding.

Baumgarten divides ethics into the cajoling and the sullen.

The impulsive grounds of morality must be appropriate to it. Motives must be so united to morality that they harmonize with it, that is to say, they must have an equal dignity. Action as such is immaterial : it is the source of it which matters. It is ethical cajolery to consider virtuous behaviour as a refined way of making the best of life. Virtuous conduct is not necessarily the acme of ethics. Virtue can undoubtedly be a rule of prudence and a source of satisfaction. Thus many dispense charity to the poor because it gives them pleasure to see the joy on the faces of the recipients. But if we do good because of the advantage or pleasure which we derive from the act, the ground of impulse is not moral. Many people boast of their good deeds though the reasons which move them are of the wrong kind. A thing which is good does not need bolstering up on false grounds. Virtue is good in itself and does not need false support. It is, for instance, false that virtue brings with it many pleasures in this life. A virtuous disposition is just as likely to increase the pain of this life. A man may know that he is virtuous, and yet find himself in straitened circumstances. Were he not virtuous, he could bear it better, in the knowledge that he deserved to suffer. As it is, he is virtuous and hungry, and he cannot still his hunger with his virtue.

Ethics must not be commended by such cajoleries.

Reverence accompanies her when she is presented in her purity, and she becomes the object of supreme approbation and supreme desire. Cajoleries only weaken, instead of strengthening the motive. Morality must not lower herself. Her own nature must be her recommendation. All else, even divine reward, is as nothing beside her, for only morality makes us worthy of happiness. Moral grounds of impulse ought to be presented by themselves and for themselves : everything else should be kept separate, even motives of benevolence. Heretofore morality has been comparatively ineffective, because it has never been purely expounded. Moral philosophers and ministers of religion have so far failed to present and recommend it unalloyed. And yet it gains when so presented ; the appeal of its own intrinsic worth is greater than when it is alloyed with sensuous excitation and inducement. Coquetry debauches instead of commending itself, and when ethics plays the flirt she courts the same fate. Beauty, simple and modest, is infinitely more appealing than all the arts and allurements of coquetry. It is the same with moral goodness. It is more potent and appealing in its simple purity than when it is bedecked with allurements, whether of reward or of punishment. The lesson of morality must be learnt : it ought not to be mixed with solicitations and sensuous incentives ; it must be taught apart and free from these ; but when the rules of morality in their absolute purity have been firmly grasped, when we have learnt to respect and value them, then, and only then, may such motives be brought into play. They ought not, however, to be adduced as reasons for action, for they are not moral and the action loses in morality on their account ; they ought to serve only as *subsidiaria motiva* calculated to overcome the inertia of our nature in the face of purely intellectual conceptions. Having done their work of overcoming this inertia, they ought then to give way to the truly genuine moral motives. In other words, the function of the sensuous mot ves should be merely that of overcoming greater sensuous obstacles so that understanding can again bear rule. But to mix inextricably moral and non-moral considerations is a terrible perversion of which many are still guilty.

The man who grasps the pure moral idea finds it extraordinarily effective : it incites him more than any sensuous stimulus. This helps greatly in our efforts to command moral conduct and should be particularly borne in mind in the education of children. In this way men become capable of a pure judgment and a pure taste in questions of good conduct. If we mix it with other drinks we are unable to taste the pure wine. So it is with morality. If we are to appreciate it, we must keep it pure and free from admixtures which are only in the way.

Opposed to this coquettish ethics is the morose ethics which is also called misanthropy. This misanthropic ethics sets moral conduct in opposition to all pleasures, as the coquettish ethics mingled the two. The ethics of moroseness assumes that all amenities of life and all pleasures of the senses are opposed to morality. It might seem at first that this type of ethics is more mistaken than the other, but such is not the case. It bases itself on man's pride and is productive of lofty deeds. For the sake of one noble deed man is expected by it to sacrifice all amenities of life. It goes wrong, of course, in holding that pleasure and morality are inconsistent with each other. Nevertheless, its very error in this respect leads it to differentiate between morality and the pleasures of life, and this separation between morality and pleasure. must be accounted greatly to its credit. If, therefore, ethics had to choose between the one kind of error and the other, it were better if the choice fell on the error of the ethics of moroseness. It sacrifices, to be sure, many charms and amenities, but these would in any case be dispensed with as inconsistent with the refined and loftier taste to which it would give rise. There is something which commands the highest respect in this misanthropical ethics. Its morality is strict and precise. But its hostility to pleasure is a mistake. To correct it, we must remember that morality and happiness are two elements of the Supreme Good, that they differ in kind, and that, whilst they must be kept distinct, they stand in necessary relation to one another. The moral law contains within it a natural promise of happiness : it tells me that if I conduct myself so as to be worthy of happiness I may hope for it ; here are the springs of morality and morality thus has a necessary relation to happiness. The contrary is also true. There is no promise of happiness to any one except by way of moral conduct, so that happiness has a bearing on morality. Happiness is not a ground, not a principle of morality, but a necessary corollary of it.

The point in favour of the ethics of cajolery is that it combines happiness (which, however, is but a natural consequence of morality) with morality ; that in favour of morose ethics is its insistence on pride ; it is proud in its renunciation of all happiness; but to renounce happiness is to differentiate it from morality in a transcendental and unnatural way.

Baumgarten next discusses a type of ethics which he terms *ethica deceptrix* or ethics of illusion. The illusion consists in taking for actual what is in fact ideal. Whatever involves mere appearance is an illusion, for appearance is the opposite of truth. But if ethics is to be illusory, the illusion must itself be moral, but yet deceptive. It will therefore envisage a perfection, but a perfection to which we cannot attain, because it is not proportionate to human nature. Consciousness of oneself, for instance, as the principle of all men's well-being would be a source of great joy, but of a joy to which we cannot attain. Man does not naturally possess the highest degree of moral perfection. The highest perfection we associate with the Supreme Being and the highest moral perfection would, therefore, consist in communion with the Supreme Being. An immediacy of union with such a Being, were it possible, would be the highest moral perfection to which we could attain. This, however, is an ideal which is beyond our reach, although Plato actualized it. Such ethics is fanciful and visionary.

NATURAL RELIGION

Natural religion should, strictly, form the concluding chapter of ethics : it should set the seal upon the treatment of the subject, pursuing the Idea of moral perfection and giving it completion. In religion all our morality ought to reach its fulfilment in respect of its object. Nevertheless, Baumgarten chooses to deal with religion in advance, and as we have already explored the concept of ethics sufficiently for the purpose, and as it does not matter greatly whether we follow Baumgarten or leave religion to the end, we propose not to depart from his arrangement.

Natural religion is no rule of morality. Religion is morality applied to God. It is ethics applied to theology. What knowledge of God, and therefore what theology ought to be made the basis of natural religion?

Natural religion is practical. It includes natural knowledge of our duties in respect of the Supreme Being. Accordingly, religion is the combination of ethics and theology, and religion without morality is an impossibility. Nevertheless, there exist religions which are devoid of morality, and there are human beings who think they possess a religion though they have no morality. These religions consist only of an external *cultus* and observances. Their adherents are assiduous and careful in cultivating a behaviour towards God which they think prudent and calculated to please him, but they have no morality. Such practices are as far from being religion as observance of the civil law and of royal ceremonial. Religion must be not only theological but also moral. But what kind of theology is necessary as a basis for religion? Ought it, for instance, to concern itself with the question whether God is a Spirit and whether He is omnipresent and pervades all space? No. Such questions as these belong to the sphere of speculative theology and are extraneous to that theology which is requisite to natural religion. An Egyptian priest built himself an image of God, and when this was taken from him he said that he had been deprived of his god: with the image before him he could in some measure represent God to himself; without it he was helpless. But to enable us to do our duty it does not matter what notions we have of God provided only they are a sufficient ground for pure morality. The theology which is to form the basis of natural religion must contain one thing, the condition of moral perfection. We must conceive a Supreme Being whose laws are holy, whose government is benevolent and whose rewards and punishments are just. In short, the theology of natural religion need only postulate a holy lawgiver, a benevolent ruler and a just judge, and assuming all these functions to be supplied by one being, we have the conception of God required by the theology which is to be the basis of natural religion. Here we have the moral attributes of God. His natural attributes are necessary only in so far as they increase the effectiveness of the moral attributes. The omniscience, omnipotence, omnipresence and unity of the Supreme Being are the conditions requisite to His moral attributes, and relate only to them. The being who is the most holy and the most benevolent must be omniscient if He is to give heed to that inner morality which depends upon our dispositions. For that reason, too, He must be omnipresent. But the principle of morality is inconceivable except on the assumption of a supremely wise will which must be one and so must be the will of a single being. This constitutes the essence of the theology of natural religion. Its sources are to be found not in speculation, but in sound reason. Speculation is necessary to satisfy our craving for knowledge : for purposes of religion, for the purpose of knowing what we ought to do and what to leave undone, no more is necessary than that which sound reason can grasp and recognize.

Let us examine the sources of this theology. A clear exposition of morality of itself leads to the belief in God. Belief in this philosophic connexion means not trust in a revelation, but trust arising from the use of the reason, which springs from the principle of practical morality. This belief in a God is so deeply ingrained in our moral feeling that no speculative counter-arguments can eradicate it, for the pre-eminent consideration in morality is purity of disposition, and this consideration would lose its force if there existed no being to take notice of it. Without belief in the existence of such a being man could not possibly attain to and be conscious of the highest moral worth. Only God can see that our dispositions are moral and pure, and if there were no God, why ought we to cherish these dispositions ? Our conduct might be the same, we might still go on doing good, but not from any pure motive ; we might be guided by considerations of honour or pleasure to benevolent actions ; the action would be the same as if the disposition were moral because the analogues of morality are identical with it in the event. It is, therefore, impossible to cherish morally pure dispositions without at the same time conceiving that these dispositions are related to the Supreme Being to whom alone they can be an open book. More than this, we cannot be moral without believing in God. Thus, in order to believe in God it is not necessary to know for certain that God exists. All moral precepts would be meaningless if there were no being to maintain them. This is the representation of God from moral concepts.

The outstanding characteristic of natural religion is its simplicity. Its theology is such that the least intelligent amongst us can grasp it as completely as the most thoughtful and speculative. Apart from its simple rudiments there are other things in theology, but these are no concern of natural religion and serve only to satisfy our thirst for knowledge. Religion and morality must go hand in hand. The philosophers of old did not appreciate this.

Religion is the application of the moral laws to the knowledge of God, and not the origin of morals. For let us imagine a religion prior to all morality : then this would imply a relation to God, and would therefore consist in recognizing Him as a mighty lord whom we should have to placate. All religion assumes morality, and morality cannot, therefore, be derived from religion. All religion which does not assume morality, consists in a *cultus externus*, in service and praise. All pagan religions were of this kind : they were not based on morality, and God to them was fearful and jealous and had to be placated with flattery and incense.

The basis of religion must, therefore, be morality. Morality as such is ideal, but religion imbues it with vigour, beauty, and reality. It would indeed be splendid if all men were righteous and moral, and the thought might induce us to be moral. But ethics tells us that we ought to be moral in and for ourselves, no matter whether others are moral or not ; it tells us in effect to pursue the Idea of morality apart from any hope of being happy. But this

is impossible ; and as without a Being to give actuality
to the Idea, morality would be merely ideal, it follows that
there must exist a Being to give vigour and reality to the
moral laws, and this Being must be holy, benevolent and
righteous.   Without such a representation ethics is merely
an Idea.   It is religion which gives weight to morality :
it ought to be its motive.   Hence we see that he who has
so conducted himself as to be worthy of happiness can
hope to be happy because a Being exists who can make
him so.   Here we have the first consequence of religion :
it is a natural corollary of morality in religion and does
not require any theology.   Religion stands in no need of
any speculative study of God.

We are obliged to be moral.   Morality implies a natural
promise :   otherwise it could not impose any obligation
upon us.   We owe obedience only to those who can protect
us.   Morality alone cannot protect us.   ' Blessedness is an
obligation' is an identical proposition, because all our moral
actions secure through religion *completudo*.   Without religion obligation is motiveless.   Religion supplies the condition under which the binding force of the laws can be thought.
But how then are we to explain that there exist men who do
good though they have no religion ?   They do so not from
principle but for sensual reasons.   It is quite *commode* to
be honest and to tell the truth, for it needs no reflection
and no scheming to say that a thing is as it is.   Such men
do not act on principles, but from designs to good which
belong to sensibility.   But let such a man find himself
in a difficult situation, let vice come along smiling tempt-
ingly and let him be in a position in which he can transgress
without losing his good name, then if he has no religion to
support him he is in a bad way.   It is far best to acknowledge our moral need of God.

Baumgarten draws an unfortunate distinction between
inner and outer religion.   This in effect amounts to differ-
entiating between religious disposition and religious observance.   But there is no such thing as outer religion.   All
religion is inner, it is entirely a matter of disposition ; all
outward action is either a means to or an expression of the
religion within us : no outward act can be a religious act ;
acts of religion are within us, because true religion is purely

a matter of disposition. Our entire conduct is religious
if every one of our activities is accompanied by religion.
Inner religion thus constitutes the whole of religion. Piety
consists in good conduct whose impulsive ground is the
will of God. Actions done on this ground are pious ; those
performed because of their intrinsic goodness are moral
or virtuous. The distinction between piety and virtue
resides, therefore, not in the action but in the grounds of
impulse. Not only does piety not exclude virtuous grounds,
it demands them. God's own inherent goodness commits
us to goodness : His will is that we should do good from a
good disposition ; He looks to the disposition and to inner
goodness. It follows, therefore, that the proper ground of
action should be virtue and morality, and not the divine
will directly. The divine will is the motive to action, not
the ground of it. Religion is not concerned to secure the
performance of actions, without respect to the ground and
intention of their performance, but to secure that they are
done from a certain disposition. Religious observance—
that is the proper observance of the means to religion—
constitutes a pious man : to be God-fearing a man must
be something more, there must be a certain punctiliousness
in his observance ; to be scrupulous he must bear in mind
that there is a divine judge. Actions which are virtuous
for the sake of religion are pious ; those which are vicious
in the name of religion are godless.

We can draw a distinction between supernatural religion
and supernatural theology. We can have a supernatural
or revealed theology and yet have a religion which is
natural. This is so when the theology contains only such
duties in regard to the Supreme Being as are obvious to
our reason. On looking around us we do in fact find that
men have a natural religion and a supernatural theology ; were their religion supernatural it would require
supernatural support ; in point of fact, however, men
carry out only those duties which their reason can appreciate naturally.

Natural religion differs from supernatural religion, but
the two are not inconsistent : the latter supplements the
former. Natural religion employs that knowledge of
God of which man's reason is capable and it is bound up

with morality ; supernatural religion brings in the further factor of higher divine aid. Supernatural religion contains much that is calculated to make up for man's deficiencies. But man can be held to account for everything which he can bring about naturally and by his own powers, and he can, therefore, make himself worthy of having his defects made good only if he puts his natural powers to proper use and conducts himself worthily. Hence we see that supernatural religion is not opposed to natural religion, but completes it. Natural religion is true but incomplete. It enables us to recognize how much lies within our own powers and accordingly the measure of our responsibility ; and provided our conduct complies with this condition, and only then—that is, provided we make good use of natural religion—do we render ourselves fit and worthy to have our deficiencies and imperfections made good by the means of supernatural religion. There can, therefore, be no supernatural without a natural religion : the former presupposes the latter. No man can hope for supernatural help unless he behaves as he naturally ought to. It is not feasible to cast aside natural religion and simply to adopt supernatural religion and so to hope for support from above. One might perhaps dispense with natural theology and have immediate recourse to supernatural and revealed theology, but not so with religion. Supernatural religion is the supplement of natural religion, and the latter is the necessary condition of our becoming worthy of being perfected ; it is the totality of moral conduct, and it is only by such conduct that we can be worthy of a higher aid. Were we to put natural religion aside, supernatural religion would become purely passive : man would have to leave everything to God and would himself have no say and nothing to do, for everything that happened would happen supernaturally. If, then, our actions are to be imbued with morality we must first have natural religion. Every one of us must, therefore, possess a natural religion which can be imputed to him and by which he renders himself worthy to be perfected.

ERRORS OF RELIGION

Errors of religion must be distinguished from errors of theology. The former affect morality, the latter our knowledge of God. Those that corrupt morality are termed *heresy*; those that affect theology and are corruptions of theory are called *heterodoxy*. It is a question of theory on the one hand and morality or religion on the other. We can have theological errors which have no bearing on religion; it is possible for us to have a very anthropomorphic conception of God and yet to have a religion which is very good. Religion can be good even though it be imperfect, and any natural religion can be good; but to cast aside our natural forces and surrender ourselves to the supernatural is a religion of the indolent.

Both in theology and in religion, but particularly in theology, we are handicapped by ignorance. This is because the concept of God is an Idea which we must regard as the limiting concept of reason, and as the totality of all derivative concepts. To this concept I seek to attribute all properties, provided that they are not contradictory. To define this Idea is beyond us. Our theological ignorance may be great; yet it is to be regarded as of no consequence so far as religion and morality are concerned. At all times there have been errors in men's theological speculations, which, however, in no way affected religion, but were something apart from it. There are, however, aspects of our knowledge of God which greatly influence our conduct and in respect of which we must guard against errors creeping into religion. Moral errors affect religion and we must be, and are, very sensitive to them.

Theological errors ought to be avoided as far as possible. How is this to be done? Mainly by leaving dogmatic judgments severely alone. If we refrain from judging dogmatically we shall not fall into error. We ought, for instance, to avoid such investigations as those into the omnipresence of God; it should suffice that we know that God is the pattern of moral perfection and that He looks to morality, that He is good and just and will see to it

that our fate will be such as our conduct deserves ; if we
do not go beyond this we shall not fall into error ; there
is no need to have recourse to dogmatic judgment.

The first and foremost theological error is *atheism*. This
can be twofold, viz. godlessness and denial of God. Godlessness consists in not knowing God ; denial of God in
asserting dogmatically that there is no God. If a man
lacks knowledge of God, he does not necessarily lack
morality in his actions ; he merely does not know that a
God exists ; if he knew he would have religion. The case
of such a godless man is, therefore, not hopeless. On the
other hand we have the man who knows that there is a
God and yet is so wicked that he lives as though there
were no God : in his case it were better if he did not know
of God, for then there might be excuse for him ; his actions
do not lack religion, but are contrary to it. Again, a man
may be an atheist in theory and not in practice ; he may
confine his atheism to the sphere of pure speculation and
in practice be a theist and honour God ; his error is one
of theology and not of religion ; such a man used in the
past to be accounted wicked, but need not necessarily be
so ; his reason is corrupted, but not his will. Spinoza was
of this type : he behaved like a religious man ; his heart
was good ; he merely trusted too much to speculative
reasoning and he could easily have been brought to the
truth. Atheism is a theological falsehood of the kind
which influences morality and religion. It deprives rules
of good conduct of their motive power. There exist also
other kinds of theological error which, however, need not
be discussed here as they appertain less to ethics than
to *theologia rationalis*. But with regard to the theoretical mention must be made of a twofold possibility
of error. We have on the one hand sophistication and
superstition, and on the other fanaticism and blasphemy ;
the first two relate to knowledge of God, the last two to
the heart ; they represent the limits of aberration.

Sophistication consists in the attempt to deduce the
knowledge of God (which is the basic principle of religion)
by rational necessity and to apprehend and prove its
necessity. There is no need for this. In religion the
knowledge of God is properly based on faith alone. If we

regard God as the principle of morality, the holy lawgiver, the benevolent ruler and the just judge, this is all that is needed for a belief in God as a basis of religion, and it is not necessary for this belief to be susceptible of logical proof. Thus sophistication is the error of refusing to accept any religion not based on a theology which can be apprehended by our reason. But theology which is needed only for the purposes of religion need not be comprehended and proved—for that matter neither Spinozism, nor Atheism, nor Deism, nor Theism are susceptible of proof. All that we require is a reasonable and adequate hypothesis through which everything else can be sufficiently determined in accordance with rules of the understanding. Such a hypothesis is necessary, for otherwise the mind can form no conceptions, either of the order of nature or of the purposive, nor can it apprehend the ground of obedience to the moral law. But if we assume the existence of a holy lawgiver, etc., we have the necessary hypothesis. There is then no point in entering upon any speculative controversy, nor of reading books which maintain the contrary. For this cannot help me, nor can it move me in my faith. As soon as these matters become controversial, I lose all basis of firm principle. What am I to do then? It amounts to a decision to set aside the principles of the moral law and become a rogue. But the moral law issues its commands. I recognize that it is good to yield obedience to it. But if there were no Supreme Ruler the law would have no worth and no validity. Therefore I shall take counsel from no grounds of speculation, but from my necessity. Only so can my demand be satisfied. Sophistication in religious matters is a dangerous thing; our reasoning powers are limited and reason can err and we cannot prove everything. A speculative basis is a very weak foundation for religion; if religion is to rest on a secure basis all sophistication must be given a wide berth.

Superstition, on the other hand, is an irrational thing. It is not a matter of principles, but of method. If we allow our religious judgments to be based on fear, or on report, or on respect for persons, we give way to superstition and our religion has then no sure and reliable foundations. Superstition is constantly creeping into religion. Rather than follow the maxims of reason, man has a tendency to derive from sensibility what should be derived from an intellectual principle. Thus if religious observance, which is only a means to religion, is taken as a principle, religion is superstitious. Religion must be grounded in reason, though not in sophistication. If we leave the maxims of reason, and allow ourselves to be guided by the sensibility, we become superstitious; on the other hand to be led by mere speculation in religious knowledge is sophistication. Superstition and sophistication are both harmful to religion. Religion is based on faith alone, and faith stands in no need of logical demonstrations, but is itself justified in postulating its content as a necessary hypothesis.

Religion is also liable to two extremes of aberration which have their source in disposition: blasphemy and fanaticism. If a man does not take a serious view of religion and even goes so far as to regard it as something absurd which deserves to be treated with contempt, he is a blasphemer. Religion is too important to be a subject for ridicule. A judge trying a man for his life will not scoff at him: it is an important matter, the man's life is at stake and ridicule is out of place. So it is always with religion: whatever may be its particular absurdities in detail, it is no matter for ridicule; the devotees of any particular religion attach great importance to it. Their whole future welfare depends upon it, and if they indulge in absurdities they are to be pitied rather than ridiculed. But religion as such is so important a matter that to scoff at it as such is a dreadful offence. Nevertheless, we ought not immediately to conclude that a man who discusses religion whimsically is necessarily a scoffer. He may have real religious feeling, but he allows his wit free play, and the butt of his ridicule is not so much religion as certain persons. It is, to be sure, not a proceeding which merits approval, but the culprit is not a blasphemer. He is guilty of thoughtlessness, of lack of sufficient consideration.

Fanaticism exceeds all limits of the maxims of reason. Whilst superstition keeps within the maxims of reason, fanaticism goes beyond them. The principles of superstition are sensual; those of fanaticism mystical and hyperphysical. Both provoke the scoffer. When a man scoffs at religion he is generally provoked either by superstition or by fanaticism ; and though his ridicule is not seemly, it may be nevertheless a means of making the fanatical and the superstitious see their folly and of correcting their religious outlook.

Superstition is the antithesis of sophistication or rationalism, but in the practical conduct of religion the two things which stand in opposition to each other are piety and bigotry. Bigotry, like sophistry, is a game, and it is far from being the same as devoutness. Piety, which is practical, consists in obeying the divine laws for the reason that God wills it ; bigotry is zeal in the worship of God which uses words and expressions of devotion and submission in order to win God's favour. To construe this as worship of God is an abomination ; for in so doing we believe that morality is unnecessary and that we can win God over to our side by flattery ; we imagine God to be like an earthly lord and we treat Him as such ; we seek to please Him with flattery, praise and obsequious servility. Devoutness is an indirect relation of the heart to God, which seeks to express itself in action and to make the knowledge of God work effectually upon the will. It is not an activity, but a method of securing readiness in action. It is action, the putting into practice of the moral law, the doing of what God wills us to do, that constitutes true religion. Devoutness supplies the exercise by which we acquire the requisite skill in such action. By means of it we seek to have the knowledge of God so impressed upon us that it acts as an incentive to us to give effect to and practise the moral law. A man ought not, therefore, to be condemned for being devout and trying thereby to prepare himself for the performance of well-disposed deeds. But as devotional exercises are meant for the purpose of acquiring the habit of doing good, it is absurd to refuse to help some one in misfortune who comes for help when we are engaged in prayer and must not be disturbed. Here is an opportunity of doing a good deed—just the sort of thing for which devotion is meant to prepare—and the opportunity should be seized. Devotion as a separate pursuit, as an occupation in itself, has no point. We do not need it when once we have, by constantly doing good, reached the point at which we may believe that our knowledge of God is sufficiently strong within us to make us continue doing good. This is the true fear of God, which manifests its effects continuously in our conduct. We see, therefore, that the fear of God can be expressed in actions alone, and not in devoutness.

UNBELIEF

Baumgarten examines unbelief before he has considered belief. We shall expound this concept so far as it is necessary to our ethical investigation.

Belief has two meanings, the one historical, the other moral. In its historical meaning belief is a readiness to give assent to testimony. Many men are intellectually incapable of this form of belief through inability to appreciate the evidence. Men's historical judgments differ, even where the data are identical, and it is impossible to convince a man by means of something to which he gives no credence (e.g. newspaper reports). Historical belief thus exhibits discrepancies, for which we can discover as little ground as for differences in taste. Take, as an instance, Bulenger's[1] belief that the seven kings in Rome represent the seven planets. Even, therefore, in the historical field there is a tendency to unbelief. Man is more inclined to doubt and to investigate than to approve and acknowledge ; he finds it safer to postpone judgment. This tendency has its roots in the understanding, and also in the fact that we wish to guard against error, because we know that we are apt to be misled by reports, even apart from any malicious intention. Yet to close all the approaches to knowledge is the way to ignorance. But as historical belief has its seat in the understanding and not in the will, and as we are engaged in examining only the morality of things, we are not at present concerned with this aspect of belief. We are, however, concerned

[1] J. C. Bulenger (1558–1628), a Jesuit who wrote *Opusculorum Systemata*, 1621.

with the other, the moral acceptation of the term. Moral belief is belief in the actuality of virtue ; moral unbelief is disbelief in the actuality of virtue.

To believe that virtue is an Idea is the attitude of misanthropy ; it is a mask donned by vanity for its own self-satisfaction. In its extreme form it would deny even the semblance of virtue in man ; it would deny the existence of righteousness and deprive man of all incentive to become righteous. It is an evil thing to throw doubt upon the existence of virtue, the germ of good in man. Many learned men have done so in order to bring home to men their degeneracy, and to disabuse them of the notion that they are virtuous. It is none the less a hateful expedient. The very purity of the moral law bears sufficient witness to the imperfections of man ; but he who seeks out the seed of evil in man is almost an advocate of the devil. Thus did a certain Hofstede, in criticizing *Bélisaire*,[1] try to undermine virtue. How could this benefit religion ? It were far better that when, for example, the character of Socrates is, truly or fancifully, depicted in my hearing in glowing terms as the acme of virtue, I should endeavour to perfect that picture rather than rummage around to find faults in it. For would not that uplift my soul and induce me to fashion myself on his virtue ? But whoever preaches the non-existence of virtue, of the germ of what is good in man, implies thereby that we are all rogues by nature and that no man is to be trusted who is not enlightened by the grace and the help of God. Yet those who so argue forget that such a society of fundamentally evil human beings would be altogether unworthy of God's aid. For just as the angelical and divine conception of good is of something wholly free of evil, so also the conception of satanic evil is pure in its kind, being the conception of something wholly free of any germ of good, even of any will to good. How then could it be possible that men cut out on such a pattern could receive God's aid ? God would have to recreate them, not help and support them. It follows, therefore, that there must be virtue in man.

[1] J. P. Hofstede (1716–1803) : *De Belizarius van Marmontel beoordeld* (1769), a criticism of Marmontel's novel *Bélisaire* (1766).

The purity of the moral law is enough to suppress any self-conceit on the score of his virtue. Therefore we must believe in virtue. If not, the worst of thieves would be as good as his neighbour : each would have in him the seeds of thieving, and only circumstances have made the one and not the other into a thief. Many have asserted that the predisposition in man is not to good but to evil. This is moral unbelief, and only one man, Rousseau, has engaged himself to maintain the contrary.

The second form of unbelief is religious, and is based on a denial that there exists a Being who assigns not only the proper outcome to our good conduct, but also to our good dispositions whatever reward seems adequate to His good pleasure. A moral law commands that good dispositions should govern our actions; its equity constrains us to accept its peculiar stringency, so that we have a holy law. But our compliance with it is not so pure. Our actions fall far short of its perfection, so that they appear blameworthy even in our own eyes—unless indeed we dull and dismiss the judge who dwells within us and who judges in accordance with it. Men conscious of this would in the long run have to give up observing such a law, since they could not face so holy and just a judge. But though weighed in the scales of the moral law man finds himself wanting, his belief that his moral insufficiency will be made good by Heaven meets his need. Let us cherish none but good dispositions ; let us exert ourselves to the utmost of our powers to comply with the moral law ; we can then hope that Heaven will find the means to make up our deficiency, and by our very endeavours we shall become worthy of the support and aid of Heaven. Any one who has this belief has religious belief in so far as concerns conduct. This is the first part of religious belief ; the second, which is to be regarded merely as a consequence of the first, is that if we have so behaved we may hope for reward. There thus exists a form of unbelief in natural religion, and the cause of all religious ceremonies is this unbelief. Men think that ceremonies can take the place of morality, and they seek to win God over by non-moral actions. If then there is absence of true religious belief, men, instead of believing that their deficiency will be made good by Heaven, have recourse to ceremonies, pilgrimages, flagellations and fastings, hoping thereby themselves to make good their deficiency, and omitting the very things by which alone they could render themselves worthy of divine aid and support.

To edify is to produce by means of devotion a frame of mind disposing to action and practice. One can give oneself up to devotion without edification ; for ' to edify ' means, etymologically, ' to build ', and the singular building we have to construct is the temple of the dispositions to moral conduct. This edifice is founded on the knowledge of God, who imparts life, vigour, and impulsive force to the laws of morality. Edification is thus the effectual working of devoutness, the perfecting of an effective, practical disposition of the heart to act in accordance with God's will. A preacher is said to be edifying, not in the sense that he is actually constructing something, but that he makes possible the construction of a system of active, practical dispositions. But as yet he has not built ; the results are not yet achieved ; his hearers can judge whether their edification is real only by the course of their subsequent life, and the preacher by the consequences which his edification produced. It is not words, gestures and voice that matter : the criterion is the power of the sermon to erect in the minds of the audience an edifice of the fear of God. Edification implies much. To be edified is to have raised within us a structure of divine holiness.

Let us, with Baumgarten, consider further the theoretical and the practical knowledge of God, of which we have already made mention. Speculation concerning God is a wide subject, but it does not appertain to the sphere of religion, for religion must be practical. Theology, indeed, can contain speculative elements, but to religion these must remain foreign. Accordingly, he who wishes to teach aright will omit from religion all speculation, the better to enable man to concentrate his attention on the practical. Hypercriticism and subtleties are obstacles to religion : they divert us from the practical. But how are we to judge whether a particular question is religious or speculative ? Here is our criterion ; if, whatever the answer, it will make no difference to our actions, the question is not religious but speculative ; if the rule of our conduct is unaffected by it, the problem is not religious but speculative.

Baumgarten discusses contentment with the divine will. We may be submissive and patient because we must, because we cannot alter things and complaint is in vain. We appear content, but our contentment has no moral quality. Contentment with the divine will consists in ready and joyful acquiescence in God's rule. It must be absolute and universal—whatever the circumstances in which we might find ourselves, be these good or bad. But is such contentment possible ? We must guard against making man a hypocrite, for it is contrary to his nature to live in want and wretchedness and yet to thank God for it. If I thank God for my state, it follows that I must be content, and I cannot, therefore, be wretched. But how can I be grateful to God for that which I wish had not happened ? And yet is it not possible to have peace and contentment, great though our wretchedness and trouble may be ? We might be sad and yet content without feeling that we ought to thank God for our lot. Not our senses but our reason might recognize—and this, too, gives us a basis of belief—that the ruler of the world does nothing without purpose. Thereby we find consolation in, though not for, the evils of life, a solid contentment with the course of life as a whole. Our gratitude to God may take one of two forms. We may be grateful for His extraordinary guidance or else for His general providence. The first is an impertinent meddling of our judgment with His rule and purpose, but the second conforms to the modesty which we ought dutifully to observe in our judgment of God's ways. The ways of God are the divine intentions which determine the government of the world. We should not seek to define these in detail ; we must be content to judge *generaliter* that therein holiness and righteousness bear rule. It is presumption to attempt to particularize the ways of God, to try to define His intentions. It is equally presumptuous to say, when some event occurs which pleases us (such as a lucky win in a lottery), that we have been singled out by God for it. The event is certainly

part of God's providential scheme of things, but it is presumptuous to claim to have been specially selected by God
for fortune's favours.   God's intentions and purposes are
universal in their nature, and an event may be the concomi-
tant of a wider, not the result of an *ad hoc* intention.   There
are people who ascribe each individual occurrence to God's
special providence and say that God has showered benefits
and happiness upon them, thinking themselves in this to
be God-fearing.   They believe that this is to be religious.
They believe that respect for God consists in assuming that
each and every thing has been individually, specially and
directly ordained by Him.   The universality of Providence
includes everything, and therefore it is better not to seek
to determine particularly in our conversation the purposes
of God.   In the course of the world taken as a whole everything is grounded in His good providence, and we may
hope that everything, in general, happens in accordance
with the foresight of God.   Universal Nature, not particular
circumstances ought to evoke our thankfulness ; for though
the latter touch us more nearly, the former attitude is a
nobler one.   Our duty is renunciation, resignation to the
will of God.   We resign our will to another if we are conscious
of his superior understanding and feel that his intentions
are for our good.   Of course, we have reason to leave ourselves entirely in God's hands, to let His will hold sway ;
but this does not imply that we ought to do nothing,
leaving Him to do all.   We must do what is in our power ;
we must do what we ought ; the rest we should leave to
God.   That is true submission to the divine will.

TRUST IN GOD AND THE CONCEPT OF FAITH

We shall now take belief in the sense that, if we do
our best, if we do what lies in our power, we may hope
that God, in His wisdom and goodness, will make up our
shortcomings.   Faith, then, denotes trust in God that He
will supply our deficiency in things beyond our power,
provided we have done all within our power.   Humility

and modesty, combined with resignation, are the characteristics of such belief. The only demand it makes upon
us is to do our duty to the best of our ability and for the
rest to hope, without defining our hope more closely.
This form of belief may be described as absolute; it is
practical. Practical faith does not consist in saying: ' If
only I trust implicitly in God He will do what I want ';
but rather in saying: ' I will myself do all I can, and if I
then leave myself in God's hands, He will strengthen my
weaknesses and make up my shortcomings as He knows
best.' The confidence of the flesh is that trust in God
whereby we hope to move Him to satisfy our carnal desires.
Carnal purposes are all those which concern the satisfaction
of an inclination which is directed upon the sensible. Our
trust is carnal when we ourselves determine the earthly
purposes of our inclination. If we do, we have no right to
expect that our trust, when it relates to the satisfaction
of our inclinations, could be an impulsive ground of the
divine activity. The purposes of the Godhead must be
determined by God. How should we dictate the purpose
of the world? Morality, the holiness of man and his
eternal happiness on the condition of morality, is the sole
object of spiritual trust. This is a sure basis on which to
build an unconditional trust. A carnal trust Baumgarten
calls *tentatio Dei*, i.e. putting God to the test to see whether
our trust might not be for Him a ground of impulse to
fulfil our carnal purposes. It is an attempt through trust
in God to determine the divine counsels in accordance
with our own will. I cannot, in reason, trust and rely that
God will do aught which does not fall within the compass
of the general plan laid down by His wisdom; and, as I
cannot know His plan, it is a presumptuous trust which
determines the purposes of God's government of the world
and assumes that my foolish desire falls within the scheme
of the divine wisdom. Whosoever, therefore, tries to influence God, through temporal wishes, to turn aside from
the supreme wisdom of His plan and satisfy the wishes of an
individual puts God to the test and offends Him. What
then can be said of him who believes this to be true faith ?
In order that our trust should not run counter to God's wise
plan it must be a wise trust. We must trust that God will

do that which conforms to His wisdom and, as we know naught of this, we must place our trust in Him absolutely and unconditionally, trusting quite generally that He will in His goodness and holiness give us His support in our moral undertakings and bestow happiness upon us.

Our bearing towards God must be characterized by reverence, love and fear—reverence for Him as a holy lawgiver, love for His beneficent rule, and fear of Him as a just judge.

We show our reverence by regarding His law as holy and righteous, by due respect for it, and by seeking to fulfil it in our disposition. We may honour a person outwardly, but reverence springs from the disposition of the heart. The moral law is in our eyes worthy of the highest esteem and honour. When, therefore, we think of God as its author, we must honour Him in terms of supreme moral worth, and while we may be struck with wonder in contemplating God and overawed by His greatness and infinity, while we may be conscious of our own littleness before Him, our reverence can take no other than the moral form. So in the case of men, though ability and industry awake our admiration, we do not revere them on these counts. We reverence them only on the moral plane.

We can love God for His beneficent rule, and only for that. His perfections are marvellous but not lovable ; they are for Himself ; and as we can love only those who can benefit us, we love God only for His goodwill towards us.

Fear of God is not rooted in His holiness and goodness, but in His unerring justice. God must be feared as a just judge. To fear God is not the same as to be afraid of Him. We are afraid of God when we have transgressed and feel guilty, but we fear Him when we are so disposed to conduct ourselves that we can stand before Him. He who fears God so conducts himself that he has no cause to be afraid. To fear God is thus the way to avoid the need to be afraid of Him.

Fear of God can be filial or slavish. It is filial when combined with love for Him and when we keep His commandments willingly, from a good disposition ; it is slavish

when our obedience to His precepts is unwilling, or if we
have transgressed, or feel inclined to transgress, against
His commandments. When we harbour any such inclination, our consciousness of it makes us afraid in anticipation.

It is not good to talk of imitating God. God tells us to
be holy, not meaning that we ought to imitate Him, but
that we ought to strive to approximate to the unattainable ideal of holiness. We cannot imitate what is specifically different from us ; but we can be obedient and
compliant. Our archetype is not a pattern which we
must reproduce, but a rule to which we should conform.

PRAYER

There is a widespread opinion that, as God knows our
wants better than we do ourselves, there is no need
to pray. Objectively, prayer is certainly unnecessary.
Whether or not we express our creature-wishes in words,
God knows them ; He is well aware of our needs and of
the nature of our dispositions ; His all-seeing eye pene-
trates into our innermost souls and reads our thoughts.
As far as God is concerned, therefore, it is unnecessary
for us to declare ourselves, and pointless to enter into
verbal explanations of our dispositions and wishes. Only
those who are ignorant of our demands require to have
them formulated and explained. Subjectively, however,
prayer is necessary. It is necessary for our own sakes,
and not in order that God, who is the object and direction of our prayer, be made cognizant of something and
be moved to grant it. To grasp and comprehend his
concepts man must clothe them in words : if, therefore,
he wants to produce for himself a lively representation of
his pious wishes and of his trust in God, he must have
recourse to words.

But prayer is unnecessary, in either the objective or
in the subjective sense, where the object is not to induce
a moral disposition, but the satisfaction of our wants.
Take, for example, the case of a man in distress. God
sees his distress, so that it is objectively unnecessary for

him to pray, and he himself stands in no need of any
lively representation of his distress, so that it is subjectively
unnecessary for him to pray. Thus the purpose of prayer
can only be to induce in us a moral disposition ; its purpose can never be pragmatic, seeking the satisfaction of
our wants. It should fan into flame the cinders of morality
in the inner recesses of our heart ; it is a means of devotion, which in turn is a practice the object of which is to
impress the knowledge of God upon our hearts with a view
to action. Prayers are devotional exercises.

To wish to converse with God is absurd : we cannot
talk to one we cannot intuit ; and as we cannot intuit
God, but can only believe in him, we cannot converse
with him. The uses of prayer are thus only subjective.
It is a weakness in man that to give his thoughts expression
he must put them into words, and accordingly, when
praying, he holds converse with himself and puts his
thoughts into words so that he may not err, thus adopting
a paradoxical but none the less, from the subjective point
of view, a necessary expedient for giving his soul strength.
Frequently ordinary people can only pray aloud. They
are incapable of silent thought, and loud prayer impresses
them ; but persons accustomed to unfold their minds in
silence stand in no need of praying aloud, and if their
moral and devotional disposition is sufficiently intense
they do not require the letter of the prayer but only the
spirit of it. Those whose minds are practised in harbouring
Ideas and dispositions can discard the aid of words and
formal expression. Subtract these from prayer, and what
remains ? Only the spirit of prayer, the sense of devotion,
the guide-line leading the heart to God by way of faith,
by way of the trust we place in Him that He will complete
the imperfection of our morality and make us partakers
of blessedness. The spirit of prayer subsists without
the letter. The letter is to no purpose as far as God is
concerned, for he reads our thoughts, but formal prayer
does not on that account stand condemned. Though the
letter is in itself dead, yet formal prayer has nevertheless
great value to the individual when it is uttered with
solemn and impressive ceremony, as, for example, in
church. Prayer in church so transforms man's moral

outlook that on recognizing his normal self he is ashamed. Admitted that it is illogical to enunciate one's wishes to God, to whom all things are known, that the need to clothe one's dispositions in the sound of words is a human weakness, yet this is the means best suited to man's limitations. It is the spirit of the prayer alone which matters.

The Gospels contain a protest against loud public prayer offered at the street corner. The standard form of prayer, the Lord's Prayer, contains only our barest necessities and teaches us that prayer should relate to the disposition and that wordy prayer is wrong. No prayer must be a determining, defining prayer except the one which touches the moral dispositions. This prayer can be categorical and unconditional: for other things I must pray conditionally. The condition must be an admission on my part that my prayer may possibly be foolish and detrimental to me. Reason, therefore, dictates that our prayer should not be definitive, but that we should place our needs in general in the wise hands of God, and accept from Him what He may choose to give us. As, however, man is weak, the Gospels permit conditional prayer in earthly affairs. Definitive prayers must be regarded as presumptuous. They breathe a perverse conceit; for if there was a chance that God should grant my particular requests, I might well be terrified. How should I know that I had not unwittingly called down upon myself some great misfortune? Definitive prayers are unbelieving. If I attach a condition to my prayer, I doubt the certainty that it will be completely granted. Had I no such doubt, I would not attach the condition. The prayer of faith cannot be definitive, but must be general. Whosoever sets God a task, and desires fulfilment in his own fashion, has no trust in God. The spirit of prayer, which teaches us skill in good conduct, is the perfection that we seek after, and the letter is but a means to secure the spirit. Thus, prayers are not to be regarded as a special way of serving God, but only as a means of awakening within us the spirit of devotion. We do not serve God with words, ceremonies and gestures: we serve Him only by actions which reflect our devotion to Him. Prayer trains us to act aright: it is merely an exercise for good action, but is not in itself such an action. We must divest it of all practical goodness to arrive at the purest concept of prayer, which is then seen to be good as a means. If, then, prayer has no higher value than that of a means to an end, it cannot be regarded as a peculiar service of God and intrinsically good. To do so is superstition. An error is more excusable than a superstition in religion. Erroneous religion can be corrected, but a superstition is not only empty but is opposed to the reality of religion.

Prayer appears to be a presumptuous act and an act of distrust in God. It seems to imply distrust in God's knowledge of what is good for us. Continuous, unremitting prayer may be construed as an attempt to coerce God by constant begging into granting our desires. We may ask, then, whether such unremitting prayer is of avail. If the prayer is offered in faith, in the spirit and not merely in the letter, trust in God supplies a ground for the granting of the request ; but the specification of the object of the prayer is no such ground ; the object of the prayer must be general and not particular ; the wisdom of God must be accorded its widest scope. Prayer may be said to be general when we ask to be made worthy of all benefits which God is ready to bestow upon us. Only such prayer can be granted ; for it is moral and in harmony with the wisdom of God. In temporal matters a specific plea is unnecessary. It can only be made subject to the condition 'if God thinks fit', and this very condition annuls the specification. But though specific pleas are unnecessary, man, who is a helpless, poor creature, ignorant of what the future holds in store for him, cannot be blamed if, for example, when in danger at sea, he offers a determinate prayer. It is the cry of distress of a helpless creature, and merits a favourable hearing in so far as trust in God is a ground of impulse for God either to grant the prayer or to provide aid in some other form. For all this, he has no right to believe that God will simply grant him what he asks.

We pray in faith when we pray for something which we may reasonably hope that God will grant. Prayers should, therefore, be confined to objects which we are convinced

are such as God would be willing to grant. This, however, can only apply to spiritual objects. If, then, we
pray for these with the purest disposition, our prayers
arise from faith and we are then worthy to receive the
support which makes up for our moral infirmity. If,
however, we pray for temporal goods, we cannot in reason
hope that God will grant them, and our prayer is, therefore,
not grounded in faith. It has been said that every prayer
uttered in faith will be heard. This is true, but the statement is identical with what has been said above, that we
should pray only for those things which we may hope that
God will grant. Thus if we ask, for example, that length
of life shall be given to us, our prayer is not in faith, since
we cannot reasonably hope that God will grant it. Thus,
also, when men, trusting in God, fervently pray for material
benefits hoping to gain their ends by the fervency of their
prayer, such prayer is not in faith. In faith we can only
pray to be made worthy of God's goodness. In this
respect we can believe with assurance that God will hear
our prayers.

Thus the spirit of prayer must be distinguished from
the letter of it. The spirit of prayer is a devout and
godly disposition. The letter is necessary to us only in
order to awaken within us the spirit of prayer. To pray
is thus an act of devotion. If our practice of prayer is
directed towards awakening in us an active and practical
disposition which manifests itself in our conduct, then our
prayer is devout.

Baumgarten speaks of purity of religion. A thing can
be said to be pure in one of two meanings : either in that
it is unmixed, or else in that it is undefiled. A pure religion,
as opposed to one which is mixed, means a religion consisting solely in dispositions which are directed towards
God and imply morality. A mixed religion, in so far as
it appeals to the senses, is one which is merely a means to
morality. But as man is sensuous and the religious appeal
to his senses has its uses, it can be said that man can have
no pure religion. The basis of religion and the ideal to
be aimed at must, however, be the pure Idea and there
must be a strong background of morality.

Baumgarten goes on to speak of religious zeal. Zeal is

a resolute and steadfast will to pursue of set purpose and to reach the aim in view. Such zeal is commendable in all things ; but if in religion it signifies a passionate pursuit of everything in it, then it is blind zeal ; and if in anything in life we should keep our eyes open it is in religion. In religion, therefore, there is no room for zeal, but only for serious determination.

Simple, as opposed to artificial, piety signifies that the means employed must bear a precise relation to the importance of the end. Religion should keep in view nothing but the end. Theology needs erudition ; religion calls for simplicity. A practical atheist is he who lives in such a way as to give the impression of not admitting the existence of God. To call a man who simply gives no thought to the question a practical atheist is to exaggerate the implication of the phrase. Of a practical atheist one must be able to say that he is godless, for godlessness is a kind of shameless wickedness which defies the fear of punishment which the representation of God inspires in us. Sophistication, bigotry and superstition are deviations from religion. Mention has already been made of them. Bigotry mistakes the letter for the spirit of religion. Superstition consists in the representation by which we accept, as grounds of reason, maxims which are essentially opposed to reason. Religious superstition is for the most part religious delusion. Fanaticism is an illusion of the inner sense whereby we believe ourselves to be in fellowship with God and with other spirits.

DE CULTU EXTERNO

We have drawn a distinction between fear of God and service of God, and religious acts can be classified under these two headings as God-fearing acts and acts of service to God.

Anthropomorphism causes us to interpret our duties towards God by analogy with our duties towards man. We believe ourselves to be serving God in proclaiming reverentially that we are His humble subjects and by

praising and honouring Him. It is true that we can do
a service to any individual, however great and important
he may be ; every subject can do an act of service to his
lord. Some acts of service are nothing more than assurances given by us that we are willing and ready to perform
any service we may be called upon to perform, e.g. when
paying court we simply present ourselves and express
our readiness to do anything which would please the person
to whom we pay court. Princes are anxious to have
honour paid to them and regard it as real service. Men
apply this idea of service to God. They pay court to
Him and declare themselves eager to do humbly and
loyally any act of service which would please Him, and
they believe that these expressions of honour in themselves constitute an act of service to God. This has given
rise to the view that, in order to keep men in practice,
God has promulgated certain commands which in themselves are empty and serve only as disciplinary exercises
intended to keep men constantly attuned to service.
Thus fasts, pilgrimages and penance, which we find in
some religions, are meant to evince man's readiness to do
what is commanded ; but they are merely observances,
devoid of any moral quality, and they help no one. There
is no religion but contains such observances in plenty.
The totality of acts which have no other purpose than that
of proving eagerness to comply with God's commands is
called the service of God ; but true service does not consist
of observances and external usages : it is to be found in
sanctified dispositions put into practice in our everyday
activities. God-fearing is he who holds God's holy law
in veneration and reflects this in his acts. Thereby God
is served. Thus we serve God not by particular acts, but
in all our activities ; our service must be incessant and
must embrace our whole life ; service of God does not
consist of particular acts performed at particular times.
The fear of God and the service of God consists not in a particular activity, but in the form of all activity. There are,
indeed, acts of religion which men believe to be a direct
service to God; but in this they err. The effect of our
activities cannot reach beyond this world ; we cannot
affect God in any way. We can only dedicate our dis-

positions submissively to Him. There are therefore no God-ward activities of religion, whereby we can show God a service. Devotional exercises are not intended in any way to please God and do Him service, but only to strengthen in us the dispositions of our souls to please God by our actions in our lives. Prayer, like all other sensuous means, is merely a preparatory exercise to make our dispositions practical. True service of God is a life purified by the true fear of God. Accordingly, we do not enter a church to serve God there : we do so in order to prepare ourselves to serve Him in our lives. We must carry out in practice outside the church the preparations we have made within it, and so devote our lives to God's service.

Religious worship consists of moral exercises and of mere observance. Under the head of moral exercises fall prayers, sermons and certain physical acts intended to strengthen our faith and to give an impetus to our moral actions. But the more worship is overloaded with observance, the more devoid it is of moral exercises. Religious worship is no direct service of God : it is only a means of exercising the human mind in dispositions to behave in all things in accordance with God's will, and in that lies its value. Man, however, is liable to mistake the means for the end. This most serious error, this evil in which all religions share, is not due to their nature, but to this tendency in man. It is an illusion of religion, the illusion which regards what has value as the means as itself the service of God, by taking the means of serving God as itself the fear and the service of God. But to serve God in act and to acquire dispositions which are sanctified is very difficult. Such dispositions compel men to do violence to their inclinations, and require to be cherished constantly. A limited number of laws, fasts, pilgrimages and such-like things does not impose any incessant duty upon us : these things last a while, and once they are done with we are again free ; we can then do what we please ; we can even engage in a little deceit, for the time for observance will come again and we shall then by submissive penitence make good the fault. Little wonder then that in a choice between religious worship and moral disposition, with its tedious burden of constant watchfulness, man prefers the former and has made religion a plaster for his conscience and for curing (so, at least, he believes) the ill done by his sins against God. In fact, the *cultus* is an invention of man. It gives him two strings to his bow : he can please God either by moral conduct or by religious observance, and it enables him to substitute the easier method—that of religious observance—for the more difficult. Thus it comes that the less punctilious men are in their moral conduct the more punctilious they are in religious worship. They would substitute observance for morality. It is accordingly imperative that those who teach the masses should do their utmost to stamp out this kind of abuse. In so far as God is concerned, the cult of observances is of no value. These are only of value to ourselves, and then only as a means of strengthening in us dispositions which our actions should express out of love to God. But how are we to know that we are using the *cultus* only as a means ? Only by taking heed in our lives that a moral disposition and the fear of God is to be found in our conduct.

The term outward religion is contradictory. Religion must be inward ; actions may be outward, but they do not constitute religion and they in nowise serve God ; actions directed to God are nothing but means for strengthening the disposition of surrender to God, and for developing our skill in following His holy law, so that our lives and our actions should find favour in His sight. Outward observance (*cultus externus*) comprises outward expedients for fanning within us the flame of good dispositions whose expression should be seen in our everyday deeds. Such outward expedients, which have an inward effect of inspiring and invigorating the inner dispositions, representations and cognitions, do in fact exist. A large congregation engaged with one voice in dedicating their dispositions in holiness to God is a case in point. To regard this, however, as in itself rendering a service to God is a dreadful illusion. It is a misconception which has done untold harm to religion. Man's moral conduct leaves much to be desired. Not only are there serious imperfections and flaws in his good deeds, but he also often consciously and wilfully transgresses against the divine law. He cannot, therefore, hope to face a just and holy judge, who cannot forgive vice *simpliciter*. But since we know that God is good and benevolent, may we not expect that He will forgive our vices if we pray fervently to Him and implore His forgiveness ? No. A benevolent judge is unthinkable. A judge must be just ; a ruler can be benevolent. Were God to forgive vice, He might also tolerate it and exempt it from punishment. In other words, God might at will allow and tolerate vice, but in that case the moral law would be the creature of arbitrary will, and this it is not. It is as necessary and as eternal as God Himself. Divine justice must reward good conduct and punish bad with unerring precision. God's will is immutable. We cannot, therefore, hope that if we implore and supplicate God He will grant us everything ; for then it would not be good conduct but prayer and appeal which would matter. A benevolent judge is thus unthinkable : the conception is absurd ; if we ask a judge to be benevolent, it is as if we asked him to blind himself for the nonce and allow himself to be bribed with flattery and supplication. But then such clemency could only be meted out to individuals, and would therefore need to be kept secret. If it were universally known, all would demand to be dealt with on the same lines. This would bring the law into contempt. Prayer cannot, therefore, bring about exemption from punishment. The holy law implies of necessity that punishment should fit the crime. But in view of man's moral infirmity, is there to be no help for him ? Assuredly there is. He can place his hope in a benevolent ruler. He cannot hope that punishment of his vices will be remitted ; for then the divine will, as revealed in the moral law, would not be holy. But he can hope that God, the benevolent ruler, will show His goodness not in the physical field alone, where indeed good conduct in itself brings good results in its train, (a fact which is itself an evidence of God's benevolence), but also in the moral field. For though man cannot hope to be relieved of moral demands, nor of the consequences of his transgressions, God reveals His goodness in the resources through which He supplements the failings of our natural infirmity: If, for our part, we do all that lies within our power, we can hope for God's completion, that we may stand before His righteousness and not be found wanting by His holy law. We cannot know—neither do we need to know—in what manner and by what aids God will make good our shortcomings, but we can hope that He will do so. In lieu of indulgent justice we have true justice with something more besides. But as—however well-intentioned they might be—men have yet invariably felt themselves more guilty in their own eyes than in the eyes of God, they have thought that God must do everything for them or else pardon all their sins. They accordingly made use of outward expedients to obtain God's favour and they had recourse to prayer. They curried favour. We thus have two forms of religion : the one the religion of currying favour, the other the religion of a good life. The latter consists in the endeavour punctiliously to observe God's holy law from the heart in the hope that God will provide a completion for our infirmity. He who has this form of religion does not curry favour with God, but leads the good life. The religion of currying favour is injurious and contrary to the very concept of God. It is a system of make-up and disguise, in which, under the false appearance of religion and outward service of God, whereby they think to make good their evil past, men proceed to a renewal of their sinning in the hope that once again they can make it good by external means. But of what benefit to a merchant, for instance, are his morning and evening devotions if, as soon as they are over, just back from matins, he proceeds to cheat some unwary buyer, and goes on, over and above, to thank God for the blessing of the day in a couple of fervent collects at the church door in passing ? Is that not merely an attempt to cheat God by jesuitical dodges ? There is common ground here between reason and the Gospels as seen in the example of the two brothers of whom the one (*complimentarius*) curried favour of his father and with alacrity promised to obey his father's will, but did it not, while the other made difficulties, but nevertheless did his duty towards his father. Such a religion of currying favour is worse than no religion at all, for there is no help for it. A word may at times lead a godless man on to the right road, but not the hypocrite. All these remarks are simply an attempt to show that the external forms of religion, the *cultus*, have no value whatsoever so far as God is concerned and are simply a means to an end for ourselves.   They are intended as a warning against the belief that the *cultus externus* can make up for our moral imperfections.   These are rendered adequate to the holiness of the law by means known only to God.

EXAMPLE AND PATTERN IN RELIGION

An example is a given concrete instance of a universal proposition of reason.   For propositions à priori we require proofs that they exist also *in concreto*; otherwise they subsist only in the understanding and must be reckoned as *fictiones*.   Thus a plan of government, the product of reason, must be capable of demonstration through an example, to show that it is possible *in concreto*. We may ask, then, whether morality and religion admit of examples.   Whatever is apodeictic à priori needs no example, because I apprehend its necessity à priori.   Thus mathematical propositions do not require examples.   An example in such a case is no part of the proof ; it merely serves as an illustration.   On the other hand in the case of concepts which are derived from experience we cannot know whether they are possible until an example is before us *in concreto* in a given case.   All cognitions in morals and religion permit of substantiation by reason à priori. The necessity to behave in such-and-such a manner and in no other, we apprehend à priori.   Accordingly, in matters of religion and of morality no examples are necessary.   It follows that there can be no patterns in religion, since the ground, the first principle of behaviour must lie in the reason, and is not to be deduced à posteriori.   For experience provides not a single example of honesty, of righteousness, or of virtue ; yet reason tells us that we ought to be honest, righteous, and virtuous.   In fact, morality and religion cannot be judged by examples ; the examples themselves can only be judged good or bad by reference to universal principles.   The archetype lies in the understanding. If, then, saintly people are presented to me as models of religion, I must not imitate them, be they ever so holy ; I must judge them rather by universal rules of morality. There are, indeed, examples of righteousness, of virtue, and even of holiness, such as the Example set before us in the Gospels, but this Example of the earthly life does not serve as our ground of judgment ; rather we judge it by the holy law. If it conforms to the holy law, then only do we recognize that it is an example of holiness. Examples serve for our encouragement and emulation. They should not be used as patterns. If we see a thing *in concreto* we cognize it the more clearly. But there is a reason for men's proneness to imitation in religious matters. Men imagine that if they conduct themselves as do the majority of their kind they can coerce God into forgiving them ; for as God cannot punish all men He must forgive all. Moreover, men like to retain the beliefs of their ancestors ; for in that case their ancestors and not themselves are to be blamed for anything which may be wrong, and so long as man can transfer blame to another he is satisfied. Men think that by this means they guard themselves against responsibility. Thus a man who changes his religion and goes over from the religion of his parents and ancestors to another is counted foolhardy. He is thought to be committing a very dangerous act since thereby he takes all blame upon himself. If we take what is universal in religion and so is common to all religions, namely pleasing God through the dispositions of our hearts, carrying out His holy law, and hoping that in His goodness God will supplement our weakness, then there is no reason why every individual should not follow the religion of his forefathers ; so long as he does not believe that he can please God more by the *cultus* of his own than by that of any other religion, it can do him no harm. Let the observances be what they may, so long as they are not regarded as anything more than a means of awakening within us a godly disposition ; but let them be regarded as in themselves a service to God and serious harm ensues. And under such conditions one religion is as harmful as another.

STUMBLING-BLOCKS

An example is not for copying, but for emulation.
Precepts, not the example of others, should be the ground
of our actions. If, however, others have demonstrated the
practical possibility of a moral act, we should follow their
example and endeavour to do the same and not let others
forestall us. On the whole, examples are desirable. Their
absence gives us an excuse. ' Life is like that ', we say.
But an example encourages us to emulation. If we can
point to a man and say : ' Look at that man's life ! ' we
are encouraged to follow his example. A bad example,
however, is a stumbling-block, and gives occasion for two
evils, its imitation as a pattern and excuse. Thus the
example set by men of eminence and by ecclesiastics is
liable to be copied ; and although we ought not to copy
in religion we do so nevertheless. But if an example
furnishes an excuse for the inexcusable, we have a
scandalum. Just as man is averse from doing his duty
single-handed and prefers to share it with others, so would
he also rather not stand alone in his wickedness ; and the
more examples of the kind there are at hand the more we
like it, for the greater is then the field of reference available
to us.

Scandala are either *data* or *accepta*. We speak of
scandalum datum if it must inevitably have a detrimental
effect on the morals of others. It is true that I can
scarcely be blamed if another mistakes and misapplies
what I have done and it corrupts his morals, although
I meant it otherwise and it had no immoral effect in me ;
but, though I am not liable for his misconstruction, I
ought none the less to exercise restraint to avoid giving
occasion for any such *scandalum*. If, however, I cannot
avoid giving occasion to such a *scandalum acceptum* except
by acting insincerely and by turning a deaf ear to my
own conscience, then I need not do so. My actions must
be upright and unaffected ; and, if in order not to give
offence I were to do a thing which I am convinced is
wrong, I should be doing violence to my own conscience.

If, for instance, my conscience tells me that to prostrate oneself before images is idolatry and I happen to find myself in a place where this is being done, I should, if I did it in order not to offend another, offend my own conscience. Sorry though I should be to be a stumbling-block to others, I could not help myself. In order not to give cause for offence to our weaker brethren, who are prone to imitate us, we are called upon for circumspection and restraint. At the same time we ought not to mock at religious doctrines, which are only indirectly contrary to morality; we ought to respect them; for let the religion be what it may, it is still worthy of our respect as a human discipline. Our conduct should tend not to schism but to unity in religion.

Religion has two constituents : the honour of God and the love of God. There are two ways of showing honour to a person : practically, by doing his will; and as a flatterer, by outward marks of esteem, by ceremonial and by praise. We cannot honour God in this latter manner, by assurances of our esteem, and so on; we can only honour Him practically, by our acts. We honour God if, recognizing the debt of honour we owe Him as the Law-giver, we comply with His holy and divine law and do His commandments, which are worthy of all honour, with a ready will. We love God practically if we take pleasure in doing His commandments, because they are worthy of love; we love Him if we love His law and fulfil it lovingly. Superstition has given rise to the false idea of honouring God, fanaticism to the false idea of loving God.

What is meant by praising God ? To frame for ourselves a lively representation of God's greatness as the ground of impulse for our will to live in accordance with His holy will. The endeavour to apprehend the perfection of God necessarily pertains to religion, which exists to strengthen and invigorate our souls to live in accordance with God's holy will. On the other hand, we may ask how the praise of God contributes towards this ? The praise of God by word and psalm (the medium by which we express our concepts) serves only to intensify our practical reverence of God. It is, therefore, of subjective but of no objective value ; the profit is to ourselves and

not to God ; we do not profit God by uttering His praises.
We praise God only if we use His perfections and the
glorifying of them as a ground of impulse to awaken in
us dispositions to practical goodness. We cannot admit
any inclination in God to be praised by us. Besides, we
cannot adequately comprehend God's greatness, and the
conceptions by which we think to praise Him are very
faulty. All our eulogies fall short of the perfection of
God. Their value is thus only subjective ; but it is
thereby also indirectly objective. If man could be taught
the habit of feeling in his heart the true reverence of
God, this would be better than teaching him to recite
a few hymns of praise—words and formulae which he
utters but does not feel. But how can we instil in ourselves such a conception of God as will produce this reverence in our hearts ? Not by expressions ; not by prescribed
forms of praise, hymning the perfection of God. They
are greatly mistaken who think that the formulae extolling
God's goodness and His omnipotence constitute the praise
of God. But in order that we should feel the greatness
of God in our hearts we must be able to intuit it, and it
would, therefore, be a great advantage if, instead of a
religious community being taught by general concepts to
respect the omnipotence of God, it were led to appreciate
(and of this all men are capable) the works of God, such
as His infinite universe which contains many worlds peopled
with rational creatures. Such representations of the
greatness of God have a greater effect upon our souls than
have all manner of songs of praise. Men believe, however,
that songs of praise in themselves please God. None the
less every kind of observance, in so far as it aims at
winning favour, is reprehensible ; methods such as these
might deceive men, but not God. Observances must in
every case be designed to quicken the soul and fill it
full of good dispositions. They are no part of religion ;
they are only means to it. True religion is the religion
of the fear of God and of a good life. If a man's actions
show no signs of it, he has no religion, let him say what
he will.

Signs of religion are of two types, essential indications
and doubtful indications. An example of the first type

is conscientiousness of life ; a characteristic of the doubtful kind is, for instance, observance of religious ceremonial. But because religious ceremonial falls within the doubtful category, it need not on that account be altogether rejected, for it is a sign of man's endeavour to become, by means of it, imbued with godly dispositions ; and it is a doubtful sign only in the judgment of others, not in one's own. Each of us can tell whether he makes use of religious worship as a means to true religion, or if he treats it as a direct service of God. He himself can have no doubt about it, but others cannot share that certainty. He can feel in his heart that he worships to awaken godly dispositions in himself, but he can prove that this is so only by his conduct in life.

DEVOUTNESS AND THE FEELING OF SHAME

No man feels shame for his piety and his fear of God, unless it be that he finds himself in wholly wicked and wholly defiant company ; he is then ashamed of his conscience, in the way that one might feel ashamed of one's honesty among rogues ; but in the company of moral men no one feels ashamed of being truly God-fearing. Not so, however, in the matter of devoutness. We feel that this is only a question of observance and not of religion, and therefore the more righteous a man is the more liable he is to feel a sense of shame when surprised at his devotions ; a hypocrite will feel no such shame— he rather courts being seen. It is for that reason that the Gospels tell us to go into our chamber to pray ; for if a man thinks that his neighbour, however unjustifiably, misconstrues his actions, he feels ashamed. If, for example, something is lost in a room where several persons are congregated, and if questions are asked and one person is looked at, he blushes.

The first cause of the feeling of shame is the desire not to be taken for a hypocrite. The second cause is as follows. We do not know God by intuition but by faith.

Thus we could without any feeling of shame refer in
conversation to God as the object of faith. We might
say, for instance, " May God in His goodness guide the
training of my children to such-and-such an outcome."
But let us assume that some one present were suddenly
to uplift his hands and pray for this, we should be taken
aback, although he would be saying exactly the same
thing as we had expressed in conversation. Why should
this be so ? Because the object of faith has been turned
into an object of intuition. Now faith is undoubtedly
no less vigorous a faculty than intuition. But we address
God as though He were before our eyes. God is no object
of intuition ; He is an object of faith and must not be
approached except as such. In approaching Him by a
form of prayer, we treat Him as an object of intuition
which is then the intuition of a fanatic. In expressing
a wish, however, we treat God as an object of faith. Why
then pray ? Because in praying in seclusion we can
compose our soul by the imitation of intuition. There is
something *pathetic*, however, in praying in church, for
then we are in fact turning the object of faith into the
object of intuition. But a preacher can pray to God
as the object of faith. In a religious assembly it is permissible to arouse *pathemata* ; in a secular assembly it
would be fantastic.

CONFESSION OF FAITH : ITS LIMITATIONS
AND CONDITIONS

This is best elucidated by examples. In those foreign
countries in which religion is superstitious, there is no need
to declare one's religion. If in my opinion ceremonies
such as prostration before saints impede religion, and I
happen to be in a place where this is done and at a moment
when all are engaged in prostrating themselves before an
image, I might as well join them and do so myself : it
does me no harm ; I need not declare my own religion,
for God looks to the bowed heart and not the bowed
knee. Neither is it a *status confessionis* if I comply with

local religious customs to save my life. Thus Niebuhr [1] relates that travellers who go to Mecca to witness Moham- medan ceremonies must allow themselves to be circumcised or be killed. This actually happened to a Frenchman. Why should I not submit to circumcision, particularly if I thereby save my life? It can do me no harm; and if a religion has compelled a man to accept it, that is no proof that the religion is true. But it is a *status con- fessionis* if I am forced to declare my dispositions, and with oaths and protestations, to accept opinions which are false, and which I believe to be false, and to abjure those which I am bound to hold in high esteem. I may say: 'My friends, I will accept your customs as and when you please, but to frame new dispositions in an instant,—that won't do. I cannot make up my mind so quickly, and I must not, therefore, give you any declara- tion of my dispositions.' Whosoever renounces his religion is either a renegade or an apostate. A man can be an apostate without being a renegade; he may forsake his religion from conviction, as Spinoza did, for instance, when he left the Jewish faith. Such a man is not a renegade.

The name of God is taken in vain, and so abused, by hypocrites and profligates; but we should not imme- diately assume that a man is profligate because, for instance, we have heard him curse. Often the gentlest of human beings do so as a matter of habit, and a drill-sergeant calls down damnation upon the heads of his soldiers, not because he thinks that he can order the forces of damnation to do his bidding, but in order to add emphasis to his words of command.

Here ends our dissertation on natural religion; we now turn to the discussion of essential morality.

DUTIES TO ONESELF

We have dealt at length with questions appertaining to natural religion, and we now proceed to deal similarly with

---

[1] Carsten Niebuhr's work on Arabia, 1772, p. 24. Kant's memory has played him false.

essential morality and with our proper duties towards everything in the world. First amongst these duties is the duty we owe to our own selves.

My duty towards myself cannot be treated juridically; the law touches only our relations with other men; I have no legal obligations towards myself; and whatever I do to myself I do to a consenting party; I cannot commit an act of injustice against myself. What we have to discuss is the use we make of liberty in respect of ourselves. By way of introduction it is to be noted that there is no question in moral philosophy which has received more defective treatment than that of the individual's duty towards himself. No one has framed a proper concept of self-regarding duty. It has been regarded as a detail and considered by way of an afterthought, as an appendix to moral philosophy, on the view that man should give a thought to himself only after he has completely fulfilled his duty towards others. All moral philosophies err in this respect. Gellert [1] hardly even deserves mention here; it does not even occur to him to touch upon the question; he is constantly harping on benevolence and charity, the poet's hobby-horses. Just as an innkeeper gives a thought to his own hunger when his customers have finished eating, so a man gives a thought to himself at the long last for fear that he might forget himself altogether! Hutcheson, too, although his thought is more philosophic, does not pass this test. The reason for all this is the want of a pure concept, which should form the basis of a self-regarding duty. It was taken for granted that a man's duty towards himself consisted, as Wolff in his turn defined it, in promoting his own happiness. In that case everything would depend on how an individual determined his own happiness; for our self-regarding duties would consist in the universal rule to satisfy all our inclinations in order to further our happiness. This would, however, militate seriously against doing our duty towards others. In fact, the principle of self-regarding duties is a very different one, which has no connexion with our well-being or earthly happiness. Far from ranking lowest in the scale of precedence, our

[1] C. F. Gellert, *Moralische Vorlesungen*, 1770, 2 vols.

duties towards ourselves are of primary importance and should have pride of place ; for (deferring for the moment the definition of what constitutes this duty) it is obvious that nothing can be expected from a man who dishonours his own person. He who transgresses against himself loses his manliness and becomes incapable of doing his duty towards his fellows. A man who performed his duty to others badly, who lacked generosity, kindness and sympathy, but who nevertheless did his duty to himself by leading a proper life, might yet possess a certain inner worth ; but he who has transgressed his duty towards himself, can have no inner worth whatever. Thus a man who fails in his duty to himself loses worth absolutely ; while a man who fails in his duty to others loses worth only relatively. It follows that the prior condition of our duty to others is our duty to ourselves ; we can fulfil the former only in so far as we first fulfil the latter. Let us illustrate our meaning by a few examples of failure in one's duty to oneself. A drunkard does no harm to another, and if he has a strong constitution he does no harm to himself, yet he is an object of contempt. We are not indifferent to cringing servility ; man should not cringe and fawn ; by so doing he degrades his person and loses his manhood. If a man for gain or profit submits to all indignities and makes himself the plaything of another, he casts away the worth of his manhood. Again, a lie is more a violation of one's duty to oneself than of one's duty to others. A liar, even though by his lies he does no harm to any one, yet becomes an object of contempt, he throws away his personality ; his behaviour is vile, he has transgressed his duty towards himself. We can carry the argument further and say that to accept favours and benefits is also a breach of one's duty to oneself. If I accept favours, I contract debts which I can never repay, for I can never get on equal terms with him who has conferred the favours upon me ; he has stolen a march upon me, and if I do him a favour I am only returning a *quid pro quo* ; I shall always owe him a debt of gratitude, and who will accept such a debt ? For to be indebted is to be subject to an unending constraint. I must for ever be courteous and flattering

towards my benefactor, and if I fail to be so he will very
soon make me conscious of my failure ; I may even be
forced to using subterfuge so as to avoid meeting him.
But he who pays promptly for everything is under no
constraint ; he is free to act as he please ; none will
hinder him. Again, the faint-hearted who complain
about their luck and sigh and weep about their misfortunes are despicable in our eyes ; instead of sympathizing
with them we do our best to keep away from them. But
if a man shows a steadfast courage in his misfortune,
and though greatly suffering, does not cringe and complain but puts a bold face upon things, to such a one our
sympathy goes out. Moreover, if a man gives up his
freedom and barters it away for money, he violates his
manhood. Life itself ought not to be rated so highly as
to warrant our being prepared, in order only not to lose
it, to live otherwise than as a man should, i.e. not a life
of ease, but so that we do not degrade our manhood.
We must also be worthy of our manhood ; whatsoever
makes us unworthy of it makes us unfit for anything,
and we cease to be men. Moreover, if a man offer his
body for profit for the sport of others—if, for instance,
he agrees in return for a few pints of beer to be knocked
about—he throws himself away, and the perpetrators who
pay him for it are acting as vilely as he. Neither can we
without destroying our person abandon ourselves to others
in order to satisfy their desires, even though it be done to
save parents and friends from death ; still less can this
be done for money. If done in order to satisfy one's own
desires, it is very immodest and immoral, but yet not
so unnatural ; but if it be done for money, or for some
other reason, a person allows himself to be treated as a
thing, and so throws away the worth of his manhood.
It is the same with the vices of the flesh (*crimina carnis*),
which for that reason are not spoken of. They do no
damage to anyone, but dishonour and degrade a man's
own person ; they are an offence against the dignity of
manhood in one's own person. The most serious offence
against the duty one owes to oneself is suicide. But
why should suicide be so abominable ? It is no answer
to say ' because God forbids it '. Suicide is not an abomina-

tion because God has forbidden it ; it is forbidden by God because it is abominable.   If it were the other way about, suicide would not be abominable if it were not forbidden ; and I should not know why God had forbidden it, if it were not abominable in itself.   The ground, therefore, for regarding suicide and other transgressions as abominable and punishable must not be found in the divine will, but in their inherent heinousness.   Suicide is an abomination because it implies the abuse of man's freedom of action : he uses his freedom to destroy himself.   His freedom should be employed to enable him to live as a man.   He is free to dispose as he pleases of things appertaining to his person, but not of his person ; he may not use his freedom against himself.   For a man to recognize what his duty is towards himself in this respect is far from easy : because although man has indeed a natural horror of suicide, yet we can argue and quibble ourselves into believing that, in order to rid himself of trouble and misery, a man may destroy himself.   The argument makes a strong appeal ; and in terms of the rule of prudence suicide may often be the surest and best course ; none the less suicide is in itself revolting.   The rule of morality, which takes precedence of all rules of reflective prudence, commands apodeictically and categorically that we must observe our duties to ourselves ; and in committing suicide and reducing himself to a carcase, man uses his powers and his liberty against himself.   Man is free to dispose of his condition but not of his person ; he himself is an end and not a means ; all else in the world is of value only as a means, but man is a person and not a thing and therefore not a means.   It is absurd that a reasonable being, an end for the sake of which all else is means, should use himself as a means.   It is true that a person can serve as a means for others (e.g. by his work), but only in a way whereby he does not cease to be a person and an end.   Whoever acts in such a way that he cannot be an end, uses himself as a means and treats his person as a thing.   Man is not free to dispose of his person as a means ; and in what follows we shall have more to say on this score.

The duties we owe to ourselves do not depend on the

relation of the action to the ends of happiness. If they did, they would depend on our inclinations and so be governed by rules of prudence. Such rules are not moral, since they indicate only the necessity of the means for the satisfaction of inclinations, and cannot therefore bind us. The basis of such obligation is not to be found in the advantages we reap from doing our duty towards ourselves, but in the worth of manhood. This principle does not allow us an unlimited freedom in respect of our own persons. It insists that we must reverence humanity in our own person, because apart from this man becomes an object of contempt, worthless in the eyes of his fellows and worthless in himself. Such faultiness is absolute. Our duties towards ourselves constitute the supreme condition and the principle of all morality; for moral worth is the worth of the person as such; our capacities have a value only in regard to the circumstances in which we find ourselves. Socrates lived in a state of wretchedness; his circumstances were worthless; but though his circumstances were so ill-conditioned, yet he himself was of the highest value. Even though we sacrifice all life's amenities we can make up for their loss and sustain approval by maintaining the worth of our humanity. We may have lost everything else, and yet still retain our inherent worth. Only if our worth as human beings is intact can we perform our other duties; for it is the foundation stone of all other duties. A man who has destroyed and cast away his personality, has no intrinsic worth, and can no longer perform any manner of duty.

Let us next consider the basis of the principle of all self-regarding duties.

Freedom is, on the one hand, that faculty which gives unlimited usefulness to all other faculties. It is the highest order of life, which serves as the foundation of all perfections and is their necessary condition. All animals have the faculty of using their powers according to will. But this will is not free. It is necessitated through the incitement of *stimuli*, and the actions of animals involve a *bruta necessitas*. If the will of all beings were so bound to sensuous impulse, the world would possess no value. The inherent value of the world, the *summum bonum*, is freedom in accordance with a will which is not necessitated to action. Freedom is thus the inner value of the world. But on the other hand, freedom unrestrained by rules of its conditional employment is the most terrible of all things. The actions of animals are regular; they are performed in accordance with rules which necessitate them subjectively. Mankind apart, nature is not free; through it all there runs a subjectively necessitating principle in accordance with which everything happens regularly. Man alone is free; his actions are not regulated by any such subjectively necessitating principle; if they were, he would not be free. And what then? If the freedom of man were not kept within bounds by objective rules, the result would be the completest savage disorder. There could then be no certainty that man might not use his powers to destroy himself, his fellows, and the whole of nature. I can conceive freedom as the complete absence of orderliness, if it is not subject to an objective determination. The grounds of this objective determination must lie in the understanding, and constitute the restrictions to freedom. Therefore the proper use of freedom is the supreme rule. What then is the condition under which freedom is restricted? It is the law. The universal law is therefore as follows: Let thy procedure be such that in all thine actions regularity prevails. What does this restraint imply when applied to the individual? That he should not follow his inclinations. The fundamental rule, in terms of which I ought to restrain my freedom, is the conformity of free behaviour to the essential ends of humanity. I shall not then follow my inclinations, but bring them under a rule. He who subjects his person to his inclinations, acts contrary to the essential end of humanity; for as a free being he must not be subjected to inclinations, but ought to determine them in the exercise of his freedom; and being a free agent he must have a rule, which is the essential end of humanity. In the case of animals inclinations are already determined by subjectively compelling factors; in their case, therefore, disorderliness is impossible. But if man gives free rein

to his inclinations, he sinks lower than an animal because
he then lives in a state of disorder which does not exist
among animals. A man is then in contradiction with
the essential ends of humanity in his own person, and so
with himself. All evil in the world springs from freedom.
Animals, not being free, live according to rules. But free
beings can only act regularly, if they restrict their freedom
by rules. Let us reflect upon the actions of man which
refer to himself, and consider freedom in them. These
spring from impulse and inclinations or from maxims and
principles. It is essential, therefore, that man should
take his stand upon maxims and restrain by rules the free
actions which relate to himself. These are the rules of
his self-regarding duties. For if we consider man in
respect of his inclinations and instincts, he is loosed from
them and determined by neither. In all nature there is
nothing to injure man in the satisfaction of his desires ;
all injurious things are his own invention, the outcome
of his freedom. We need only instance strong drink and
the many dishes concocted to tickle his palate. In the
unregulated pursuit of an inclination of his own devising,
man becomes an object of utter contempt, because his
freedom makes it possible for him to turn nature inside
out in order to satisfy himself. Let him devise what he
pleases for satisfying his desires, so long as he regulates
the use of his devices ; if he does not, his freedom is
his greatest misfortune. It must therefore be restricted,
though not by other properties or faculties, but by itself.
The supreme rule is that in all the actions which affect
himself a man should so conduct himself that every exercise
of his power is compatible with the fullest employment of
them. Let us illustrate our meaning by examples. If I
have drunk too much I am incapable of using my freedom
and my powers. Again, if I kill myself, I use my powers
to deprive myself of the faculty of using them. That
freedom, the principle of the highest order of life, should
annul itself and abrogate the use of itself conflicts with
the fullest use of freedom. But freedom can only be in
harmony with itself under certain conditions ; otherwise it
comes into collision with itself. If there were no established
order in Nature, everything would come to an end, and

so is it with unbridled freedom. Evils are to be found, no doubt, in Nature, but the true moral evil, vice, only in freedom. We pity the unfortunate, but we hate the vicious and rejoice at their punishment. The conditions under which alone the fullest use of freedom is possible, and can be in harmony with itself, are the essential ends of humanity. It must conform with these. The principle of all duties is that the use of freedom must be in keeping with the essential ends of humanity. Thus, for instance, a human being is not entitled to sell his limbs for money, even if he were offered ten thousand thalers for a single finger. If he were so entitled, he could sell all his limbs. We can dispose of things which have no freedom but not of a being which has free will. A man who sells himself makes himself a thing and, as he has jettisoned his person, it is open to anyone to deal with him as he pleases. Another instance of this kind is where a human being makes himself a thing by making himself an object of enjoyment for some one's sexual desire. It degrades humanity, and that is why those guilty of it feel ashamed. We see, therefore, that just as freedom is the source of virtue which ennobles mankind, so is it also the root of the most dreadful vices—such as, for instance, a *crimen carnis contra naturam*, since it can devise all manner of means to satisfy its inclinations. Some crimes and vices, the result of freedom (e.g. suicide), make us shudder, others are nauseating ; the mere mention of them is loathsome ; we are ashamed of them because they degrade us below the level of beasts ; they are grosser even than suicide, for the mention of suicide makes us shudder, but those other crimes and vices cannot be mentioned without producing nausea. Suicide is the most abominable of the vices which inspire dread and hate, but nausea and contempt indicate a lower level still.

Not self-favour but self-esteem should be the principle of our duties towards ourselves. This means that our actions must be in keeping with the worth of man. The legal maxim, *Neminem laede*, can be said to apply in this connexion in the form *Noli naturam humanam in te ipso laedere*. There are in us two grounds of action ; inclinations, which belong to our animal nature, and humanity, to which the inclinations must be subjected. Our duties to ourselves are negative; they restrict our freedom in respect of our inclinations, which aim at our own welfare. Just as law restricts our freedom in our relations with other men, so do our duties to ourselves restrict our freedom in dealing with ourselves. All such duties are grounded in a certain love of honour consisting in self-esteem; man must not appear unworthy in his own eyes; his actions must be in keeping with humanity itself if he is to appear in his own eyes worthy of inner respect. To value approbation is the essential ingredient of our duties towards ourselves.

The better to appreciate our duties to ourselves, let us imagine the evil consequences of failure in these duties. They will be found to be most prejudicial to man. It is, of course, the inner baseness, and not the consequences, which is the principle of the action, but the consequences enable us to appreciate better the principle of the duties. Because we have freedom and the faculty to satisfy our inclinations by all manner of devices, if we did not restrain our freedom we should destroy ourselves. If it be argued that this is a rule of prudence, the answer is that the consequences must first be given before we can derive our prudence from them. There must, therefore, be a principle that man shall restrict his freedom, and this principle is a moral one.

We shall now examine separately the several duties man owes to himself, with particular reference to the conditions under which he lives as an intelligent being.

First there is the universal duty which devolves upon man of so ordering his life as to be fit for the performance of all moral duties. This demands that he should establish in himself principles and moral purity and strive to act in accordance with them. This in turn demands that he shall prove and examine himself to see whether his dispositions also are morally pure. The springs of disposition must be examined to discover whether they are honour or illusion, superstition or pure morality. Neglect to do this is exceedingly detrimental to morality. If men were to examine the grounds of their religion and actions, they would find that honour, compassion, prudence and habit were more conspicuous in them than morality. This self-examination must be constant. It is true that the special procedure must be intermittent, but we ought constantly to watch ourselves, and exercise a certain vigilance, *vigilantia moralis*, in our actions. This watch-fulness ought to be directed upon the purity of our disposition and the strictness of our actions.

Moral fancies may infect either the moral law or our moral actions. On the one hand we may imagine that the moral law is indulgent as far as we are concerned; on the other hand, we may fancy that our moral accomplishments are in perfect keeping with the moral law. The first delusion is more harmful than the second; for should we imagine that our accomplishments conform to the perfection of the moral law, it is easy to have our misapprehension corrected by regarding the purity of the moral law; but if we assume that the moral law is indulgent, our conception of it is false and we fashion such maxims and principles that our actions in their turn can possess no moral goodness.

PROPER SELF-RESPECT

Humility, on the one hand, and true, noble pride on the other, are elements of proper self-respect; shamelessness is its opposite. We have reason to have but a low opinion of ourselves as individuals, but as representatives of mankind we ought to hold ourselves in high esteem. In the light of the law of morality, which is holy and perfect, our defects stand out with glaring distinctness and on comparing ourselves with this standard of perfection we have sufficient cause to feel humble. But if we compare ourselves with others, there is no reason to have a low opinion of ourselves; we have a right to consider ourselves as valuable as another. This self-respect in comparison with others constitutes noble pride. A low opinion of oneself in relation to others is no humility; it is a sign of a little spirit and of a servile character. To flatter oneself that this is virtue is to mistake an imitation for the genuine article; it is monk's virtue and not at all natural; this form of humility is in fact a form of pride. There is nothing unjust or unreasonable in self-esteem; we do no harm to another if we consider ourselves equal to him in our estimation. But if we are to pass judgment upon ourselves we must draw a comparison between ourselves and the purity of the moral law, and we then have cause to feel humble. We should not compare ourselves with other righteous men who, like ourselves, model themselves on the moral law. The Gospel does not teach humility, but it makes us humble.

Our self-esteem may arise from self-love and then it is favour and partiality towards ourselves. This pragmatic self-respect in accordance with rules of prudence is reasonable and possible inasmuch as it keeps us in confidence. No one can demand of me that I should humiliate myself and value myself less than others; but we all have the right to demand of a man that he should not think himself superior. Moral self-esteem, however, which is grounded in the worth of humanity, should not be derived from comparison with others, but from comparison with the moral law. Men are greatly inclined to take others as the measure of their own moral worth, and if they find that there are some whom they surpass it gives them a feeling of moral pride; but it is much more than pride if a man believes himself perfect as measured by the standard of the moral law. I can consider myself better than some others; but it is not very much only to be better than the worst, and there is really not much moral pride in that. Moral humility, regarded as the curbing of our self-conceit in face of the moral law, can thus never rest upon a comparison of ourselves with others, but with the moral law. Humility is therefore the limitation of the high opinion we have of our moral worth by comparison of our actions with the moral law. The comparison of our actions with the moral law makes us humble. Man has reason to have but a low opinion of himself because his actions not only contravene the moral law but are also lacking in purity. His frailty causes him to transgress the law, and his weakness makes his actions fall short of its purity. If an individual takes a lenient view of the moral law, he may well have a high opinion of himself and be conceited, because he judges himself by a false standard. The conceptions which the ancients had of humility and all moral virtues were impure and not in keeping with the moral law. The Gospel first presented morality in its purity, and there is nothing in history to compare with it. But if this humility is wrongly construed, harm may result ; for it does not bring courage, but the reverse. Conscious of his shortcomings, a man may feel that his actions can never attain to the level of the moral law and he may give up trying, and simply do nothing. Self-conceit and dejection are the two rocks on which man is wrecked if he deviates, in the one direction or the other, from the moral law. On the one hand, man should not despair, but should believe himself strong enough to follow the moral law, even though he himself is not conformable to it. On the other hand, he ought to avoid self-conceit and an exaggerated notion of his powers ; the purity of the moral law should prevent him from falling into this pitfall, for no one who has the law explained to him in its absolute purity can be so foolish as to imagine that it is within his powers fully to comply with it. The existence of this safeguard makes the danger of self-conceit less than that of inertia grounded in faith. It is only the lazy, those who have no wish to do anything themselves but to leave it all to God, who interpret their religion thus. The remedy against such dejection and inertia is to be found in our being able to hope that our weakness and infirmity will be supplemented by the help of God if we but do the utmost that the consciousness of our capacity tells us we are able to do. This is the one and indispensable condition on which we can be worthy of God's help, and have a right to hope for it. In order to convince man of his weakness, make him humble and induce him to pray to God for help, some writers have tried to deny to man any good disposition. This can do no good. It is certainly right and proper that man should recognize how weak he is, but not by the sacrifice of his good dispositions, for if he is to receive God's help he must at least be worthy of it. If we depreciate the value of human virtues we do harm, because if we deny good intentions to the man who lives aright, where is the difference between him and the evil-doer? Each of us feels that at some time or other we have done a good action from a good disposition and that we are capable of doing so again. Though our actions are all very imperfect, and though we can never hope that they will attain to the standard of the moral law, yet they may approach ever nearer and nearer to it.

CONSCIENCE

Conscience is an instinct to pass judgment upon ourselves in accordance with moral laws. It is not a mere faculty, but an instinct; and its judgment is not logical, but judicial. We have the faculty to judge ourselves logically in terms of laws of morality; we can make such use as we please of this faculty. But conscience has the power to summon us against our will before the judgment-seat to be judged on account of the righteousness or unrighteousness of our actions. It is thus an instinct and not merely a faculty of judgment, and it is an instinct to judge, not in the logical, but in the judicial sense. A judge passes judgment; he does not merely form a judgment. The difference is that he has the right to judge *valide*, and to give legal effect to his judgment. Thus his judgment has force of law, and is a sentence. The judge must either condemn or acquit, not merely form a judgment. If our conscience were merely an impulse to form a judgment, it would be, like other faculties of which we are possessed (e.g. the impulses to compare ourselves with others, or to flatter ourselves), a faculty of knowledge. We all have an impulse to pat ourselves on the back for good actions done in accordance with rules of prudence. We likewise reproach ourselves for imprudent conduct. Thus we all have an impulse to flatter and blame ourselves in accordance with rules of prudence. But this tendency to praise and blame oneself is not conscience, though it is analogous to it and men often mistake it for conscience. A criminal lying under sentence of death frets and worries

and reproaches himself severely, but mainly for the imprudence which led to detection. He imagines that it is his
conscience which reproaches him for his immorality; but
it is not the pangs of conscience that he feels; for, had he got
off scot-free, he would have felt no qualms, and if he had
a conscience he would feel its reproach in any event. We
must, therefore, differentiate between the judgment of
prudence and the judgment of conscience. Many people
have only a semblance of conscience which they imagine
is conscience itself. Death-bed repentance is a case in
point. Such repentance is often enough not remorse for
the immorality of behaviour, but for the folly of actions
which, now that the judgment-seat is near, make it impossible to stand before the judge. Vices bring their
own punishments, and these punishments bring home to
us the criminality of the acts; a man, therefore, who feels
disgust with his past vices does not know whether his
loathing is due to the punishments or to the criminality
of his offences. He who has no immediate loathing for
what is morally wicked, and finds no pleasure in what is
morally good, has no moral feeling, and such a man has
no conscience. He who goes in fear of being prosecuted
for a wicked deed, does not reproach himself on the score
of the wickedness of his misdemeanour, but on the score
of the painful consequences which await him; such a
one has no conscience, but only a semblance of it. But
he who has a sense of the wickedness of the deed itself, be
the consequences what they may, has a conscience. We
must guard against confusion here: reproaches for the
consequences of imprudence must not be confused with
reproaches for breaches of morality. It is important in
practice that a teacher, for instance, should look to see
whether his pupil repents a deed from a true sense of its
wickedness, or whether he feels remorse because he must
soon face a judge before whom, on account of his action,
he cannot hope to stand. Repentance which manifests
itself for the first time on the death-bed has no moral
worth: its motive is the nearness of death; if the approach
of death were not feared there would probably be no
repentance. The penitent in such a case may be likened
to the unlucky gambler who fumes and rages against

himself for his folly and tears his hair. He has no qualms about the vice; he hates its consequences. We ought not to be misled into consoling and comforting a man for such a semblance of conscience.

Prudence reproaches; conscience accuses. If a man has acted unwisely and reproaches himself for his imprudence no longer than is necessary for him to learn his lesson, he is observing a rule of prudence and it must be accounted to him for honour, for it is a sign of strength of character. But the accusation of conscience cannot be so readily dismissed, neither should it be; it is not a matter of the will, and the capacity to dismiss the accusation of a remorseful conscience is no evidence of strength of character, but rather of wickedness and religious impenitence. A man who can at will dismiss the accusations of conscience is a rebel, like the man who can disregard the accusation of his judge, over whom the judge has no power. Conscience is an instinct to judge with legal authority according to moral laws; it pronounces a judicial verdict, and, like a judge who can only punish or acquit but cannot reward, so also our conscience either acquits or declares us guilty and deserving of punishment. The judgment has validity if it is felt and enforced. Two consequences follow from this. The first effectual expression of this judicial verdict which has the force of law is moral repentance; the second, without which the sentence is inoperative, is action in accordance with the judicial verdict. If it does not result in practical endeavour to do what is demanded for the satisfaction of the moral law, the conscience is but an idle conscience, and however penitent we may be the penitence is vain so long as we do not satisfy the debt we owe to the moral law; for even *in foro humano* a debt is not satisfied by penitence, but by payment. Preachers must, therefore, impress upon their hearers that, whilst they must repent for their transgressions against their duties to themselves, though they cannot remedy these, in the case of injustice done to others mere repentance is not enough: it must be followed by endeavour to remedy the injustice. Whining and lamentation are as useless *in foro divino* as they are *in foro humano*. The history of death-bed repentances can, of course, show

no instance of such practical repentance—a proof that it
neglects an essential element.

The court of justice of our conscience can conveniently
be compared with an ordinary law-court. We find in our
hearts a prosecutor, for whom there would be no place
unless there were also a law. This law, which is based on
reason and not on sentiment, is incorruptible and incon-
testably just and pure ; it is the moral law, established
as the holy and inviolable law of humanity. Beside these
there is equally an advocate within us, called Self-love,
who brings forward many an argument in our defence,
and whose pleas the prosecutor in his turn endeavours to
refute. Lastly we find a judge within us who either
condemns or acquits. It is impossible to blind his judgment. To refuse to appear before the bar of conscience
is easier. Once we appear, the judge pronounces imparti-
ally, and his verdict falls normally upon the side of truth.
If not, it must be because he judges by false principles of
morality. Except on the death-bed, when they listen
more eagerly to the accuser, men lend a readier ear to
their defender. A good conscience demands a pure law,
for the accuser must be on the watch, whatever we do ;
and in judging our actions we must judge justly and
morally and must have strength of conscience to give
effect to the valid judgment. The conscience must have
its operative, and not merely its speculative, principles ;
and to make its judgments operative it must be strong
and command respect. Where is the judge who would
be content to do no more than lecture and make judicial
pronouncements ? Judicial pronouncements must be put
into operation.

Let us consider wherein the just conscience differs from
one that is at fault. An error of conscience can be either
an *error facti* or an *error legis*. If a man's conscience errs
and he acts in accordance with it, his acts may be at fault,
but they cannot be accounted to him for a transgression.
There are *errores culpabiles* and *errores inculpabiles*. In
respect of his natural obligations no man can be at fault ;
the natural moral laws must be known to all ; they are
contained in our reason ; no man can, therefore, err innocently in respect of them, and in the case of natural

laws there can be no innocent errors; but it is otherwise with positive laws; here we can have *errores inculpabiles*, and a *conscientia erronea* may give rise to actions which are not culpable. In respect of the natural law there can be no *errores inculpabiles*. But what is a man to do when a positive and a natural law conflict? Take, for instance, the case of a man who is taught by his religion to execrate adherents of other religions, or that of a man who is told by Jesuits that good can come from knavery. Such a man would not be acting in accord with his conscience; the natural law is known to him, and he is aware that he ought on no account to act unrighteously. The verdict of natural conscience being in conflict with the verdict of instructed conscience, he must obey the former. All positive laws are conditioned by the natural law, and they cannot, therefore, rightly contain anything which conflicts with it. To plead the excuse of an erring conscience is a serious matter, for in this way we could shift the responsibility for a great deal; but we are also accountable for our errors. In talking of a natural conscience, Baumgarten would appear to be contrasting ' natural ' with ' revealed '; but all conscience is natural, although it may be based on a supernatural or a revealed law. Conscience is the representative within us of the divine judgment-seat : it weighs our dispositions and actions in the scales of a law which is holy and pure ; we cannot deceive it, and, lastly, we cannot escape it because, like the divine omnipresence, it is always with us. Since, then, conscience is the representative within us of divine justice, we must not hurt or injure it. We might contrast *conscientia naturalis* and *conscientia artificialis*. Many have argued that conscience is a work of art and education, and that it judges and sentences by force of habit ; but if this were the case, men with a conscience not so tutored and practised could escape the stings of conscience ; there are, however, no cases of this. It is obvious that art and instruction can only bring into fruition that for which we have a natural aptitude, so that if our conscience is to judge we must have a prior knowledge of good and evil. Yet a cultivated mind need not be followed by a cultivated conscience. Thus conscience is synonymous with natural conscience ;

and if we are to draw distinctions it should be between conscience before, during, and after the act. Before the act the conscience has power enough to dissuade a man from committing the act, during the act it is stronger, and it is strongest of all after the act. Before the act conscience must still be weak; for the act has not yet been committed, and we feel weaker in the presence of an unsatisfied inclination which is still strong enough to withstand conscience. During the act conscience becomes stronger; and then, when inclination is satisfied, and has become too weak to withstand conscience, conscience is at its strongest. We can see from the case of passion that after satisfying his strongest desire, a man is even overcome by a feeling of disgust, because a strong passion, once satisfied, becomes too languid to offer opposition, so that conscience is at its strongest, and remorse follows. But a conscience which does no more than this is incomplete; the law demands satisfaction.

Conscientia concomitans, or conscience accompanying the act, is gradually weakened by usage, so that in the long run man becomes as used to his vices as to tobacco smoke. In the end his conscience loses all its authority, the court of justice ceases to function and decide, and the accuser has no longer any task to perform. Some burden their conscience with many matters of negligible importance (*adiaphora*); they ask it to resolve problems of a quibbling nature, such as whether it is right to tell a lie in order to make an April fool of a person, or whether a rite or ceremony should be performed in this or that manner. This is casuistry, and it produces a micrological conscience. The subtler conscience is in such matters of detail, the worse is it in matters of practical importance, and people with such consciences are notoriously wont to concern themselves with speculations arising from positive law and to give themselves a free hand in everything else. If a person is capable of reproaching himself for his sins, his conscience is said to be alive; but on the other hand, if a man searches needlessly for evidences of evil in his conduct, his conscience is melancholy. Conscience should not lord it over us like a tyrant; we do no hurt to our conscience by proceeding on our way cheerfully; tormenting consciences in the long run become dulled and ultimately cease to function.

SELF-LOVE

The love which takes delight in others is the judgment of delight in their perfection ; the love which takes delight in ourselves, or self-love, is an inclination to be well-content with ourselves in judging our own perfection. *Philautia*, or moral self-love, is not arrogance or moral self-sufficiency. *Philautia* and arrogance differ in that the former is merely an inclination to be satisfied with one's *perfections*, whereas the latter is an unwarranted claim to merit ; whilst the one pretends to be possessed of more moral perfections than it has, the other claims nothing and is merely satisfied with itself and does not take itself to task ; the one is proud of its moral perfections, the other is not, simply believing itself blameless and innocent. Arrogance is a harmful fault. *Philautia* tests itself by the moral law, not by taking it as a guide, but through examples, and so finds cause for self-satisfaction. The examples of moral men are criteria taken from experience ; but the moral law is a criterion of the reason. If we make use of the first of these criteria the result is either *philautia* or arrogance. We have arrogance if we take a narrow and indulgent view of the moral law, or if the moral judge within us is not impartial. The less strict our view of the moral law and the less strictly the judge within us judges us, the more arrogant we are apt to be.

Self-love differs from self-esteem. Esteem refers to intrinsic worth ; love to the bearing which worth has on welfare. We esteem that which has intrinsic worth, and we love that which has worth through its bearing on something else. Thus intellect has intrinsic worth irrespective of the purposes to which it is applied. He who does his duty, who does not degrade his person, is estimable ; he who is sociable is lovable. We can judge ourselves to be worthy either of esteem or of love. The man who believes himself kindhearted, who thinks that he would gladly help other men if he were only rich (and if he is, in fact, rich, if he were still richer—as rich as so and so, for what he has he needs badly himself, as all miserly people believe), such a man judges himself to be lovable. On the other hand, the man who believes that he is fulfilling the essential ends of humanity, thinks himself worthy of esteem. If a man believes himself kindhearted and promotes the welfare of all mankind by empty wishes, he is a prey to *philautia*. That a man should wish himself well is natural ; but it is not natural that he should have a good opinion of himself. Men fall into *philautia* or arrogance according to their temperaments. Gellert's philosophy is full of talk of love and kindness and friend-ship—the hobby-horses of all moralists ; such philosophy conduces to self-love. But man is required to be worthy, not so much of love, as of respect and of esteem. A con-scientious and righteous man who is impartial and will accept no bribe, is not an object of love, and because he is conscientious in the matter of what he accepts, he will have few opportunities to act with magnanimity and love, and he will consequently not be thought lovable by his fellows. But he finds happiness in being considered by his fellows worthy of esteem ; virtue is his true, intrinsic worth. A man might therefore be an object of esteem without being an object of love, because he refuses to curry favour. We can also love a bad man without in the least respecting him. Whatever increases self-love ought to be rejected from moral philosophy, and only that ought to be commended which makes one worthy of respect, e.g. doing one's duty to oneself, righteousness and conscien-tiousness ; these things may not make us objects of love, but we can hold our head high, though not defiantly, and look men straight in the eye, for we have worth. This is not arrogance, for we do not strain the standard of the moral law. By that standard we feel humble ; by the standard of comparison with other men we can regard ourselves as worthy of respect. Moral *philautia*, which gives a man a high opinion of himself in respect of his moral perfections, is detestable ; it springs up when we preen ourselves upon the goodness of our disposition, and think to promote the welfare of the world by empty wishes

and romantic ideas. We love the Hottentot and would
fain do good to him, but give no thought to our neighbour
because he is too near us. *Philautia* is unpractical, and
consists of wishes which merely shrivel the heart. Self-
lovers are generally milk-sops, not solid and practical ; the
arrogant are at least practical.

In man's moral court of justice there exists a type of
sophistication to which self-love gives rise. Our inner
advocate becomes a pettifogger, expounding the law
sophistically to our advantage. More than this, he grows
deceitful and cheats about the facts. All his sophistries
serve but to undermine his credit with us, so that we
look upon him as a twister. Only a weak man fails to
appreciate this. Our pettifogger engages in all manner of
legal quibbles ; he makes use of the letter of the law for
his own purposes ; when dealing with facts he pays no
heed to disposition, but only to external circumstances ;
he deals in probabilities. This theory of moral probability
is a means of self-deception whereby a man persuades
himself that he has been acting on principle and rightly.
There is nothing worse, nothing more abominable than the
artifice that invents a false law to enable us, under the
shelter of the true law, to do evil. A man who has transgressed against the moral law, but still recognizes it in its
purity, can be improved because he still has a pure law
before his eyes ; but a man who has invented for himself a favourable and false law has a principle in his
wickedness, and in his case we can hope for no improvement.

A man may compare himself with others and esteem
only himself. This is moral egoism. We ought not to
measure our worth by comparing ourselves with others,
but with the standard of the moral law. To compare ourselves with others is to use a fortuitous standard, which
may lead to a very different estimate of our worth. We
may conclude that we are of lesser value than others.
This makes us hate them and produces envy and jealousy.
Parents sow the seeds of these in their children when they
do not bring them up by the principles of morality, but
constantly point to other children as examples. Envy
and jealousy are thus engendered in them ; because if

these others did not exist, they themselves would not be regarded as inferior.

To love oneself alone in comparison with others is moral solipsism, which belongs properly to the sphere of duties towards others and not of duties to ourselves.

SELF-MASTERY

The principle of self-mastery is universal respect for one's own person in relation to the essential ends of humanity or human nature. This is the principle of duties to oneself, and the objective condition of morality. The self-regarding duties are conditions under which alone the other duties can be performed. But what is the subjective condition of the performance of duties to oneself ? Here is the rule : Seek to maintain self-mastery ; thou wilt then be fit to perform thy self-regarding duties. There is in man a certain rabble of acts of sensibility which has to be vigilantly disciplined, and kept under strict rule, even to the point of applying force to make it submit to the ordinances of government. This rabble does not naturally conform to the rule of the understanding, yet it is good only in so far as it does so conform. Man must have discipline, and he disciplines himself by the rules of prudence. We often wish to stay a little longer in bed, but force ourselves to get up because we see that it is necessary. Again, we often would like to go on eating or drinking, but refrain, because we see that it would be harmful.

This discipline is the executive authority of the prescription of reason over the acts whose origin is in sensibility. It is the pragmatic discipline of prudence. But we must have yet another form of discipline—moral discipline, the endeavour to master and control our sensuous acts not by prudence but by the moral laws. Moral discipline derives its authority from these laws, and provides the condition under which alone we can perform our duties to ourselves. It follows, therefore, that self-mastery is one's highest duty to oneself. It consists in the ability to subject all our principles and faculties to

our free will. This can be done in two ways : by the rule
of prudence, or by the rule of morality. It is true that
every rule of prudence depends upon the rule of the
understanding, but in the case of the rule of prudence,
the understanding is a servant of the sensibility; it provides the means for satisfying inclination, because of its
subordination to the ends of sensibility. But real self-
mastery is moral. In its sovereignty it issues categorical
laws to the sensibility, unlike pragmatic self-mastery,
where the understanding uses one element of sensibility
to counter another. To exercise a sovereign authority
over ourselves we must invest morality with the highest
authority over us; it must rule our sensibility. Can
man govern himself, if he will ? Since it rests with
ourselves, it appears that we can, and we think it easier to
obtain mastery over ourselves than over others. Yet,
indeed, the very fact that it is ourselves we seek to master
makes it difficult ; for then our powers are divided ;
sensibility is in conflict with understanding, whereas if
we wish to obtain mastery over others we marshal all
our forces for the task. Furthermore, we have to contend
with another source of difficulty. The moral law contains
precepts, but no motives ; it lacks the executive authority
of moral feeling. Moral feeling does not distinguish
between good and evil. It is a motive to action which
arises when sensibility is in harmony with understanding.
In moral matters men can have a sound judgment, but no
feeling ; they recognize that an act is evil and deserves
punishment, but they nevertheless commit it. Now self-
mastery depends on the strength of our moral feeling. To
govern ourselves well, we must weaken the opposing forces.
To do this we must divide them. It follows that we must
first of all discipline ourselves. By repeated endeavour we
must stamp out the tendency which arises from sensuous
motive. He who wishes to discipline himself morally,
must watch himself carefully ; he must at frequent intervals
give to the judge within him an account of his deeds ; by
constant practice he will strengthen the moral grounds of
impulse, through self-cultivation he will acquire a habit
of desire and aversion in regard to what is morally good
and bad. In this way his moral feeling will be cultivated,

since morality will acquire strength and motives. These motives will weaken and overcome his sensibility, and in this way self-mastery will be achieved. Without disciplining his inclinations man can attain to nothing. Therefore in self-mastery there resides an immediate worth, for to be lord of oneself is to be independent of all things. Where no such mastery exists, there is anarchy. But the anarchy is not absolute ; there is moral anarchy, but prudence takes the place of morality and rules in its stead. Self-control by the rules of prudence is merely a semblance of self-mastery.

The power of the soul over all our faculties and circumstances to make them submit to its free and undetermined will is autocratic. Man must give this autocracy its full scope ; otherwise he becomes a plaything of other forces and impressions which withstand his will and a prey to the caprice of accident and circumstance. If he surrenders authority over himself, his imagination has free play ; he cannot discipline himself, but his imagination carries him away by the laws of association ; he yields willingly to his senses, and, unable to curb them, he becomes their toy and they sway his judgment. Leaving aside inclination and passion, we need only consider the arbitrariness of man's intellectual position, if his thought is not under his own control. Every man must, therefore, secure that his powers and his condition submit to the authority of his free will. Our authority over ourselves is both productive and disciplinary. As executive authority it can, in spite of every obstacle, compel us to produce certain effects, in which event it has might. As directing authority it can only guide the forces of character. Thus, for instance, a motive to slothfulness within us cannot be suppressed by the directing but only by the compulsive authority. Again, if we have prejudices, it is not enough to guide our hearts ; we must use the force of authority, or we shall be carried away by them. Man has strength to guide his heart, but not to dominate it, and even if there is no rebellious element in our hearts, in the absence of rules it can only be guided. Our sensibility is a kind of rabble without law or rule ; it requires guidance even if it is not rebellious. In our powers, however, there is an

element of habit which resists the dominion and free will
of the thinking subject. Voluptuousness and laziness, for
instance, must not merely be guided but dominated. Our
autocracy is, therefore, the power to compel our hearts to do
our bidding in spite of every obstacle. Autocracy implies
not merely directing authority, but mastery over oneself.

Baumgarten, in enumerating the duties towards ourselves, falls into an error which we must touch on here.
He includes in his list all human perfections, even those
which relate to our talents. He speaks of the perfection
of all the powers of the soul. On this argument, logic
and all sciences which go to perfect the understanding and
satisfy our thirst for knowledge, would need to be included ;
but there is nothing moral in these. Morality does not tell
us what we ought to do in order to become perfect in the
skilled use of our powers ; any such precepts are merely
pragmatic, they are rules of prudence for amplifying our
powers because this conduces to our welfare. But when
speaking of morality we must exclude everything which
has no bearing on the perfecting of our inner worth, maintaining in our own person the dignity of humanity, and
subjecting everything to our own will, in so far as our will
directs our actions in conformity with the essential ends of
humanity. All of Baumgarten's rules and propositions
in which he lays down our duties to ourselves, and all his
definitions, are tautological. A practical proposition is
tautological, when no performance can follow from it ;
when it specifies means by which what is demanded cannot
be produced ; when it comprises conditions which are
identical with the given conditions and demands. The
problem is tautologically resolved when conditions reappear
in the solution which were already comprised in its statement. All practical sciences à priori, with the exception
of mathematics, contain tautological propositions. Practical logic is full of them ; it states conditions which have
been stated by theoretical logic. It is the same with
moral philosophy, which does not indicate the means for
fulfilling the condition required. This is a common error,
not confined to Baumgarten ; and if we cannot correct it
fully, we will at least show wherein it consists. This will
enable us to notice the gaps in the sciences, and make their

filling up a possibility. We should not even notice them if we believed that there were none but that everything was perfect.

To promote the perfections of one's talents is, therefore, not a part of the duties to oneself which Baumgarten discusses at length on philosophical lines. We can perform our duties to ourselves without speculation and with but an imperfect comprehension. All embellishments of the mind are its luxuries; they appertain to the *melius esse*, but not to the *esse* of it. But to have a healthy mind in a healthy body is a duty to oneself, and in so far as the perfections of our mental powers are bound up with the essential ends of mankind, it is a duty to ourselves to promote them. All our mental powers and characteristics can have a bearing upon moral conduct.

The autocracy of the human mind, with all the powers of the soul in so far as they have a bearing on morality, is the principle of our duties towards ourselves, and on that very account of all other duties. Let us survey the powers of the mind which bear on moral conduct in order to see how we are to apply to them our autocracy, our capacity to keep them under the control of free will. Let us take imagination first. Our most vivid images and fancies are not produced by the allurement of objects, but by our own power of imagination. We must therefore exercise our authority over it lest it provide us with riotous and capricious images. The objects which give rise to the images are not always before us, but the images which we carry with us can be ever present, causing us to offend and trespass in our duties towards ourselves. If, for instance, we give our imagination free play in sensual pleasures, to the extent of even giving it reality, vices are created which are contrary to nature and involve most serious offences against the duties we owe to ourselves. Our imaginings have intensified the allurement of the object. Here our autocracy should step in to banish such imaginings completely from our mind and to prevent our imagination casting a spell over us by representing objects which we cannot attain. This is our duty to ourselves in so far as imagination is concerned.

With regard to the senses generally, as they outwit and

cheat the understanding, we can do nothing else than
outwit them in turn by doing our best to offer to the mind
an alternative entertainment to that offered by the senses.
We must try to occupy the mind with ideal pleasures,
with which all polite learning and literature are concerned.
The relation of wit to morality does not fall within the
scope of our self-regarding duty to further our own perfection. The sportiveness of the mind must produce a
pleasure which touches ourselves and not the forces of
duty.

Baumgarten includes observation of oneself amongst
the duties towards oneself. We keep ourselves under
observation not by eavesdropping but by watchful attention to our actions. The effort to know ourselves and so
to discover whether we are good or bad must be made in
the practical business of living, by examining our actions
to see whether they are good or bad. The supreme rule
is this : Give good, practical proof of yourselves in your
lives by your actions ; not by set prayers, but by doing
good acts, by work and steadiness, and in particular by
righteousness and active benevolence towards your neighbour; then you can see whether you are good. Just as
one does not get to know a friend from conversation, but
from having dealings with him, so also it is not easy to
get to know oneself from any opinion one has about oneself. In any case it is not so easy to know oneself. Thus
many people do not know that they are stout-hearted
and have courage until an opportunity occurs to show
it in act. Again, a person is often disposed to an action
without knowing whether he could actually perform it.
Thus, for instance, many people think to themselves that
they would do this or that magnanimous action if they
won a substantial prize in a lottery, and if perchance they
do win it, nothing comes of their good intentions. So it
is with the evil-doer who, faced with death, is full of
honourable and upright dispositions ; they may be so,
but he does not know himself ; he does not know whether,
if the threat of impending death were removed, he would
act in accordance with them ; in the state in which he
finds himself he cannot imagine himself saved ; but in
point of fact if he continued to live he would continue to

be a rogue, for, although he has the power to change, he cannot do so all at once. Self-knowledge, therefore, always comes to man little by little.

Let us now consider something which approaches ever nearer and nearer to autocracy, and which includes *suspensio judicii*. In our judgments there must be so much of autocracy that we should be able to defer them if we will and not driven to declare our judgment on good grounds of persuasion. To defer coming to a decision shows great strength of mind, whatever the decision. Thus, for instance, it is a strong mind which can delay coming to a decision in a matter of choice until fully convinced. If I receive a letter which angers me greatly and I answer it on the spot, my answer will show much evidence of my anger, but if I can defer my reply to the following day, I will approach it from a different point of view. *Suspensio judicii* is thus an important factor in autocracy. In active pursuits we show our autocracy by keeping our mind active and efficient under the burden of work, contented whatever the nature of the work, satisfied with itself, conscious of having sufficient strength to carry out the work without vexation, and strong to overcome the discomfort of the work. We must, therefore, have the resolution to persist firmly in what we have undertaken and to give short shrift to the whisperings of procrastination. Presence of mind is also included in autocracy. It is the unity and harmony of our mental powers which reveals itself in the process of carrying the business through. It is a gift which not all of us have; it depends upon natural talent, but for all that it can be strengthened by practice.

We shall next consider the self-regarding duties in such matters as pleasure, desire and aversion, satisfaction and dissatisfaction.

Ills are the opposite of well-being—wickedness the opposite of good conduct. Wickedness arises from our freedom and is produced entirely by our conduct; but ills can also be produced by nature. With regard to all the ills in the world man ought to show himself steady, resolute and calm of mind; but not so in regard to wickedness; only a profligate mind and an infamous character can remain calm and composed in the face of wickedness, for such an attitude merely intensifies the evil; wicked acts ought rather to be accompanied by a consciousness of spiritual pain. But a mind which faces ills and misfortune steadily and cheerfully makes man more worthy. To submit to physical ills and to be the toy of accident and circumstance is contrary to the dignity of man, and there is no need for it; there is a source of strength in man's character which enables him to withstand all ills. The means for the cultivation of steadfastness of mind consists in the removal of that false appearance which lurks in the supposed goods of life and in the common acceptation of happiness. The greatest source of happiness and unhappiness, of well-being and wretchedness, of satisfaction and dissatisfaction is to be found in the comparison with other men. If every one in the town had nothing but bread and water for food and drink, I should be satisfied with so simple a diet and would submit to it with a cheerful mind; but if every one else were able to enjoy sumptuous repasts and I alone had to live in a wretched state, I should feel unhappy and regard it as a misfortune. Thus good and ill-fortune depend upon ourselves and upon the mental attitude we adopt towards them. For let us consider the happiness of this life, and we find that it consists in an illusion. The beggar at the door is often happier than the king on his throne; life is short and all happiness fleeting; we shudder at the thought of some great misfortune, but when it befalls us we find it bearable; we have no claim upon fortune, but regard ourselves as unfortunate because before the blow fell we were always happy and have been so pampered that we look upon every diminution of our happiness as a fresh misfortune. Yet contemplation of these things makes us realize that we can readily dispense with a good deal and maintain a virtuous and cheerful frame of mind in whatever ill befalls us. We cannot claim greater happiness in this life. God has placed us on the stage of this world, provided us with all the materials for our welfare and with freedom to use them as we please, and everything depends on how men divide these benefits among themselves. Of this task men doubtless make a sorry mess. Let us then accept the benefits of life as we have received them, let us be satisfied with God's universal wisdom and care and not allow misery and misfortune to weigh upon us. The man in wretched circumstances who faces his condition with a resolute and cheerful heart, who sets it at nought since there it is and he cannot alter it, is not miserable ; the wretched man is he who thinks himself so ; and he is also malicious because he envies others their good fortune. Thus a wicked ruler once said : ' God hates the unfortunate, for otherwise he would not let him linger in misfortune ; we therefore promote God's intentions if we make the unfortunate still more unfortunate.' But by turning this malicious idea round we can say that he who regards himself as unfortunate and unhappy deserves to be hated ; while he who in his misfortune shows a cheerful and resolute heart and maintains a calm courage even when he has lost everything, possesses a value in himself, and deserves our sympathy instead. To keep the soul free from the wickedness of envy we must try to bear every misfortune, and when once it has befallen us, to extract from it the advantage which can be derived from every misfortune. It rests with us to put ourselves in the proper humour— a humour is a wilfully chosen disposition—in which to contemplate the world and its fortunes and to pass judgment upon them.

With regard to the guidance of the mind in respect of the emotions and passions, we must distinguish these from feelings and inclinations. A man can have feeling and inclination for something without having emotion and passion. If the feelings and passions are so bound up with the reason that their soul is in harmony with reason, they can quite well be in keeping with our duties towards ourselves. These duties and the dignity of humanity demand that man should have no passion or emotion, but though this is the principle it is open to question whether man can really achieve so much. In his work man must be thorough, regular and resolute and must beware of giving way to the heat of passion. No man is sane when swayed by passion ; his inclination is blind and cannot be in keeping with the dignity of mankind. We must, therefore, altogether avoid giving way to passion, and the rule laid down by the Stoics in this regard is correct. The most ungodly of all passions is that of religious fervour, because it makes man think that under the cloak of piety he can do all manner of things.

To sum up, the autocracy of the mind over all mental powers and faculties must be regarded as the principal condition of observing our duties towards ourselves. The maxims of our conduct must, of course, be well weighed, and it is worse to do evil from maxims than from inclination. But good actions must be done from maxims.

Finally, we must mention that Baumgarten speaks of victory over oneself, but there need be no question of any such victory if man governs himself so well that he prevents mutiny and disorder in his mind and preserves peace therein (by peace in this connexion we do not mean satisfaction with everything, but orderly government and unity). If he does that there is no conflict in his mind and consequently there can be no victory. It is far better that man should so govern himself that he need gain no victory over himself.

DUTIES TOWARDS THE BODY IN REGARD TO LIFE

What are our powers of disposal over our life ? Have we any authority of disposal over it in any shape or form ? How far is it incumbent upon us to take care of it ? These are questions which fall to be considered in connexion with our duties towards the body in regard to life. We must, however, by way of introduction, make the following observations. If the body were related to life not as a condition but as an accident or circumstance so that we could at will divest ourselves of it ; if we could slip out of it and slip into another just as we leave one country for another, then the body would be subject to our free will and we could rightly have the disposal of it. This, however, would not imply that we could similarly dispose of our life, but only of our circumstances, of the movable goods, the furniture of life. In fact, however, our life is entirely conditioned by our body, so that we cannot conceive of a life not mediated by the body and we cannot make use of our freedom except through the body. It is, therefore, obvious that the body constitutes a part of ourselves. If a man destroys his body, and so his life, he does it by the use of his will, which is itself destroyed in the process. But to use the power of a free will for its own destruction is self-contradictory. If freedom is the condition of life it cannot be employed to abolish life and so to destroy and abolish itself. To use life for its own destruction, to use life for producing lifelessness, is self-contradictory. These preliminary remarks are sufficient to show that man cannot rightly have any power of disposal in regard to himself and his life, but only in regard to his circumstances. His body gives man power over his life ; were he a spirit he could not destroy his life ; life in the absolute has been invested by nature with indestructibility and is an end in itself ; hence it follows that man cannot have the power to dispose of his life.

SUICIDE

Suicide can be regarded in various lights ; it might be held to be reprehensible, or permissible, or even heroic. In the first place we have the specious view that suicide can be allowed and tolerated. Its advocates argue thus. So long as he does not violate the proprietary rights of others, man is a free agent. With regard to his body there are various things he can properly do ; he can have a boil lanced or a limb amputated, and disregard a scar ; he is, in fact, free to do whatever he may consider useful and advisable. If then he comes to the conclusion that the most useful and advisable thing that he can do is to put an end to his life, why should he not be entitled to do so ? Why not, if he sees that he can no longer go on living and that he will be ridding himself of misfortune, torment and disgrace ? To be sure he robs himself of a full life, but he escapes once and for all from calamity and misfortune. The argument sounds most plausible. But let us, leaving aside religious considerations, examine the act itself. We may treat our body as we please, provided our motives are those of self-preservation. If, for instance, his foot is a hindrance to life, a man might have it amputated. To preserve his person he has the right of disposal over his body. But in taking his life he does not preserve his person; he disposes of his person and not of its attendant circumstances; he robs himself of his person. This is contrary to the highest duty we have towards ourselves, for it annuls the condition of all other duties; it goes beyond the limits of the use of free will, for this use is possible only through the existence of the Subject.

There is another set of considerations which make suicide seem plausible. A man might find himself so placed that he can continue living only under circumstances which deprive life of all value; in which he can no longer live conformably to virtue and prudence, so that he must from noble motives put an end to his life. The advocates of this view quote in support of it the example of Cato. Cato knew that the entire Roman nation relied upon him in their resistance to Caesar, but he found that he could not prevent himself from falling into Caesar's hands. What was he to do? If he, the champion of freedom, submitted, every one would say, "If Cato himself submits, what else can we do?" If, on the other hand, he killed himself, his death might spur on the Romans to fight to the bitter end in defence of their freedom. So he killed himself. He thought that it was necessary for him to die. He thought that if he could not go on living as Cato, he could not go on living at all. It must certainly be admitted that in a case such as this, where suicide is a virtue, appearances are in its favour. But this is the only example which has given the world the opportunity of defending suicide. It is the only example of its kind and there has been no similar case since. Lucretia also killed herself, but on grounds of modesty and in a fury of vengeance. It is obviously our duty to preserve our honour, particularly in relation to the opposite sex, for whom it is a merit; but we must endeavour to save our honour only to this extent, that we ought not to surrender it for selfish and lustful purposes. To do what Lucretia did is to adopt a remedy which is not at our disposal; it would have been better had she defended her honour unto death; that would not have been suicide and would have been right; for it is no suicide to risk one's life against one's enemies, and even to sacrifice it, in order to observe one's duties towards oneself.

No one under the sun can bind me to commit suicide; no sovereign can do so. The sovereign can call upon his subjects to fight to the death for their country, and those who fall on the field of battle are not suicides, but the victims of fate. Not only is this not suicide; but the opposite, a faint heart and fear of the death which threatens by the necessity of fate, is no true self-preservation; for he who runs away to save his own life, and leaves his comrades in the lurch, is a coward; but he who defends himself and his fellows even unto death is no suicide, but noble and high-minded; for life is not to be highly regarded for its own sake. I should endeavour to preserve my own life only so far as I am worthy to live. We must draw a distinction between the suicide and the victim of fate. A man who shortens his life by intemperance is guilty of imprudence and indirectly of his own death; but his guilt is not direct; he did not intend to kill himself; his death was not premeditated. For all our offences are either *culpa* or *dolus*. There is certainly no *dolus* here, but there is *culpa*; and we can say of such a man that he was guilty of his own death, but we cannot say of him that he is a suicide. What constitutes suicide is the intention to destroy oneself. Intemperance and excess which shorten life ought not, therefore, to be called suicide; for if we raise intemperance to the level of suicide, we lower suicide to the level of intemperance. Imprudence, which does not imply a desire to cease to live, must, therefore, be distinguished from the intention to murder oneself. Serious violations of our duty towards ourselves produce an aversion accompanied either by horror or by disgust; suicide is of the horrible kind, *crimina carnis* of the disgusting. We shrink in horror from suicide because all nature seeks its own preservation; an injured tree, a living body, an animal does so; how then could man make of his freedom, which is the acme of life and constitutes its worth, a principle for his own destruction ? Nothing more terrible can be imagined ; for if man were on every occasion master of his own life, he would be master of the lives of others ; and being ready to sacrifice his life at any and every time rather than be captured, he could perpetrate every conceivable crime and vice. We are, therefore, horrified at the very thought of suicide ; by it man sinks lower than the beasts ; we look upon a suicide as carrion, whilst our sympathy goes forth to the victim of fate.

Those who advocate suicide seek to give the widest interpretation to freedom. There is something flattering in the thought that we can take our own life if we are so minded ; and so we find even right-thinking persons defending suicide in this respect. There are many circumstances under which life ought to be sacrificed. If I cannot preserve my life except by violating my duties towards myself, I am bound to sacrifice my life rather than violate these duties. But suicide is in no circumstances permissible. Humanity in one's own person is something inviolable ; it is a holy trust ; man is master of all else, but he must not lay hands upon himself. A being who existed of his own necessity could not possibly destroy himself ; a being whose existence is not necessary must regard life as the condition of everything else, and in the consciousness that life is a trust reposed in him, such a being recoils at the thought of committing a breach of his holy trust by turning his life against himself. Man can only dispose over things ; beasts are things in this sense ; but man is not a thing, not a beast. If he disposes over himself, he treats his value as that of a beast. He who so behaves, who has no respect for human nature and makes a thing of himself, becomes for everyone an Object of freewill. We are free to treat him as a beast, as a thing, and to use him for our sport as we do a horse or a dog, for he is no longer a human being ; he has made a thing of himself, and, having himself discarded his humanity, he cannot expect that others should respect humanity in him. Yet humanity is worthy of esteem. Even when a man is a bad man, humanity in his person is worthy of esteem. Suicide is not abominable and

inadmissible because life should be highly prized ; were
it so, we could each have our own opinion of how highly
we should prize it, and the rule of prudence would often
indicate suicide as the best means.   But the rule of morality
does not admit of it under any condition because it degrades
human nature below the level of animal nature and so
destroys it.   Yet there is much in the world far more
important than life.   To observe morality is far more
important.   It is better to sacrifice one's life than one's
morality.   To live is not a necessity ; but to live honourably while life lasts is a necessity.   We can at all times go
on living and doing our duty towards ourselves without
having to do violence to ourselves.   But he who is prepared to take his own life is no longer worthy to live at
all.   The pragmatic ground of impulse to live is happiness.
Can I then take my own life because I cannot live happily ?
No !   It is not necessary that whilst I live I should live
happily ; but it is necessary that so long as I live I should
live honourably.   Misery gives no right to any man to
take his own life, for then we should all be entitled to take
our lives for lack of pleasure.   All our duties towards ourselves would then be directed towards pleasure ; but the
fulfilment of those duties may demand that we should
even sacrifice our life.

Is suicide heroic or cowardly ?   Sophistication, even
though well meant, is not a good thing.   It is not good
to defend either virtue or vice by splitting hairs.   Even
right-thinking people declaim against suicide on wrong
lines.   They say that it is arrant cowardice.   But instances
of suicide of great heroism exist.   We cannot, for example,
regard the suicides of Cato and of Atticus as cowardly.
Rage, passion and insanity are the most frequent causes
of suicide, and that is why persons who attempt suicide
and are saved from it are so terrified at their own act that
they do not dare to repeat the attempt.   There was a
time in Roman and in Greek history when suicide was
regarded as honourable, so much so that the Romans
forbade their slaves to commit suicide because they did
not belong to themselves but to their masters and so were
regarded as things, like all other animals.   The Stoics
said that suicide is the sage's peaceful death ; he leaves

the world as he might leave a smoky room for another, because it no longer pleases him ; he leaves the world, not because he is no longer happy in it, but because he disdains it. It has already been mentioned that man is greatly flattered by the idea that he is free to remove himself from this world, if he so wishes. He may not make use of this freedom, but the thought of possessing it pleases him. It seems even to have a moral aspect, for if man is capable of removing himself from the world at his own will, he need not submit to any one ; he can retain his independence and tell the rudest truths to the cruellest of tyrants. Torture cannot bring him to heel, because he can leave the world at a moment's notice as a free man can leave the country, if and when he wills it. But this semblance of morality vanishes as soon as we see that man's freedom cannot subsist except on a condition which is immutable. This condition is that man may not use his freedom against himself to his own destruction, but that, on the contrary, he should allow nothing external to limit it. Freedom thus conditioned is noble. No chance or misfortune ought to make us afraid to live ; we ought to go on living as long as we can do so as human beings and honourably. To bewail one's fate and misfortune is in itself dishonourable. Had Cato faced any torments which Caesar might have inflicted upon him with a resolute mind and remained steadfast, it would have been noble of him ; to violate himself was not so. Those who advocate suicide and teach that there is authority for it necessarily do much harm in a republic of free men. Let us imagine a state in which men held as a general opinion that they were entitled to commit suicide, and that there was even merit and honour in so doing. How dreadful everyone would find them. For he who does not respect his life even in principle cannot be restrained from the most dreadful vices ; he recks neither king nor torments.

But as soon as we examine suicide from the standpoint of religion we immediately see it in its true light. We have been placed in this world under certain conditions and for specific purposes. But a suicide opposes the purpose of his Creator ; he arrives in the other world as one who has deserted his post ; he must be looked upon as a rebel against God. So long as we remember the truth that it is God's intention to preserve life, we are bound to regulate our activities in conformity with it. We have no right to offer violence to our nature's powers of self-preservation and to upset the wisdom of her arrangements. This duty is upon us until the time comes when God expressly commands us to leave this life. Human beings are sentinels on earth and may not leave their posts until relieved by another beneficent hand. God is our owner ; we are His property ; His providence works for our good. A bondman in the care of a beneficent master deserves punishment if he opposes his master's wishes.

But suicide is not inadmissible and abominable because God has forbidden it ; God has forbidden it because it is abominable in that it degrades man's inner worth below that of the animal creation. Moral philosophers must, therefore, first and foremost show that suicide is abominable. We find, as a rule, that those who labour for their happiness are more liable to suicide ; having tasted the refinements of pleasure, and being deprived of them, they give way to grief, sorrow, and melancholy.

CARE FOR ONE'S LIFE

We are in duty bound to take care of our life ; but in this connexion it must be remarked that life, in and for itself, is not the greatest of the gifts entrusted to our keeping and of which we must take care. There are duties which are far greater than life and which can often be fulfilled only by sacrificing life. Observation and experience show that a worthless man values his life more than his person. He who has no inner worth sets greater store by his life ; but he who has a greater inner worth places a lesser value upon his life. The latter would sacrifice his life rather than be guilty of a disgraceful action ; he values his person more than his life. But a man of no inner worth would act basely rather than sacrifice his life. He certainly preserves his life, but he is no

longer worthy to live; he has, in his person, disgraced
human nature and its dignity. But is it consistent that
the man who places a lesser value upon his life should
command a greater value in his person ? There is something obscure about this, though the fact is clear enough.
Man looks upon life, which consists in the union of the
soul with the body, as a contingent thing, and rightly so.
The principle of free action in him is of a kind which
insists that life, which consists in the union of soul and
body, should be held in low esteem. Let us take an
example. Assume that a number of persons are innocently
accused of treachery, and that whilst some of them are
truly honourable, others, although innocent of the particular accusation levelled against them, are contemptible
and of no real worth ; assume further that they are all
sentenced together, and that each of them has to choose
between death and penal servitude for life ; it is certain
that the honourable amongst them would choose death,
and the vile ones the galleys. A man of inner worth
does not shrink from death ; he would die rather than
live as an object of contempt, a member of a gang of
scoundrels in the galleys ; but the worthless man prefers
the galleys, almost as if they were his proper place. Thus
there exist duties to which life must be subordinated, and
in order to fulfil them we must give no countenance to
cowardice and fears for our life. Man's cowardice dishonours humanity. It is cowardly to place a high value
upon physical life. The man who on every trifling occasion fears for his life makes a laughing-stock of himself.
We must await death with resolution. That must be of
little importance which it is of great importance to despise.

On the other hand we ought not to risk our life and hazard
losing it for interested and private purposes. To do so
is not only imprudent but base. It would, for instance,
be wrong to wager for a large sum of money that we would
swim across some great river. There is no material benefit
in life so great that we should regard it as a duty to risk
our life for it. But circumstances do exist in which men
risk their lives from motives of interest. A soldier does
so in the wars ; but his motives are not of private interest,
but of the general good. But seeing that human beings

are so constituted that they war against each other, men
are to be found who devote themselves to war merely as
a profession. How far we should value our life, and how
far we may risk it, is a very subtle question. It turns
on the following considerations. Humanity in our own
person is an object of the highest esteem and is inviolable
in us ; rather than dishonour it, or allow it to be dishonoured, man ought to sacrifice his life ; for can he
himself hold his manhood in honour if it is to be dishonoured
by others ? If a man cannot preserve his life except by
dishonouring his humanity, he ought rather to sacrifice
it ; it is true that he endangers his animal life, but he can
feel that, so long as he lived, he lived honourably. How
long he lives is of no account ; it is not his life that he
loses, but only the prolongation of his years, for nature
has already decreed that he must die at some time ; what
matters is that, so long as he lives, man should live honourably and should not disgrace the dignity of humanity ;
if he can no longer live honourably, he cannot live at all ;
his moral life is at an end. The moral life is at an end
if it is no longer in keeping with the dignity of humanity.
Through all the ills and torments of life the path of morality
is determined. No matter what torments I have to suffer,
I can live morally. I must suffer them all, including the
torments of death, rather than commit a disgraceful action.
The moment I can no longer live in honour but become
unworthy of life by such an action, I can no longer live
at all. Thus it is far better to die honoured and respected
than to prolong one's life for a few years by a disgraceful
act and go on living a rogue. If, for instance, a woman
cannot preserve her life any longer except by surrendering
her person to the will of another, she is bound to give up
her life rather than dishonour humanity in her own person,
which is what she would be doing in giving herself up as
a thing to the will of another.

The preservation of one's life is, therefore, not the highest
duty, and men must often give up their lives merely to secure
that they shall have lived honourably. There are many
instances of this ; and although lawyers may argue that to
preserve life is the highest duty and that *in casu necessitatis*
a man is bound to stand up for his life, yet this is no matter

of jurisprudence.   Jurisprudence should concern itself only
with man's duties to his neighbour, with what is lawful
and unlawful, but not with duties towards oneself; it
cannot force a man on any occasion to give up his life;
for how could it force him?   Only by taking his life from
him.   Of course, lawyers must regard the preservation of
life as the highest duty, because the threat of death is
their most powerful weapon in examining a man.   In any
event, there is no *casus necessitatis* except where morality
relieves me of the duty to take care of my life.   Misery,
danger and torture are no *casus necessitatis* for preserving
my life.   Necessity cannot cancel morality.   If, then, I
cannot preserve my life except by disgraceful conduct,
virtue relieves me of this duty because a higher duty here
comes into play and commands me to sacrifice my life.

DUTIES TOWARDS THE BODY ITSELF

The body belongs to the self and is included in the
general laws of freedom which lay down our duties.   The
body is entrusted to us and our duty in respect of it is
that our mind should first discipline the body and then
look after it.   The body must first be disciplined, because
it contains principles which affect the mind and can change
its condition.   The mind must, therefore, ensure that it
establishes an autocracy over the body so that the latter
cannot change the mind's condition.   The mind must gain
such mastery over the body that it can guide and direct
it in accordance with moral and pragmatic principles and
maxims.   This demands a discipline, a discipline which is
only negative; the mind need only secure that the body
does not exercise any compulsion upon it; it cannot well
prevent the body affecting it.   Much depends on the body
in matters of our faculty of knowledge, of our faculty of
desire and aversion, and of the passions.   If the mind
does not exercise a proper mastery over the body, the
habits which we allow the body to acquire can become
necessities; and if the mind does not repress the propensity of the body the latter can gain dominance over it.

This mastery of the mind over the body, or, in other words, of intellect over sensuality, can well be compared to a state with a good or a bad government. The discipline can be of one of two kinds : we may have to strengthen the body, or we may have to weaken it. Some visionary moralists have preached the doctrine that everything is to be gained by weakening and destroying the whole sensibility of the body. We ought, they said, to deny ourselves everything that tends to promote the pleasures of the senses in order to suppress the animal nature of our body and anticipate here on earth the life of the spirit which we hope one day to attain ; by gradually divesting ourselves of all sensibility, the body would approach more and more to the spiritual life. This may be termed the mortification of the flesh, an expression unknown to the heathen world. These practices, by which men sought to free themselves from the fetters of the body, were called *exercitia coelestica*. But there is no virtue in practices of the kind, such as doing penance and fasting, which merely waste the body ; they are fanatical and monkish virtues. Perfect discipline of the body consists in the ability to live in conformity with one's purpose. It is true that the body must be kept under discipline, but it should not be shattered or have its strength broken by men. We must strengthen it, harden it in every useful way, and take care of it, but without pampering ; we must not allow it to become inveterate in any of its pleasures, but must so regulate it that it is able to dispense with everything but necessaries, to be content with inferior fare and to bear up cheerfully in hardship and misfortune. The less man needs for the upkeep of his life-strength, the more is he conscious of living. We must harden our body as Diogenes did. He was a slave who had learnt nothing but resignation, and he brought up the children of his master so that, hardened against the discomforts of life, they had vigour and cheerfulness of mind and were imbued with the principle of righteousness. As has been said at the beginning of this book, Diogenes was happy not through a superfluity of the good things of the world but from lack of them and through his ability to dispense with them.

While we must discipline the body we must also care and provide for it by seeking to promote its strength, energy, vigour, liveliness, and courage. In the matter of discipline our duty is twofold: the body must be made frugal in its needs and temperate in its pleasures. We cannot deny to the body what it needs, but it is better to keep within the limits of these needs, and even to fall a little short of them, than to go beyond them and enfeeble the body and sap its powers. We must be frugal in eating and in drinking. Intemperance in drink is not a matter of quantity (we often have a desire to drink a lot of water) but of the quality and the nature of the drink; but with regard to food, men may be led to over-eat even when the food is bad. To depart in either respect from the path of moderation is a breach of our duty to ourselves. Unlike some vices, which, like the vice of telling lies, are human and not contrary to our nature, the vices of over-eating and over-drinking are bestial and degrade man. There are some vices which stand outside the pale of human nature and cannot be reconciled with the nature and character of man. These are of two kinds: bestial and satanic. By his bestial vices man degrades himself below the level of beasts; satanic vices are of a wickedness far surpassing the wickedness of man. Amongst the latter are reckoned envy, ingratitude, and malice; amongst the former we have gluttony, drunkenness, and the *crimina contra naturam*. All bestial vices are utterly contemptible; satanic vices are utterly detestable. Which of the two bestial vices, gluttony or drunkenness, is the more contemptible and the baser? Gluttony is the baser of the two, for drink promotes sociability and conversation, and inspires man, and in so far as it does so there is an excuse for it; but once it goes beyond this stage it becomes a vice, that of drunkenness. In so far, therefore, as it serves sociability, immoderate drinking, although a bestial vice, is not as contemptible as gluttony; the latter is far baser, because it neither promotes sociability, nor does it enliven the body, but is purely bestial. Secret drinking, drunkenness in solitude, is as disgraceful, for then the factor which raised it a fraction above the level of gluttony disappears.

OCCUPATION

It is by his activities and not by enjoyment that man feels that he is alive. The busier we are the more we feel that we live and the more conscious we are of life. In idleness we not only feel that life is fleeting but we also feel lifeless. Activity is part of life's sustenance. We find any empty space of time disagreeable. What then makes time agreeable to us? The pleasures of life do not fill time full, but leave it empty. The human mind abhors an empty time, and is bored and disgusted with it. The present may, indeed, seem full to us, but if we have filled it with play, etc., the appearance of fullness will be confined to the present. Memory will find it empty. For if we have done nothing in life except waste our time and we review in retrospect the span of our life, we are puzzled to know how it has passed so quickly; we have done so little in it. Time can be filled up only by action. Only when occupied are we conscious that we live; indulgence gives us a feeling of insufficiency; for what is life? Life is the faculty of spontaneous activity, the awareness of all our human powers. Occupation gives us this awareness, and the more we feel our powers the more we feel that we are alive. Feeling is but the capacity to be aware of impressions; in feeling we are passive, or only so far active as to make awareness possible. But the more active he is, the more conscious a man is of his life; he can remember it the more, because there is much to remember; and at death he feels the more that he has had fullness of life. To have had one's fill of life is not to be weary of it. Mere enjoyment leads to weariness of life; but to die having had fullness of life is possible only after a life of action, and after we have made such full and busy use of our life that at its end we are not sorry that we have lived. He who has so lived has had fullness of life; he who has done nothing, grows weary of life; he does not seem to have lived; he is bored and would fain begin to live when it is time to die. We must, therefore, fill out our span of life with activities, and we shall not then complain that whilst each period of time has been long, when we look upon the past, the time as a whole has been all too short. This is the lament of people who do nothing ; the hours drag and seem long to them because they have nothing to do ; but in retrospect time seems to have fled, and they do not know what has become of it. But not so with the busy man ; for him the hours are short and pass all too quickly whilst he is occupied ; he wonders how they have passed until he looks back and sees how much he has managed to do in the time. Man must, therefore, by constant practice preserve his life-force, that is, his energies ; his worth must be measured by what he does. Laziness reduces the degree of life. Unless man feels within him an impulse to activity, he will not even trouble to make a beginning ; and since then all moral precepts are in vain, it must be the condition of all other duties that we should be energetic and zealous, show vigour and resolution in difficult tasks, and shun procrastination. Vigour is the reverse of indolence.

All occupation is either play or work. To have no occupation is a vice ; it is better to be occupied in play than not to be occupied at all ; for by play we at least sustain our energies. But if a man has no occupation whatever, he loses some of his life-force, and by degrees grows indolent. After a while he finds it difficult to regain his former energy of mind.

Without occupation man cannot live happily. If he earns his bread, he eats it with greater pleasure than when it is doled out to him. When mail-day is over, the business-man goes eagerly to the theatre, and is more pleased and contented than if there had been no mail-day. Man feels more contented after heavy work than when he has done no work ; for by work he has set his powers in motion ; he, therefore, feels them better, and his mind is on that account more alive to pleasure. But when a man does nothing, he does not feel his life and his powers, and he is not disposed to pleasure.

Rest must be distinguished from idleness. There is something to be said for a life of rest if it comes at the end of an active life. When a man has laid down the duties of his station in the world after a busy life, he has the right to rest from the general labours of the world and from the common routine, but there is no reason why he should not find private occupations. Then his rest is the tranquillity of the sage. The rest enjoyed by the aged is no laziness, but refreshment after labour. In order to rest man must have been occupied; he who has done nothing cannot rest. Rest cannot be properly enjoyed except after occupation. After a busy day we enjoy a restful sleep; rest is not so pleasant to the man who has done nothing.

Before we leave the subject we must make some observations on the question of—

SHORTENING TIME

There are various ways of shortening the time in which we live and various expressions of it. The more attention we give to time, the more we feel that it is empty. Thus, for instance, when we watch the clock, time becomes long. But he who has something to do, does not notice time and it appears to him shorter. When our attention is absorbed by objects we do not notice time and it is short; but as soon as we direct our attention to measuring time and to observing it, it is empty for us. Our life, therefore, is the longer the more full it is.

Note.—Miles near to town seem shorter than those farther away; for as we proceed on our way our attention is diverted by many objects near town, but farther away there is nothing to see and the miles seem long. But if at the end of the journey we look back, the journey seems to have been short, because, except for a short length of it near to town, there was nothing to notice and to remember.

DUTIES TOWARDS THE BODY IN RESPECT OF SEXUAL IMPULSE

Amongst our inclinations there is one which is directed towards other human beings. They themselves, and not their work and services, are its Objects of enjoyment. It

is true that man has no inclination to enjoy the flesh of
another—except, perhaps, in the vengeance of war, and
then it is hardly a desire—but none the less there does
exist an inclination which we may call an appetite for
enjoying another human being. We refer to sexual
impulse. Man can, of course, use another human being
as an instrument for his service; he can use his hands,
his feet, and even all his powers; he can use him for his
own purposes with the other's consent. But there is no
way in which a human being can be made an Object of
indulgence for another except through sexual impulse.
This is in the nature of a sense, which we can call the sixth
sense; it is an appetite for another human being. We
say that a man loves someone when he has an inclination
towards another person. If by this love we mean true
human love, then it admits of no distinction between
types of persons, or between young and old. But a
love that springs merely from sexual impulse cannot be
love at all, but only appetite. Human love is good-will,
affection, promoting the happiness of others and finding
joy in their happiness. But it is clear that, when a person
loves another purely from sexual desire, none of these
factors enter into the love. Far from there being any
concern for the happiness of the loved one, the lover, in
order to satisfy his desire and still his appetite, may even
plunge the loved one into the depths of misery. Sexual
love makes of the loved person an Object of appetite; as
soon as that appetite has been stilled, the person is cast
aside as one casts away a lemon which has been sucked
dry. Sexual love can, of course, be combined with human
love and so carry with it the characteristics of the latter,
but taken by itself and for itself, it is nothing more than
appetite. Taken by itself it is a degradation of human
nature; for as soon as a person becomes an Object of
appetite for another, all motives of moral relationship cease
to function, because as an Object of appetite for another a
person becomes a thing and can be treated and used as
such by every one. This is the only case in which a human
being is designed by nature as the Object of another's
enjoyment. Sexual desire is at the root of it; and that
is why we are ashamed of it, and why all strict moralists,

and those who had pretensions to be regarded as saints, sought to suppress and extirpate it. It is true that without it a man would be incomplete; he would rightly believe that he lacked the necessary organs, and this would make him imperfect as a human being; none the less men made pretence on this question and sought to suppress these inclinations because they degraded mankind.

Because sexuality is not an inclination which one human being has for another as such, but is an inclination for the sex of another, it is a principle of the degradation of human nature, in that it gives rise to the preference of one sex to the other, and to the dishonouring of that sex through the satisfaction of desire. The desire which a man has for a woman is not directed towards her because she is a human being, but because she is a woman; that she is a human being is of no concern to the man; only her sex is the object of his desires. Human nature is thus subordinated. Hence it comes that all men and women do their best to make not their human nature but their sex more alluring and direct their activities and lusts entirely towards sex. Human nature is thereby sacrificed to sex. If then a man wishes to satisfy his desire, and a woman hers, they stimulate each other's desire; their inclinations meet, but their object is not human nature but sex, and each of them dishonours the human nature of the other. They make of humanity an instrument for the satisfaction of their lusts and inclinations, and dishonour it by placing it on a level with animal nature. Sexuality, therefore, exposes mankind to the danger of equality with the beasts. But as man has this desire from nature, the question arises how far he can properly make use of it without injury to his manhood. How far may persons allow one of the opposite sex to satisfy his or her desire upon them? Can they sell themselves, or let themselves out on hire, or by some other contract allow use to be made of their sexual faculties? Philosophers generally point out the harm done by this inclination and the ruin it brings to the body or to the commonwealth, and they believe that, except for the harm it does, there would be nothing contemptible in such conduct in itself. But if this were so, and if giving vent to this desire was not in itself abominable and did not involve immorality, then any one who could avoid being harmed by them could make whatever use he wanted of his sexual propensities. For the prohibitions of prudence are never unconditional; and the conduct would in itself be unobjectionable, and would only be harmful under certain conditions. But in point of fact, there is in the conduct itself something which is contemptible and contrary to the dictates of morality. It follows, therefore, that there must be certain conditions under which alone the use of the *facultates sexuales* would be in keeping with morality. There must be a basis for restraining our freedom in the use we make of our inclinations so that they conform to the principles of morality. We shall endeavour to discover these conditions and this basis. Man cannot dispose over himself because he is not a thing; he is not his own property; to say that he is would be self-contradictory; for in so far as he is a person he is a Subject in whom the ownership of things can be vested, and if he were his own property, he would be a thing over which he could have ownership. But a person cannot be a property and so cannot be a thing which can be owned, for it is impossible to be a person and a thing, the proprietor and the property.

Accordingly, a man is not at his own disposal. He is not entitled to sell a limb, not even one of his teeth. But to allow one's person for profit to be used by another for the satisfaction of sexual desire, to make of oneself an Object of demand, is to dispose over oneself as over a thing and to make of oneself a thing on which another satisfies his appetite, just as he satisfies his hunger upon a steak. But since the inclination is directed towards one's sex and not towards one's humanity, it is clear that one thus partially sacrifices one's humanity and thereby runs a moral risk. Human beings are, therefore, not entitled to offer themselves, for profit, as things for the use of others in the satisfaction of their sexual propensities. In so doing they would run the risk of having their person used by all and sundry as an instrument for the satisfaction of inclination. This way of satisfying sexuality is *vaga libido*, in which one satisfies the inclinations of others for gain. It is possible for either sex. To let one's person out

on hire and to surrender it to another for the satisfaction
of his sexual desire in return for money is the depth of
infamy. The underlying moral principle is that man is
not his own property and cannot do with his body what he
will. The body is part of the self ; in its togetherness with
the self it constitutes the person ; a man cannot make of
his person a thing, and this is exactly what happens in
vaga libido. This manner of satisfying sexual desire is,
therefore, not permitted by the rules of morality. But
what of the second method, namely *concubinatus* ? Is
this also inadmissible ? In this case both persons satisfy
their desire mutually and there is no idea of gain, but they
serve each other only for the satisfaction of sexuality.
There appears to be nothing unsuitable in this arrangement, but there is nevertheless one consideration which
rules it out. Concubinage consists in one person surrendering to another only for the satisfaction of their
sexual desire whilst retaining freedom and rights in other
personal respects affecting welfare and happiness. But
the person who so surrenders is used as a thing ; the
desire is still directed only towards sex and not towards
the person as a human being. But it is obvious that to
surrender part of oneself is to surrender the whole, because
a human being is a unity. It is not possible to have the
disposal of a part only of a person without having at the
same time a right of disposal over the whole person, for
each part of a person is integrally bound up with the whole.
But concubinage does not give me a right of disposal over
the whole person but only over a part, namely the *organa
sexualia*. It presupposes a contract. This contract deals
only with the enjoyment of a part of the person and not
with the entire circumstances of the person. Concubinage
is certainly a contract, but it is one-sided ; the rights of
the two parties are not equal. But if in concubinage I
enjoy a part of a person, I thereby enjoy the whole person ;
yet by the terms of the arrangement I have not the rights
over the whole person, but only over a part ; I, therefore,
make the person into a thing. For that reason this method
of satisfying sexual desire is also not permitted by the rules
of morality. The sole condition on which we are free
to make use of our sexual desire depends upon the right

to dispose over the person as a whole—over the welfare and happiness and generally over all the circumstances of that person. If I have the right over the whole person, I have also the right over the part and so I have the right to use that person's *organa sexualia* for the satisfaction of sexual desire. But how am I to obtain these rights over the whole person ? Only by giving that person the same rights over the whole of myself. This happens only in marriage. Matrimony is an agreement between two persons by which they grant each other equal reciprocal rights, each of them undertaking to surrender the whole of their person to the other with a complete right of disposal over it. We can now apprehend by reason how a *commercium sexuale* is possible without degrading humanity and breaking the moral laws. Matrimony is the only condition in which use can be made of one's sexuality. If one devotes one's person to another, one devotes not only sex but the whole person ; the two cannot be separated. If, then, one yields one's person, body and soul, for good and ill and in every respect, so that the other has complete rights over it, and if the other does not similarly yield himself in return and does not extend in return the same rights and privileges, the arrangement is one-sided. But if I yield myself completely to another and obtain the person of the other in return, I win myself back ; I have given myself up as the property of another, but in turn I take that other as my property, and so win myself back again in winning the person whose property I have become. In this way the two persons become a unity of will. Whatever good or ill, joy or sorrow befall either of them, the other will share in it. Thus sexuality leads to a union of human beings, and in that union alone its exercise is possible. This condition of the use of sexuality, which is only fulfilled in marriage, is a moral condition. But let us pursue this aspect further and examine the case of a man who takes two wives. In such a case each wife would have but half a man, although she would be giving herself wholly and ought in consequence to be entitled to the whole man. To sum up : *vaga libido* is ruled out on moral grounds ; the same applies to concubinage ; there only remains matrimony, and in matrimony polygamy is ruled out also for moral reasons; we, therefore, reach the conclusion that the only feasible arrangement is that of monogamous marriage. Only under that condition can I indulge my *facultas sexualis*. We cannot here pursue the subject further.

But one other question arises, that of incest. Incest consists in intercourse between the sexes in a form which, by reason of consanguinity, must be ruled out; but are there moral grounds on which incest, in all forms of sexual intercourse, must be ruled out ? They are grounds which apply conditionally, except in one case, in which they have absolute validity. The sole case in which the moral grounds against incest apply absolutely is that of intercourse between parents and children. Between parents and children there must be a respect which should continue throughout life, and this rules out of court any question of equality. Moreover, in sexual intercourse each person submits to the other in the highest degree, whereas between parents and their children subjection is one-sided; the children must submit to the parents only ; there can, therefore, be no equal union. This is the only case in which incest is absolutely forbidden by nature. In other cases incest forbids itself, but is not incest in the order of nature. The state prohibits incest, but at the beginning there must have been intermarriage between brothers and sisters. At the same time nature has implanted in our breasts a natural opposition to incest. She intended us to combine with other races and so to prevent too great a sameness in one society. Too close a connection, too intimate an acquaintance produces sexual indifference and repugnance. But this propensity must be restrained by modesty; otherwise it becomes commonplace, reduces the object of the desire to the commonplace and results in indifference. Sexual desire is very fastidious; nature has given it strength, but it must be restrained by modesty. It is on that account that savages, who go about stark-naked, are cold towards each other ; for that reason, too, a person whom we have known from youth evokes no desire within us, but a strange person attracts us much more strongly. Thus nature has herself provided restraints upon any desire between brother and sister.

CRIMINA CARNIS

Crimina carnis are contrary to self-regarding duty
because they are against the ends of humanity. They
consist in abuse of one's sexuality. Every form of sexual
indulgence, except in marriage, is a misuse of sexuality,
and so a *crimen carnis*. All *crimina carnis* are either
secundum naturam or *contra naturam*. *Crimina carnis
secundum naturam* are contrary to sound reason ; *crimina
carnis contra naturam* are contrary to our animal nature.
Among the former we reckon *vaga libido,* which is the
opposite of matrimony and of which there are two kinds :
scortatio and *concubinatus*. *Concubinatus* is indeed a *pactum,*
but a *pactum inaequale,* in which the rights are not
reciprocal. In this pact the woman surrenders her sex
completely to the man, but the man does not completely
surrender his sex to the woman. The second *crimen
carnis secundum naturam* is *adulterium*. Adultery cannot
take place except in marriage ; it signifies a breach of
marriage. Just as the engagement to marry is the most
serious and the most inviolable engagement between two
persons and binds them for life, so also is adultery the
greatest breach of faith that there can be, because it is
disloyalty to an engagement than which there can be none
more important. For this reason adultery is cause for
divorce. Another cause is incompatibility and inability
to be at one, whereby unity and concord of will between
the two persons is impossible. Next comes the question
whether incest is incest *per se,* or whether it is by the civil
law that it is made a *crimen carnis,* natural or unnatural.
The question might be answered either by natural instinct
or by reason. From the point of view of natural instinct
incest is a *crimen carnis secundum naturam,* for it is after
all a union of the sexes ; it is not *contra naturam animalium,*
because animals do not differentiate in this respect in
their practices. But on the judgment of the understanding incest is *contra naturam*.

Uses of sexuality which are contrary to natural instinct
and to animal nature are *crimina carnis contra naturam*.

First amongst them we have onanism.   This is abuse of
the sexual faculty without any object, the exercise of the
faculty in the complete absence of any object of sexuality.
The practice is contrary to the ends of humanity and even
opposed to animal nature.   By it man sets aside his person and degrades himself below the level of animals.   A
second *crimen carnis contra naturam* is intercourse between
sexus homogenii, in which the object of sexual impulse is
a human being but there is homogeneity instead of hetero-
geneity of sex, as when a woman satisfies her desire on a
woman, or a man on a man.   This practice too is contrary
to the ends of humanity ; for the end of humanity in
respect of sexuality is to preserve the species without
debasing the person ; but in this instance the species is
not being preserved (as it can be by a *crimen carnis secundum naturam*), but the person is set aside, the self is
degraded below the level of the animals, and humanity is
dishonoured.   The third *crimen carnis contra naturam*
occurs when the object of the desire is in fact of the opposite sex but is not human.   Such is sodomy, or intercourse with animals.   This, too, is contrary to the ends
of humanity and against our natural instinct.   It degrades
mankind below the level of animals, for no animal turns
in this way from its own species.   All *crimina carnis contra
naturam* degrade human nature to a level below that of
animal nature and make man unworthy of his humanity.
He no longer deserves to be a person.   From the point of
view of duties towards himself such conduct is the most
disgraceful and the most degrading of which man is capable.
Suicide is the most dreadful, but it is not as dishonourable
and base as the *crimina carnis contra naturam.*   It is the
most abominable conduct of which man can be guilty.   So
abominable are these *crimina carnis contra naturam* that
they are unmentionable, for the very mention of them is
nauseating, as is not the case with suicide.   We all fight
shy of mentioning these vices ; teachers refrain from
mentioning them, even when their intention is unobjectionable and they only wish to warn their charges against
them.   But as they are of frequent occurrence, we are
in a dilemma : are we to name them in order that people
should know and prevent their frequent occurrence, or are

we to keep them dark in order that people should not learn of them and so not have the opportunity of transgressing ? Frequent mention would familiarize people with them and the vices might as a result cease to disgust us and come to appear more tolerable. Hence our modesty in not referring to them. On the other hand, if we mention them only circumspectly and with disinclination, our aversion from them is still apparent. There is also another reason for our modesty. Each sex is ashamed of the vices of which its members are capable. Human beings feel, therefore, ashamed to mention those things of which it is shameful for humanity to be capable. These vices make us ashamed that we are human beings and, therefore, capable of them, for an animal is incapable of all such *crimina carnis contra naturam.*

DUTIES TOWARDS OURSELVES IN RESPECT OF EXTERNAL CIRCUMSTANCES

We have already said that man has in himself a source of happiness. This happiness is not due to any ability to make himself completely independent of his needs and external circumstances ; nor can man acquire such complete independence, but he may tutor himself not to need much to make him happy. To this end he must exercise an autocratic authority over his inclinations ; he must curb his inclination for things which he cannot attain or can attain only with great difficulty ; if he does so he becomes independent of them. He must further act on the principle of providing for himself the comforts of life which lie within his reach, the pleasures of the spirit. These he must cultivate in ample sufficiency. But his attitude to external things must be different. So far as these are the condition and means of wellbeing they are divisible into two classes and are of two kinds : necessaries and amenities. Those which are necessaries serve merely to support life ; the amenities do not support life, but serve to make life comfortable. The natural level of contentment depends on our bare necessities ; we can be contented when our barest needs are provided for, but we still lack comforts. Contentment is negative ; comfort is positive. So long as I find pleasure in living I am contented ; as soon as I cease to find pleasure in living I am discontented. But I may find pleasure in living even though I live in poverty and yet have none of the comforts of life. Comforts are means of welfare ; they must be dispensable ; whatever is indispensable is a necessity. What, then, is to be regarded as comfort and what as need ? What are to be looked upon as the means for the one purpose and what for the other ? What is dispensable and what indispensable ? All comforts and pleasures should be enjoyed in such a way that we can dispense with them ; we ought never to make necessities of them. On the other hand, we ought to accustom ourselves to bear resolutely all discomforts (which need be no misfortune). Thus we must learn to dispense with comfort and to bear discomfort. The ancients expressed this by the maxim *Sustine et abstine*. We ought not to deprive ourselves of all amenities and pleasures ; to deprive oneself of all enjoyment proper to human life is monkish virtue ; we ought to enjoy the good things of life, but only in such a way that we can at any time dispense with them and they do not become necessities ; we can then say that we are abstinent. On the other hand, we must learn to bear the discomforts of life and to test our strength in suffering them with patience and without losing our contentment ; if we bear with a cheerful mind and a happy disposition the ills which cannot be altered, we have strength of mind. This is the *sustine* of the ancients. We ought not to impose discomforts upon ourselves, invite every possible inconvenience and mortify ourselves with chastisements ; to do so is monkish, not philosophical virtue, which meets the ills that come upon us with a cheerful countenance so that in the end we find everything bearable. The maxim *Sustine et abstine* does not, therefore, mean a discipline, but the ability to dispense with comforts and amusements and to suffer discomforts with a cheerful courage. There are some necessaries, such as food and clothes, which we must have ; deprive us of these and we are thoroughly discontented. But there are others, the absence of which makes us dissatisfied, but which we could none the less go without. The more dependent we are on such pseudo-necessities, the more is our contentment at their mercy. Man must, therefore, discipline his mind in regard to the necessaries of life. If we wish to make a classification of needs, we may call excess of pleasure and amusement luxury, and excessive self-indulgence in comfort effeminacy. Luxury makes us dependent upon a multitude of enjoyable things. Man becomes dependent upon a multitude of pseudo-necessities ; a time comes when he can no longer procure these for himself and he becomes miserable, even to the length of taking his life ; for where luxury prevails, suicide is usually common. The prevalence of luxury limits the range of our welfare ; the prevalence of effeminacy completely saps our human strength. Luxury is riotous extravagance, effeminacy is the extravagance of self-indulgence. Riotous extravagance is active, extravagance of self-indulgence is indolent. The former has its uses ; it adds vitality and vigour to life ; horse-riding, for instance, is a luxury. But all kinds of indolent effeminacy are very harmful ; they sap the vital powers of man ; tippling, wearing silk, driving in carriages are examples of this tendency. The man who is inclined to riotous extravagance preserves his own energy, as well as that of others, but he who indulges in the refinements of indolent comfort, though he maintains the energy of others, discourages his own. The former is, therefore, preferable to the latter. The rule of *Sustine et abstine* applies both to luxury and to effeminacy. We must make ourselves independent of both ; for the more dependent man is upon luxury and comfort, the less free he is and the more prone to vice. We ought not, however, slavishly to shun all amusement, provided we enjoy it in such a manner that we can at any time dispense with it. The man who does not wrong himself or another, but does his duty, may enjoy as much pleasure as he can and will ; he will still be good-natured and fulfil the end of his creation. On the other hand, we are not called upon to impose discomforts upon ourselves and then to suffer them ; there is no merit in suffering ills which we have voluntarily taken upon ourselves and which we might have been spared ; but the ills which fate has sent us and which cannot be cured must be resolutely endured ; for fate can no more be stayed than a toppling wall. All of this, however, is in itself no virtue, just as its opposite is no vice ; it merely conditions our duties. Man cannot fulfil his duties if he cannot do without things, for he will be dulled by the temptations of his senses. He cannot be virtuous if he is not resolute in misfortune ; in order to be virtuous he must be able to suffer. That is why Diogenes said that his philosophy was the shortest cut to happiness. He went wrong in regarding as a duty what is no more than the principle that a man can be content even in such a state. The philosophy of Epicurus is not one of luxury but of manly strength. He taught that one ought to be content even with polenta and yet be able to enjoy, and enjoy with cheerfulness and serenity, social pleasures and the amenities of life. Thus these two philosophers laid hold of happiness at opposite ends. The Stoics not only did not indulge in such enjoyments but they even forbade them.

The hardships to which we must accustom ourselves and must learn to endure include work. Work is useful occupation with a purpose. There are other occupations which are not work but serve merely for pleasure. Such occupations, which entail no hardship, are pastimes. The loftier its purpose the greater the difficulties and hardships of the work. But however great its hardship we must get so accustomed to our work that it becomes play, ceases to be difficult, and entertains and pleases us. Man must, therefore, be active and industrious and must undertake difficult work readily and cheerfully ; otherwise his work will bear the marks of compulsion, and not of facility. There are men who are occupied with a purpose, and others who are occupied without a purpose ; the latter have no serious end in view and are busy idlers, which is a silly sort of trade. Play is, of course, an occupation without a serious purpose, but it is refreshment from difficult work, a recreation ; but to be constantly busy to no end is worse than not being busy at all, for it has about it an illusion of occupation. The greatest happiness a man can experience is to feel that he is the originator and builder of his own happiness and that what he enjoys he has acquired himself. Man can never be contented without work. The man who retires and frees himself from all work does not feel nor enjoy his life ; man feels that he is alive only when spontaneously active, and he is contented only when he is industrious. Occupation without a purpose is an occupation of leisure, a hobby ; in this case we are busy only to amuse ourselves. Occupation with a purpose is business ; business under difficulties is work ; work is compulsory business, to which we either compel ourselves or are compelled by others. We force ourselves if we have a ground of impulse which outweighs the hardships of the work. Many other things can compel us to work, e.g. duty. He who is not obliged to work, but works voluntarily, cannot fill up his time with such voluntary work as well as he could if he had to work from duty, because at the back of his mind there is always the thought that he is not compelled to work and need not unless he wishes. We need, therefore, to have some compulsory work.. When our work is finished we feel a sense of satisfaction of which no one who does no work is capable ; we feel that we have merit, we approve of ourselves and pat ourselves on the back that we have overcome difficulties and done our work. Man must discipline himself, and his greatest discipline lies in accustoming himself to work ; it is an incentive to virtue, because when at work he has no time for vicious thoughts. Besides, work brings its natural recompense, which those who do not work must procure for themselves by deceit and wickedness.

Philosophers have given much thought to the subject of luxury and have sought to discover whether one should approve or disapprove of it, and whether it was moral or immoral. A thing may be moral and may yet indirectly impede morality. Now luxury adds to the number of our wants and temptations and makes it increasingly more difficult to walk in the path of morality ; for the more artless and simple our desires the less likely are we to go astray in satisfying them. This luxury is indirectly an infringement of morality. On the other hand, it promotes the arts and the sciences and develops man's talents ; it thus seems to be the condition for which humanity is designed. It refines morality; for in morality both uprightness and refinement are to be looked for ; the one implies ungrudging observance, the other adds charm to this, as, for instance, in hospitality. Thus luxury tends to develop to the utmost the beauty of human nature. We must not confound it with self-indulgence. Luxury consists in variety ; self-indulgence in quantity. Intemperance is a sign of lack of taste. A wealthy miser who entertains once in a while piles up the food on his guests' plates, but gives no thought to variety. But luxury requires good taste, and is found only with people who possess that quality; by its variety it clarifies man's judgment, gives occupation to many people and vitalizes the entire social structure. From this point of view, therefore, there can be no moral objection to luxury, provided it is managed so as to keep it within the bounds of what we can afford and continue to afford. Luxury of the pampering kind, which includes effeminacy in men, delicacy in food and all voluptuousness, must be restrained. Thus the ladies are more attracted to a brave, clever and industrious man than to an overdressed fop. Provided that the former dresses passably well, provided that he does not show himself quite indifferent to and ignorant of how to dress, but dresses as befits his station in life and in the fashions of his time, he is more respected than is the man who is effeminate in his ways and foppish in dress. The ladies know that such a one gives more thought to himself than to them. Man must be manly and woman womanly; effeminacy in man pleases as little as does masculinity in woman. This type of luxury makes man effeminate, while a luxury such as hunting befits his manhood.

WEALTH

A man whose possessions are sufficient for his needs is well-to-do ; if he has sufficient not only for his needs but also for other purposes, he is a man of means ; if he has sufficient for his needs and other purposes and then to spare he is a man of wealth; if he has so much as would enable him to make others also well-to-do, he is rich. Riches are a sufficiency for luxury. On the other hand, if a man has only sufficient for his barest necessities he is poor, and if he has not sufficient even for these he is needy. Not only the man who possesses wealth values it, but others do so too. A wealthy man is highly esteemed by his fellows because of his wealth; a needy man is less respected because of his straitened circumstances. We shall soon see the reasons for this. All wealth is means, in so far as it is a means for satisfying the owner's wants, free purposes and inclinations. Wealth in excess of this is a fortune; to have a fortune is more than to have means. A fortune has two advantages. In the first place it makes us independent of others. A man who has a fortune does not need others and does not require their help. In the second place, fortune is power; it has purchasing power; it enables us to procure all that can be produced by human powers. A fortune, in the literal sense, consists of money and goods; it makes a man independent, by putting him in a position where he need serve no one and beg of none, because he can buy what he wants. Money enables a man to bring others under his power; for reasons of self-interest they will labour for him and do his bidding. By dependence upon others man loses in worth, and so a man of independent means is an object of respect. It is in the nature of things that we should respect less a man who depends upon others; but if, like an officer, he in turn makes others dependent upon him he restores the balance. For that reason a common soldier and a man-servant are less respected than an officer and a master. Since, then, money makes one independent, one gains respect by the possession of it; one has worth, needs no one and depends on no one. But in making us independent of others, money in the long run makes us dependent upon itself; it frees us from others in order to enslave us. The worth which springs from independence is only negative; the positive value of wealth arises from the power which wealth gives us. Money gives me the power to use the powers of others in my service. The ancients held that riches are not noble because it is properly the disdain of riches

that is noble.   That is true.   To the understanding the contempt of riches is noble, yet in the world of appearance
riches themselves are noble.   A rich man has great influence
upon the social structure and on the general welfare ; he
provides occupation for many people.   This does not, however, make his person noble ; but the contempt for riches
does.   Riches ennoble a person's circumstances, but not
himself.

THE ATTACHMENT OF THE MIND TO WEALTH
(GREED AND AVARICE)

To possess wealth sufficient for any purposes is in itself
pleasant.   Riches are pleasant because of what they can
provide.   They are pleasant whether I actually put them
to this use, or renounce all my purposes and retain only
the feeling that I have the means and fortune to achieve
them all if I wished.   The very possession of wealth is
pleasant because we can enjoy it when we will.   It is
merely a matter of the will, for we have the money in our
pocket.   We enjoy our fortune mentally, because we can
always enjoy it actually, if we want to.

When a man must forego something which he desires
because it is not in his power to obtain it, he feels aggrieved ;
but let him feel that he has the power to procure it and
then he finds it easy to forego.   Thus a young bachelor
feels vexed that he must forego the pleasures of the
married man ; but though the married man has the same
appetite he can forego gratifying it more easily, knowing
that he can gratify it whenever he will.   It is more painful
to have to forego gratifying a desire because it is not in
our power to gratify it, than to forego gratification when
we could gratify it if we wished.   The mere possession of
the power of gratification is pleasant.   A rich miser will
pay no heed to clothes and go in rags ; he knows that he
has the money to buy the clothes if he wishes and that
all he need do is to have them cut out and stitched up.
He sees others in their carriage and pair and thinks to
himself that he too could have his carriage and pair if he

thought it worth while.   Thus he feeds himself on the thought of pleasure, knowing that it is within his reach. He is fashionably dressed, drives about in state, eats twelve-course dinners every day, but all in thought ; for if he wished to he could do all this at any time.   The very possession of wealth enables him both to enjoy and to forego all pleasures.

The man who has enjoyed a pleasure is not nearly so pleased as the man who is still looking forward to it.   The enjoyment being over and the money spent, the hope that it can still be enjoyed is gone.   The attraction of the prospect has vanished.   A man of lesser sensibility may prefer to feed upon the prospect and to keep his money in his pocket rather than actually to enjoy the pleasure and spend his money.   A miser, with his money in his pocket, thinks to himself : ' How will I feel when the money has been expended on the pleasure ?   I shall be no better off than I am at present.   I had better keep my money in my pocket.'   He does not think of the pleasure which he would be enjoying, but of how he would feel after he has enjoyed it.   But the spendthrift thinks only of the pleasure at the moment of its enjoyment.   He cannot care about what will happen afterwards and what his feelings will be then.   In the attachment to property there is something which has the appearance of virtue ; it is a pseudo-virtue. He who has it is master of his inclination, foregoes many pleasures of his own accord, promotes thereby his health and is regular in everything.   For that reason elderly people who are miserly live longer than if they were not miserly ;   to save .money they live temperately ;   they would not be so temperate if it cost money ;   they show how good their digestion is by the way they eat and drink when some one else pays the bill.

Miserly people are despised and detested by others, and they cannot understand why.   Even those who want nothing from them despise them, and the more they deprive themselves the more they are despised.   In the case of other vices the culprit blames himself ;   he knows that he has a vice, and even though he cannot restrain himself and break himself of the vice, he sees and knows that it is a vice and heaps reproaches upon his own head ;

but in the case of avarice, it is not so. The miser does not know that his avarice is a vice and he cannot conceive how his miserly conduct can possibly be wicked. The reason is that a miser is a man who is hard and skimpy only towards himself and may act with absolute propriety towards others. He gives to none, but he takes from none. Why then, so he argues, should he be despised ? He does not harm anybody, and what he does to himself is no concern of others ; whether he eats much or little or not at all, whether he is dressed expensively or poorly, or goes in rags, hurts no one. Why should others care ? He is right in his argument, and that is why he fails to appreciate that it is a vice ; that is also why it is difficult to answer him with confidence, particularly if, as is usually the case with misers, he is not unjust to others. Misers regard themselves as quite innocent. Besides, they have an excuse for being so saving. They generally say that they save against bad times or for their relatives. But this is self-deception on their part. If the miser really meant to save for his relatives he would support them in his lifetime so as to derive pleasure from seeing them comfortably situated. Misers are also as a rule very devout. As they have no amusements and do not entertain socially, because it all costs money, their mind is occupied with anxious thoughts. They want comfort and support in their anxiety and look to God for it, by means of a fanatical devoutness, which, after all, costs nothing. They think, besides, how good and profitable it would be to have God on their side. There would be no harm in this and it would be even better than a profit of 12 per cent per annum.

Their religion is as base as their general conduct ; their sole motive is gain, and they aspire to gain the kingdom of heaven as they aspire to gain everything else. Why consider moral conduct so long as they pray fervently ? That will gain them heaven. Misers are also very superstitious. They see danger lurking everywhere, and they pray to God to protect all men from danger, but in praying for all men they have mainly themselves in mind. When a catastrophe occurs a miser weeps over the distressed victims, because he fears that he may have to contribute

to their support. A miser does not even know himself ;
he is quite unconscious of his true nature, and it is impossible to convince him of his wickedness ; he is, therefore,
incorrigible. It is possible to reclaim most wicked men,
but not misers. They are irrational and therefore rational
representations have no effect upon them. Were they
susceptible to reason, they would not be miserly ; they
would then recognize that money is valuable merely as a
means and is no immediate object of welfare. But the
miser finds a direct pleasure in money itself, although
money is nothing but a pure means. His proposal to
make use of it is a mere illusion of possibility ; it is never
realized. This illusion can never be corrected by reason,
for it would be itself irrational to offer reasonable advice
to a man suffering from a hallucination. The vice of
avarice is so irrational that we would scarcely believe it
possible did we not know from experience that it existed.
Avarice swallows up all other vices : for that very reason
it is irremediable.

Avarice arises from a process of misguided logic. We
see about us the good and pleasant things of life, and we
wish to possess and enjoy them, but because we have not
the wherewithal we make up our minds to obtain the
necessary funds by saving. We accustom ourselves to do
without one thing after another, and in the process of
time we gradually wean ourselves from all pleasures; we
cease to care for them and we become indifferent to their
very existence ; by the time that we have acquired the
means, so that the good and pleasant things are within
our reach, we have lost the taste for them and it has
given way to the taste for saving and hoarding ; we go
on saving and laying by when it is no longer necessary
for us to do so. In the days before money was invented
saving was not so easy, but the invention of money gave
an impetus to it and so to avarice. To be niggardly with
things which can be directly enjoyed and used, like food
and old clothes, is therefore the meanest kind of avarice.
But money, not being itself directly consumable and only
a means of exchange for anything whatever, is an inducement to hoarding ; for if I have a sum of money, I can
make all kinds of plans for procuring for myself all sorts

of objects and amenities in terms of which alone money is serviceable. Thus far my opportunity to spend the money as I please remains ; I can regard all the amenities of life, all the Objects of my satisfaction as things which I may still have ; but once I have spent it on one of the many things that appeal to me I am no longer a free agent ; I can no longer apply it to the acquisition of any of the other objects and amenities upon which my mind was dwelling ; they cease to be within my reach. In this way an illusion takes possession of me. If I possess a sum of money, I can think of it disjunctively, as service-able for this purpose or for that. Instead, I think col-lectively, and imagine that it can procure whatever I want. So long as the money is still in my possession the pleasant dream of having all the pleasures of life at my disposal remains, and I am by no means eager to dispel the sweet error by rational thought. In order, therefore, not to dispel the illusion that my limited hoard is a means of placing every pleasure within my reach, I come to regard it as itself the greatest pleasure because it is the repository of all pleasures which I can enjoy, in their totality, if I will. So long as I have my money I can enjoy all pleasure in prospect, but once the money is spent the infinite prospect of the other pleasures is gone. Man is thus led to look upon money as the object of the greatest pleasure, in which all other pleasures and objects lie hid. The miser's thoughts are daily the sport of this illusion, and while others enjoy life he consoles himself with the thought that he could do likewise if he were so minded. He is certainly pained at the sight of the other man enjoying himself and he begrudges him his pleasure, but when the other has spent his money and his enjoyment is over, it is the miser's turn to crow ; he still has his money and the laugh is with him.

Let us next consider avarice in relation to class, sex and age. In regard to class we find that clerics as a class are accused of being miserly. This is an accusation which could be levelled against men of learning generally, and so against the clerical profession as one of the learned professions. A minister of religion as a rule enjoys only a small income, gets into the habit of placing an inordinate value on small things, and is accordingly liable to become miserly. But the reason why scholars generally lay themselves open to accusation of meanness is as follows. Scholars follow their calling for the love of learning and not as a means of earning a fortune; they recognize that their profession is not a profitable, money-making business; not a means of livelihood like any other, which has the earning of money as its immediate object. Their income is certainly less sure than that of men who have a trade in their hands and can always earn a satisfactory living at it; they may, therefore, incline to value money and to become mean. Further, sedentary occupations tend to make people miserly; they do not go out much and lose the habit of spending; they keep away from worldly pleasures and amusements and so from the expenditure which these entail; the nature of their occupation leads them to turn for enjoyment to the pleasures that accord with their temperament, so that they learn to be abstemious. Business-men tend more to greed than to miserliness, but soldiers to neither. A soldier never knows how long and when he may be able to enjoy his fortune; he lives in uncertainty, and the soldier's profession is, moreover, very sociable. Thus there are no springs of avarice in him.

As regards sex, women are more inclined to be miserly than men. This is in keeping with the nature of woman, for the women have to be more sparing since they are spending money which they do not earn themselves. The man, who earns the money, is in a position to be the more generous.

In so far as age is concerned, youth is less inclined to be miserly than old age. Youth has the possibility open to it of acquiring almost anything, but not so old age. Now, money brings power; it is the universal means to all ends, so that even thieves, when they have collected sufficient booty, use money for the purpose of making themselves safe and securing themselves against punishment. They may even buy themselves a peerage, the easier to escape the gallows. Thus old age also tries by means of the artificial power of money to make up for its lack of physical strength and power. A further reason is the fear of old age lest it should fall upon bad times and want, for when an old man loses his all he is no longer able to earn more.   Youth can lose, can begin over again, lay fresh plans and with luck recover its position, but not so old age.   Old age must, therefore, set up a fund to secure itself against want.   The sordid miser is more often actuated by the fear of want, though in some cases the motive is a yearning for power and authority, and money is the readiest means to this end.

THRIFT

Thrift is care and scruple in the spending of one's substance.   It is no virtue ; it requires neither skill nor talent. A spendthrift of good taste requires much more of these qualities than does he who merely saves ; an arrant fool can save and put money aside ; to spend one's money with refinement on pleasure needs knowledge and skill, but there is no cleverness in accumulating by thrift.   The thrifty, who acquire their wealth by saving, are as a rule small-minded people, but amongst the spendthrifts we find men of spirit and high intelligence.

To answer the question whether miserliness or extravagance is more harmful to the State, we must leave out of account the possible infringements of the rights of others to which either might lead, the miser's grasping and the spendthrift's squandering of other people's property. Then we see that the spendthrift enjoys his life, while the miser cheats himself by his unwillingness ever to enjoy anything except in prospect.   So he leaves the world like the village idiot who does not even know that he has lived.   On the other hand, the spendthrift is incautious and improvident ; he cannot know how long he will live, and having squandered what he had he may afterwards have to live in privation.   The miser will not be reduced to this extremity ; but is there really any difference between them in this respect ?   The one deprives himself of future joys, whilst the other cheats himself of the present.   It is true that it is a hardship to live in want after one has tasted the joys of comfort, and it would be better to reverse the process, but in point of fact whilst the spend-thrift at some time of his life enjoys himself, the miser never does ; he is constantly deferring his joys, he lives ever in the future and feeds upon the prospect of pleasure. The spendthrift is a lovable simpleton, the miser a detestable fool. The former has not destroyed his better self and might face the misfortune which awaits him with courage, but the latter is a man of poor character.

But as regards their effect upon others, while the spend-thrift is preferable to the miser so long as both are alive, it is the other way about after they are dead. Misers provide foresight with the means for furthering her ends. They are machines which work in unison with universal ends in the order of things. Their labours are for the benefit of their heirs, who will be able to enter into a complete possession of their goods. Their piled-up wealth can form the basis of great enterprises which will bring it back into circulation.

Thrift is no virtue, merely prudence ; frugality, however, is a virtue. Frugality can take the form either of temper-ance or of total abstinence. It is easier to abstain altogether than to be moderate ; we can abstain without having tasted, but to be moderate means that we must already have tasted and so have whetted our appetite. It is thus hard to resist a pleasure which one has partly en-joyed, harder than to refuse one altogether. It is virtuous to abstain, but more so to be temperate. Both virtues lead to self-mastery.

THE TWO IMPULSES OF OUR NATURE AND THEIR CONCOMITANT DUTIES

Man has by nature two impulses, to be esteemed and to be loved. These impulses refer to the dispositions of others. But which of these two inclinations is the stronger ? That for esteem, and for the following reasons. Esteem regards the inner worth, love only the relative worth of our fellows. We are esteemed for our intrinsic worth ;

we are loved, because of the advantages we bring to others and the pleasure we confer. We love that by which we gain advantage; we esteem that which has worth in itself. A second reason is the greater security which respect gives us. We can be loved even though we command little respect, but if we are highly esteemed we are more secure against insults. Whether my neighbour loves me or not depends upon himself: he can love me or hate me as he pleases; but if I am a man of inner worth every one respects me; any one may love me or not, but every one who appreciates my worth must respect me. Let us consider the opposite—contempt and hate. Both are unpleasant, but it hurts one more to be treated with contempt than to be hated. The number of people who may hate me cannot be large and, though they can cause me a great deal of mischief, yet if only others recognize my worth, I will find courage and means to bear and to withstand their hate; but to be held in contempt is unbearable. A contemptible man is a universal object of disdain; no one holds him in regard, and he loses all sense of his own value. If we wish to be respected we must respect others, we must respect humanity as a whole. On the other hand, a similar duty bids us love mankind if we would ourselves be loved. We must do to others as we require that they should do to us. If we analyse further the esteem which we desire from others, we find that it is prudent not to be indifferent to the opinions of others, but to be strongly concerned about the opinions which others hold of us. This desire for the esteem of others is no desire for profit or advantage or anything of the sort. If it were, we should have, not a love, but a lust, an avarice for honour; we should be like the merchant who wants to be considered rich because it is useful to him. It is the end and not the means which must determine the names we give to things. Thus the man who saves money inordinately with a view to dissipating his hoard on show and pomp, is not miserly, but ambitious. In the same way our inclination to earn favourable opinions is not actuated by the expectation of advantage. On the contrary, it is an immediate inclination, directed to honour and nothing else. It has no advantage for its

Object. Accordingly we are said to love, not to covet honour. It is an inclination implanted in us by prudence, and no man, be he ever so great, is indifferent to what others think of him. One man may be more susceptible than another. A nobleman might pay little heed to what peasants, or even the middle classes, think of him, and a ruling prince may be indifferent to the views held of him by his subjects, but each of them will solicit the good opinions of his peers ; to these they will not be indifferent. A prince will value the esteem of another prince ; to be honoured by his subjects, over whom he holds sway and authority, is of less consequence to him, for the simple reason that he has them in his power and so attaches less importance to what they think than he does to the opinions of those over whom he has no authority ; but he will be very solicitous of his reputation with his peers. In the same way a woman of low degree is more ashamed before her equals than before her superiors ; she would rather be looked down upon by the latter than be held in contempt by her equals. But to have the respect of our superiors flatters us more than does that of our inferiors. None the less, we truly honour humanity in general only if we are not indifferent to the esteem of men of low station, if we value what the meanest of our fellows think of us as highly as we do the opinions of those of high degree.

Why are we thus impelled to value our reputation ? Because prudence teaches that we should weigh our conduct by the judgment of our fellows so that we may not act purely from self-love ; our own judgment of our conduct may have a corrupting effect, but the judgments of others are a corrective.

We must distinguish between love of honour and lust for honour. The former, compared with the latter, is negative in its nature ; it is dictated merely by our desire not to become an object of contempt ; but the lust for honour craves to be an object of surpassing esteem. The love of honour might be called *honestas*, though we should then need to distinguish it from honourableness. But the lust for honour is ambition. The man who is solicitous of his reputation may shrink from company so as not to risk incurring contempt, but the ambitious man cannot withdraw into solitude because he longs for the high esteem of others. The lust for honour implies an arrogant demand to be noticed. We never object to the love of honour, but to the lust for honour we do object. The love of honour is modest, never becoming a lust ; it is anxious for the respect of all and to escape contempt. Changed to a lust, it demands uncommon and inordinate honour. To gain the preference of others, the ambitious man sets out to force the judgments of his fellows to his own opinion. But since the judgments of others with respect to our-selves are free, the grounds for respecting us must be such that the judgments of others follow necessarily from them. A man who lusts after honour seeks to compel the judgment of others, by demanding their esteem, and in so doing he makes himself ridiculous. He encroaches upon our rights and drives us to resist him. But the man of honour whose sole desire is to be respected by his fellows, and not to be held in contempt, gains our respect ; and the more worthy he is of it and the less arrogant, the more eager are we to respect him.

Ambition can be characterized by vanity, or true love of honour, or both. To aim at gaining respect by dress, or by titles, or by any other things which are not inherent in our person, is vanity ; true ambition aims at being honoured for personal worth. All ambition, whether natural or not, ought to be restrained. We are all of us ambitious, but we must not push ourselves forward, because our ambitions would then miscarry ; for men will repel the pre-sumption that claims their favourable judgment, since they want their judgment to be free and unconstrained. What-ever has value we can prize, but we can only prefer in honour that which has the value of merit. Common men are those whose worth is of that degree which can be expected from every one ; they have no merit and are not worthy of honour ; they deserve respect and esteem, but not honour and deference. Integrity, honesty, and punc-tilious discharge of our obligations may be expected from all of us ; these qualities entitle us to respect, but not to honour and homage. That I am honest is no reason why I should be specially honoured ; I do not thereby show any excellence or outstanding merit ; but I deserve respect.

It is only in corrupt periods, in which honesty is rare, that it is held to deserve special honour ; to regard it so and to consider the honest man as one who shows outstanding merit by his honesty is a mark of degraded times. Why should it be accounted for merit seeing that it ought to be a common quality, that every one should be honest and that he who falls short of honesty by the merest fraction is already a rogue ? If a Turkish judge refuses to accept bribes he is praised for his honesty ; but to praise him is to condemn his colleagues. Aristides was called the Just ; if his righteousness deserves high praise it is because in the age in which he lived there were but few righteous men, and to praise Aristides is to condemn his age. But magnanimity and kindness are meritorious ; we cannot expect every one to be kind and generous, and men who show these qualities are highly esteemed and honoured. We respect ordinary good conduct ; we honour meritorious conduct. If we fail in our bounden duties we forfeit the respect of our fellows.

Sexual desire is natural to all of us, yet we conceal it and make a secret of it ; nature prompts us to this secrecy because by so doing we restrain this propensity or inclination, whereas if we were unabashed and talked openly about it we should find it more difficult to keep it within bounds. In the same way nature demands that we should hide our ambitions, for as soon as we make a show of them we become unreasonably presumptuous. There is an impulse in every man to honour ; this instinct is generally unselfish, though at times it is selfish. If a man seeks honour in order to improve his station in life, to get into office, or to win a wife by it, his motives are interested ; but if he has no ulterior motive and seeks only the approbation of his fellows, he is a true lover of honour.

When a man hopes that after he is dead his memory shall be respected and honoured by those he leaves behind, his impulse to honour clearly does not involve self-interest. Apart from such honour no one would devote himself to the pursuit of knowledge ; a student on a desert island would throw away his books, and search for roots instead. Is love of honour, then, the proper impulse to knowledge or not ? Providence has instilled in us the impulse to honour, to secure the conformity of our actions and procedure with the universal judgment of all men; without it we would not be guided to the same extent by considerations of the common good. Again, if we relied entirely upon our own judgment, we could not always be sure that we were not in error and that our conclusions were not wrong, as they often would be; we have, therefore, this independent impulse to compare our judgment about our own knowledge with that of others; we test it by submitting it to the examination of many minds; our cognitions must stand the test of universal reason, and of the world's judgment; thus only can we be sure that they are right, and not wrong, as for one reason or another they might well be. Others may err as well, but it is unlikely that they would fall into exactly the same trap as ourselves. We, therefore, refer our conclusions to other people at the bidding of our impulse to honour. It is true that this love of honour may subsequently degenerate into a lust for approval which, with an eye to commendation and self-glory, may lead us to strain arguments and adduce specious reasons to bolster up what is false; but in the first instance the impulse is pure and genuine. Should it degenerate, it thwarts the intention of Providence. Except under certain conditions, the lust for honour is not very natural, but the love of honour is. Without any love of honour, the sciences would lose their incentive.

But is this love of honour, in and for itself, and apart from all self-interest, to which we cannot be indifferent even when it looks beyond the grave, which is even stronger so, seeing that after death we can no longer wipe any stain from our reputation—is this love of honour in keeping with our duties towards ourselves? Is it indeed an object of self-regarding duty at all? There can be no question that it is both. Man must be a lover of honour. A man who is careless of his honour is base. Honour is the goodness of conduct as it appears. It is not enough that our conduct should be good: it must appear as good before the eyes of others. Morality, the good-will and disposition are the things from which mankind derives its worth. Here is the moral unity of mankind, and therefore each of us must see to it, not merely that our actions provide a negative example by containing nothing evil, but that they set a positive example by the presence of some real good in them. Our actions must not only be good ; they must also be set as examples before the eyes of others.

Our actions should spring from love of honour. The question then arises whether we ought to guide our conduct by our own principles or by the opinions held by others about what is worthy and unworthy. The opinions of others may arise from empirical grounds, in which case they have authority ; or from reason, when they have no authority. Thus my own reason shows me what is righteous, and I must be guided by my own principle, and not by the opinions of others ; but in matters of custom, for instance, I must follow others.

There is yet a third aspect of ambition, namely, to take what people think and say of us for the object of honour. What people think of us certainly affects our honour, but it is wrong to attach primary importance to what they say.

A man is honourable if his conduct makes him worthy of respect and not an object of contempt.

DUTIES TOWARDS OTHERS

At this point Baumgarten strays into a discussion of duties towards inanimate beings, beings which are animate but irrational, and rational beings. In fact we have only other-regarding duties towards men. Inanimate things are completely subject to our will, and our duties to animals are duties only with reference to ourselves. We shall therefore reduce all these duties to duties towards other men. They are divisible into two main groups :

1. Duties of good-will, or benevolence.
2. Duties of indebtedness or justice.

Actions falling under the first group are benevolent ; those falling under the second are righteous and compulsory.

The duties falling under the first heading do not imply any definite obligation upon us to love other human beings and to do them good. The man who loves his neighbour wishes him well, but of his own impulse ; he does so willingly and from a voluntary disposition, not because he is bound to. Love is good-will from inclination ; but there can also be good-will on principle. It follows that the pleasure we find in doing good to others may be either direct or indirect. The direct pleasure comes from doing good from obligation, when we enjoy the consciousness of having done our duty. Doing good from love springs from the heart ; doing good from obligation springs rather from principles of the understanding. Thus a man may act kindly towards his wife from love, but if his inclination has evaporated he ought to do so from obligation.

But can a moralist say that we have a duty to love others ? Love is good-will from inclination. Now whatever depends upon my inclination and not upon my will, cannot be laid upon me as a duty. I certainly cannot love at will, but only when I have an impulse to love. Duty is always a compulsion, which may be either self-imposed or else imposed upon us by others. If then we are under an obligation to be mindful of the welfare of others, on what is this obligation founded ? On principles. For let us consider the world and ourselves. The world is an arena on which nature has provided everything necessary for our temporal welfare, and we are nature's guests. We all have an equal right to the good things which nature has provided. These good things have not, however, been shared out by God. He has left men to do the sharing. Every one of us, therefore, in enjoying the good things of life must have regard to the happiness of others ; they have an equal right and ought not to be deprived of it. Since God's providence is universal, I may not be indifferent to the happiness of others. If, for instance, I were to find in the forest a table spread with all manner of dishes, I ought not to conclude that it is all for me ; I may eat, but I should also remember to leave some for others to enjoy. I ought not even to consume in its entirety any particular dish in case some one else might fancy it also. Recognizing, therefore, that Providence is universal, I am placed under an obligation to restrict my own consumption, and to bear in mind that nature's preparations are made for all of us. This is the source of the obligation to benevolence.

But let us consider the man who is benevolent from love, who loves his neighbour from inclination. Such a man stands in need of people to whom he can show his kindness, and is not content until he finds human beings towards whom he can be charitable. A kindly heart gets more pleasure and satisfaction from doing good to others than from its own enjoyment of the good things of life ; the inclination to do good is a necessity to it, which must be satisfied. It is not this kindliness of heart and temper whicht he moralist should seek to cultivate, but good-will from principles. For the former is grounded in inclination and a natural necessity, giving rise to unregulated conduct. Such a man will be charitable, by inclination, to all and sundry ; and then, if someone takes advantage of his kind heart, in sheer disgust he will decide from then onwards to give up doing good to others. He has no principle by which to calculate his behaviour. Therefore the moralist must establish principles, and commend and inculcate benevolence from obligation. When all the obligations, religious as well as natural, have been expounded, we may go on to inculcate the inclination, though never forgetting that it must be subordinated to principles. On these conditions only may we proceed to expound the motives to acts of benevolence from inclination.

Let us now consider the second group of duties towards others, namely the duties of indebtedness and justice. Here there is no question of inclination, only of the rights of others. It is not their needs that count in this connexion, but their rights ; it is not a question of whether my neighbour is needy, wretchedly poor or the reverse ; if his right is concerned, it must be satisfied. This group of duties is grounded in the general rule of right.

The chief of these duties is respect for the rights of others. It is our duty to regard them as sacred and to respect and maintain them as such. There is nothing more sacred in the wide world than the rights of others. They are inviolable. Woe unto him who trespasses upon the

right of another and tramples it underfoot! His right
should be his security; it should be stronger than any
shield or fortress. We have a holy ruler and the most
sacred of his gifts to us is the rights of man.

Let us take a man who is guided only by justice and
not by charity. He may close his heart to all appeal;
he may be utterly indifferent to the misery and misfortune
around him; but so long as he conscientiously does his
duty in giving to every one what is his due, so long as he
respects the rights of other men as the most sacred trust
given to us by the ruler of the world, his conduct is
righteous; let him give to another no trifle in excess of
his due, and yet be equally punctilious to keep no jot nor
tittle back, and his conduct is righteous. If all of us
behaved in this way, if none of us ever did any act of love
and charity, but only kept inviolate the rights of every
man, there would be no misery in the world except sickness
and misfortune and other such sufferings as do not spring
from the violation of rights. The most frequent and
fertile source of human misery is not misfortune, but the
injustice of man.

Respect for the rights of others is rooted in principle,
and as mankind is not rich in principles, Providence has
implanted in our bosoms the instinct of benevolence to
be the source of actions by which we restore what we have
unrighteously procured. We have thus an instinct to
benevolence, but not to righteousness. This impulse
makes a man merciful and charitable to his neighbour, so
that he makes restitution for an injustice of which he is
quite unconscious; though unconscious of it only because
he does not properly examine his position. Although we
may be entirely within our rights, according to the laws
of the land and the rules of our social structure, we may
nevertheless be participating in general injustice, and in
giving to an unfortunate man we do not give him a gratuity
but only help to return to him that of which the general
injustice of our system has deprived him. For if none of
us drew to himself a greater share of the world's wealth
than his neighbour, there would be no rich and no poor.
Even charity therefore is an act of duty imposed upon us
by the rights of others and the debt we owe to them.

We have considered the man who is guided only by justice and not by charity. Let us now examine the man who has no respect for the rights of others and the debt he owes to them, but habitually does even his bounden duties from benevolence. It is no use talking to such a man of right and indebtedness. He will do a great deal because he is kind ; but let any one who is in the direst need come to him demanding the repayment of a debt and address him in the ordinary terms which a creditor might use in speaking to a debtor, and although he is only asking for something to which he is fully entitled, he will chide him for a churl who will have everything by force. If our charitable friend refuses to repay the debt and thereby brings misfortune upon his debtor, not all the kind and charitable acts of his life can counterbalance his one injustice. They cannot even be taken into account, for charity is a thing apart where right and justice are concerned. We may not withhold from any one what is due to him ; having complied with this condition, we can be charitable with our surplus means.

If charity were the mainspring and sole motive of our conduct, there would be no such thing as ' mine ' and ' thine ' ; the world would be the theatre, not of reason, but of inclination, and men would not trouble to earn but would rely on the charity of their fellows. But just as children share their sweets only so long as they have enough and to spare, so could this arrangement work only if there was in the world a superfluity of wealth. It is therefore good that man must work for his happiness and welfare, and must respect the rights of others. Teachers and moralists must, therefore, concentrate as far as possible upon showing that charity is a duty which we owe to mankind and that in the last analysis it is a question of right. A man ought not to be flattered for his acts of charity lest his heart swell with generosity and desire to make benevolence the sole rule of his conduct.

Good-will and charity call for some further remarks. Good-pleasure from love cannot be made to follow a law, but good-will from obligation can. But if we do good from duty, it becomes a habit and we ultimately do it from love and inclination. If we see that a man merits praise and we speak well of him, we get so into the habit of it that in the long run we have no inclination to say anything but good of him. Thus love from inclination is also a moral virtue : commencing by doing good from obligation through habit we can end by doing it from inclination, and to this extent love can be commanded.

There are two kinds of love, the love of good-will and the love of good-pleasure. The love of good-will consists in the wish and inclination to promote the happiness of others, the love of good-pleasure in the satisfaction which we ourselves derive from appreciating the perfections of another. This good-pleasure can be either of the senses or of the intellect. The sensuous love of good-pleasure is a satisfaction in sensuous intuition from inclination. Thus the sexual impulse is a satisfaction of the senses, and is less concerned with happiness than with the community between the two persons. The intellectual love of good-pleasure is harder to conceive. It is not intellectual good-pleasure which we find it hard to represent to ourselves, but a love which consists in intellectual good-pleasure.

Which good-pleasure of the intellect is it that generates inclination ? The good dispositions of benevolence. Now we are told to love our neighbour. How are we to understand this ? The love here referred to is not the love of good-pleasure, which I can show to the veriest rascal, but the love of good-will. Now moral good-will does not consist in wishing a person well, but in wishing that he should be worthy of it ; we can thus bear good-will even to our enemies. Good-will can always be ; for I can at all times wish that my enemy should come to himself, become worthy of every happiness and attain to it. A king can bear good-will towards a rebel even though he may punish and hang him ; he may be sorry that the unfortunate man should have incurred the penalty of the law, and he may have a cordial desire that the man should make himself worthy of the happiness above, and find it waiting him in heaven. Everyone can, therefore, be enjoined to love his neighbour with the love of good-will ; but the love of good-pleasure cannot be universally ordained, since we cannot be well pleased where there is no object of esteem. But we must draw a distinction

between the man himself and his humanity.   If a man be
a rogue, I disapprove of him as a man, but however wicked
he is there is still some core of the goodwill in him, and
if I distinguish between his humanity and the man himself
I can contemplate even the rogue with pleasure.   No
rogue is so abandoned that he does not appreciate the
difference between good and bad and does not wish to be
virtuous.   The moral feeling and the goodwill are within
him, but he lacks the strength and the motive.   He may
be a most wicked wretch, but who knows what drove him
to it ?   With his temperament, his wickedness may be no
greater than a trifling fault of my own.   If I look into
his heart, I can find in him too a feeling for virtue, and
therefore in him too humanity must be loved.   It can,
therefore, be said with full justification that we ought to
love our neighbour.   We are bound not only to well-doing
but also to the love of men both with the love of good-will
and the love of good-pleasure.

Since men are objects of love, of good-pleasure, in the
sense that we ought to love humanity in them, judges
ought not when punishing criminals to dishonour their
humanity ; a miscreant should be punished, but his
humanity ought not to be violated by base punishments ;
for if another dishonours any man's humanity, it is as
though he had done so himself, as if he were no longer
worthy to be a man, so that he must be treated as an
object of universal contempt.

Thus the command to love our neighbour applies within
limits both to love from obligation and to love from inclination.   For if I love others from obligation, I acquire in
the course of time a taste for it, and my love, originally
duty-born, becomes an inclination.   There are some duties,
like this of loving from duty, that have something artificial
about them, which makes us wonder whether they can
really be obligations.   But inclination goes its own secret
way ; indeed it can do no other, because it has no principle.

Affability is simply a convention of our behaviour to
others.   It abhors anything which might give offence to
them ; it moderates our anger and checks any impulsive
infringements of their rights ; it is born of the love of mankind.   At bottom it is nothing positive, for though affable

people avoid doing hurt to others, they are not generous in promoting the welfare of others. We might expect to find affability and generosity combined, but in fact they are incompatible, because generosity demands vigour and energy of spirit, whereas affability consists only in gentleness and suavity.

To be humane is to have sympathy with the fate of others ; to be inhumane is to harbour no such feelings of sympathy. Why are certain studies called *humaniora* ? Because they have a refining influence upon men. However restricted the learning which the student absorbs, these studies, by occupying his mind, produce in him a refinement and suavity which he never loses. Thus whilst a merchant will judge the worth of a man by his possessions, a student will employ another standard.

Frankness, by which we mean the combination of candour and affability, is very popular. Geniality, courtesy, politeness and civility are simply virtue manifesting itself in small things. It is rare to find these virtues combined with strength of character. We find this rare combination in friendship and self-sacrifice. But just because of the rarity of true friendship we must guard against repeatedly calling upon a friend to help us out of our difficulties lest we become a burden to him and give him the impression that our calls upon him may be never-ending. It is better to bear one's own troubles than to worry others with them. People who complain of lack of friends are those who are selfish and ever on the look-out to turn friendship to their own advantage. Of my friends I require, not advantage, but the joy of their company and the opportunity to open my heart to them ; but courtesy I require from everyone. Social intercourse is in itself a cultivator of virtue and a preparation for its surer practice. Courtesy signifies a pleasantness sufficiently fine to enable us to please others in the smallest trifles. We show elegance when our coarsenesses have been rubbed away. We scrape and polish one another until we fit together satisfactorily. Thus arises tact, which manifests a refinement in our power of judging what is pleasing and displeasing to others.

A cold temperament is one which is unemotional and unmoved by love. A man whose spirit is never moved to impulses of kindness is said to be cold. Coldness is not necessarily a thing to be condemned. Poets, who boast an excess of warm feelings and affection, condemn it, but if a man of a cold temperament is at the same time a man of principles and of good dispositions, he is at all times reliable. A cold-blooded but well-disposed guardian, advocate, or patriot, is a man of cool deliberation who will resolutely do his utmost for our good. Wickedness, if cold-blooded, is all the worse for it, but (although this may not sound well) cold-blooded goodness is better than a warmth of affection ; because it is more reliable.

If our senses are cold we lack love ; if our blood is cold we lack affection, that is, the impulse of love. In the first case we have no feeling and are indifferent to the condition of others ; but the coolness of the blood gives regularity and order to our love.

It is a good thing to love one's neighbour: it makes us good-natured ; but how can we love him if he is not lovable ? In such a case, love cannot be an inclination, but must be a wish that he had the worth in which we could find pleasure. The inclination to wish to find others lovable is one that we ought to possess. If we seek for it, we shall surely discover something lovable in them, just as an unlovable man finds in others, because he looks for them, the qualities which make them unlovable. We ought to wish our neighbour well, but we ought also to endeavour to find him lovable. Here there is a rule to be noticed. Our inclinations to love others and wish for their happiness should not be sentimental longings. Such ineffectual cravings we should seek to avoid, and cherish only practical desires. A desire is practical when it concerns itself not so much with the end wished for as with the means to that end. I see that another is prosperous and I am pleased, but it is not his good fortune which should please me as much as the actual steps and conduct which have brought it about. Again, I see a man miserable and I feel for him ; but it is useless to wish that he might be rid of his misery ; I ought to try to rid him of it. Misfortune and ills should be regarded with displeasure, not as such, but only if they are caused by man. If a man suffers in health or sustains a loss and it is just

his fate, there is nothing more that can be said about it :
such things must happen ; but if his hurt was caused by some
one else, it should arouse our utmost displeasure.   If in
such a case there is no way in which I can be of help to
the sufferer and I can do nothing to alter his situation, I
might as well turn coldly away and say with the Stoics :
' It is no concern of mine ; my wishes cannot help him ;
for I can only sympathize with him and hope fervently
that he should be rid of his misfortune.'   Men pride
themselves that they have a kind heart because they wish
that every one might be happy ; but merely to wish is not
the sign of a kind heart ; we are kindhearted only in so
far as we actually contribute to the happiness of others :
that alone betokens a kind heart.

Moral instruction must, therefore, be based on the view
that our pleasure in seeing others happy should be synonymous with the pleasure it gives us to promote their happiness.   It follows that the object of our pleasure is not the
happiness of others in and for itself, but only in so far
as we have helped to bring it about.   Men believe that
sympathy in another's misfortune and kindness of heart
consist in wishes and feelings, but when a man is indifferent
to the wretchedness of others just in so far as he can do
nothing to change it, and troubles only where he can do
some good and be of some help, such a man is practical ;
his heart is a kind heart, though he makes no show ; he
does not wear it on his sleeve, as do those who think that
friendship consists in empty wishes, but his sympathy is
practical because it is active.

FRIENDSHIP

Friendship is the hobby-horse of all rhetorical moralists ;
it is nectar and ambrosia to them.

There are two motives to action in man.   The one—
self-love—is derived from himself, and the other—the
love of humanity—is derived from others and is the moral
motive.   In man these two motives are in conflict.   If the
purposes of self-love did not demand our attention, we would

love others and promote their happiness. On the other hand, we recognize that acts of self-love have no moral merit, but have at most the sanction of the moral law, while acts prompted by our love of mankind and by our desire to promote the happiness of the human race, are most meritorious. Yet we attach particular importance to whatever promotes the worth of our own person. Here friendship comes in ; but how are we to proceed ? Are we first, from our self-love, to secure our own happiness, and having done that, look to the happiness of our fellows ; or should the happiness of others be our first concern ? In the first case we subordinate the happiness of others to our own, the inclination towards our own happiness becomes stronger and stronger, the pursuit of our own happiness has no term, and so care for the happiness of others is altogether suppressed ; in the second case, we think of others and our own happiness loses ground in the race. If men, however, were so minded that each one looked to the happiness of others, then the welfare of each would be secured by the efforts of his fellows. If we felt that others would care for our happiness as we for theirs, there would be no reason to fear that we should be left behind. The happiness I gave to another would be returned to me. There would be an exchange of welfare and no one would suffer, for another would look after my happiness as well as I looked after his. It might seem as if I should be the loser by caring for the happiness of others, but if this care were reciprocated, there would be no loss ; and the happiness of each would be promoted by the generosity of the others. This is the Idea of friendship, in which self-love is superseded by a generous reciprocity of love.

Let us now examine the other side of the picture. Let us see what would happen if every man concerned himself only with his own happiness and was indifferent to the happiness of others. Everyone is then entitled to care for his own happiness. There is no merit in this, though it has the sanction of the moral rule. Provided that, in furthering my own, I do not hinder my neighbour in his pursuit of happiness, I commit no moral fault, although I achieve no moral merit.

But if I had to choose between friendship and self-love,

which should I choose ?   On moral grounds I should choose
friendship, but on practical grounds self-love, for no one
could see to my happiness so well as I could myself.
In either case, however, my choice would be bad. If I
chose only friendship, my happiness would suffer ; if I
chose only self-love, there would be no moral merit or
worth in my choice.

Friendship is an Idea, because it is not derived from
experience. Empirical examples of friendship are ex-
tremely defective. It has its seat in the understanding.
In ethics, however, it is a very necessary Idea. Let us
take this opportunity to define the significance of the terms
' an Idea ' and ' an Ideal '. We require a standard for
measuring degree. The standard may be either natural
or arbitrary, according as the quantity is or is not determined by means of concepts a priori. What then is the
determinate standard by means of which we measure
quantities which are determined a priori ? The standard
in such cases is the upper limit, the maximum possible.
Where this standard is employed as a measure of lesser
quantities, it is an Idea ; when it is used as a pattern,
it is an Ideal. Now if we compare the affectionate inclinations of men, we find that the degrees and proportions
in which men distribute their love as between themselves and their fellows vary greatly. The maximum
reciprocity of love is friendship, and friendship is an Idea
because it is the measure by which we can determine reciprocal love. The greatest love I can have for another is
to love him as myself. I cannot love another more than
I love myself. But if I am to love him as I love myself
I must be sure that he will love me as he loves himself,
in which case he restores to me that with which I part
and I come back to myself again. This Idea of friendship enables us to measure friendship and to see the
extent to which it is defective. When, therefore, Socrates
remarks, ' My dear friends, there are no friends ', he
implies thereby that there is no friendship which fully
conforms to the Idea of friendship. And he is right ; for
any such absolute conformity is impossible ; but the Idea
is true. Assume that I choose only friendship, and that I
care only for my friend's happiness in the hope that he

cares only for mine. Our love is mutual ; there is complete restoration. I, from generosity, look after his happiness and he similarly looks after mine ; I do not throw away my happiness, but surrender it to his keeping, and he in turn surrenders his into my hands ; but this Idea is valuable only for reflection ; in practical life such things do not occur.

But if every one cared only for himself and never troubled about any one else, there would be no friendship. The two things must, therefore, be combined. Man cares for his own happiness and for that of others also. But as in this matter no limits are fixed and the degrees and proportions cannot be defined, the measure of friendship in the mixture cannot be determined by any law or formula. I am bound to look to my wants and to my satisfaction. If I cannot secure the happiness of my neighbour otherwise than by refraining from satisfying the needs of life, no one can place upon me the obligation of looking to his happiness and showing friendship towards him. But as each of us has his own measure of need and can raise the standard at will, the point at which the satisfaction of needs should give place to friendship is indeterminate. There is no question, however, that many of our needs, or things we have made our needs, are of such a nature that we can well sacrifice them for friendship.

There are three types of friendship, based respectively on need, taste, and disposition.

The friendship of need comes about when men can trust one another in the mutual provision for the needs of life. It was the original form of friendship amongst men, and is encountered mostly in the crudest social conditions. When savages go hunting, each of them has at heart and endeavours to promote the same interests as his colleagues ; they are friends. The simpler the needs of a group of men the more frequent is this kind of friendship amongst them ; and in proportion as their needs increase the frequency of such friendship diminishes. When the stage of luxury, with its multiplicity of needs, is reached, man has so many of his own affairs to absorb his attention that he has little time to attend to the affairs of others. At that stage, therefore, such friendship does not exist ; it is not even wanted ; for if one of the participants knows that the other seeks his friendship as a means for satisfying some of his needs, the friendship becomes interested and ceases. In such friendship one of the participants may be active, the other passive ; the one may really provide for the needs of the other ; where that happens the active friend is generous and the passive friend is the reverse. That being so, no true man will importune a friend with his troubles ; he will rather bear them himself than worry his friend with them. If, therefore, the friendship is noble on both sides, neither friend will impose his worries upon the other. Nevertheless, the friendship of need is pre-supposed in every friendship, not for enjoyment, but for confidence. In every true friend I must have the confidence that he would be competent to care for my affairs and to further my necessities, though I must never demand the proof of my confidence in order to enjoy it. If I know and can assume with confidence that my friend will really help me in need, I have a true friend. But as I am also a true friend of his, I ought not to expect any such thing of him or place him in any quandary ; I must have confidence only ; rather than make demands, I ought to bear my own troubles ; he again must have the same confidence in me, but must also refrain from demanding proof. On the one hand, therefore, friendship presupposes a benevolent disposition and a helping hand in need, and on the other abstention from abusing it by making calls upon it. My friend is magnanimous in being well disposed towards me, wishing me well and being ready to help me in my need ; I, again, must be magnanimous in refraining from making demands upon him. Friendship which goes to the length of making good a friend's losses is very rare and is a very delicate and sensitive thing. The reason is that we cannot lay such demands upon another. The finest sweets of friendship are its dispositions of good-will ; and on these we must avoid encroaching. The delight of friend-ship does not consist in the discovery that there is a shilling for me in a stranger's money-box. There is another reason, that it changes the relationship. The relation of friendship is a relation of equality. A friend who bears my losses becomes my benefactor and puts me in his debt.

I feel shy in his presence and cannot look him boldly in the face. The true relationship is cancelled and friendship ceases.

The friendship of taste is a pseudo-friendship. It consists in the pleasure we derive from each other's company, and not from each other's happiness. Persons of the same station and occupation in life are less likely to form such a friendship than persons of different occupations. One scholar will not form a friendship of taste with another; because their capacities are identical; they cannot entertain or satisfy one another, for what one knows, the other knows too. But a scholar can form such a friendship with a business-man or a soldier. Provided the scholar is not a pedant and the business-man not a blockhead, each of them can talk entertainingly to the other about his own subject. I am not attracted to another because he has what I already possess, but because he can supply some want of mine by supplementing that in which I am lacking. In other words, variety and not uniformity is the source of the friendship of taste.

There remains the third type of friendship, the friendship of disposition or sentiment. There is no question here of any service, or of any demand. The friendship is one of pure, genuine disposition, and is friendship in the absolute sense. There is no proper expression in German for the friendship of sentiment. There are dispositions of the feelings which are not dispositions to actual service; on these the friendship of sentiment is based. The point of special importance is this. In ordinary social intercourse and association we do not enter completely into the social relation. The greater part of our disposition is withheld; there is no immediate outpouring of all our feelings, dispositions and judgments. We voice only the judgments that seem advisable in the circumstances. A constraint, a mistrust of others, rests upon all of us, so that we withhold something, concealing our weaknesses to escape contempt, or even withholding our opinions. But if we can free ourselves of this constraint, if we can unburden our heart to another, we achieve complete communion. That this release may be achieved, each of us needs a friend, one in whom we can confide unreservedly, to whom we can disclose completely all our dispositions and judgments, from whom we can and need hide nothing, to whom we can communicate our whole self. On this rests the friendship of dispositions and fellowship. It can exist only between two or three friends. We all have a strong impulse to disclose ourselves, and enter wholly into fellowship ; and such self-revelation is further a human necessity for the correction of our judgments. To have a friend whom we know to be frank and loving, neither false nor spiteful, is to have one who will help us to correct our judgment when it is mistaken. This is the whole end of man, through which he can enjoy his existence. But even between the closest and most intimate of friends there are still some things which call for reserve, for the other's sake more than for one's own. There can be perfect and complete intimacy only in matters of disposition and sentiment, but we have certain natural frailties which ought to be concealed for the sake of decency, lest humanity be outraged. Even to our best friend we must not reveal ourselves, in our natural state as we know it ourselves. To do so would be loathsome.

To what extent do we make things better for ourselves by making friends ? It is not man's way to embrace the whole world in his good-will ; he prefers to restrict it to a small circle. He is inclined to form sects, parties, societies. The most primitive societies are those based on family connexion, and there are men who move only in the family circle. Then there are religious sects. These also are societies, associations formed by men for the cultivation of their common religious views and sentiments. This is on the face of it a laudable purpose, but it tends to harden the heart against and to ostracize those who stand outside the pale of the particular sect ; and any tendency to close the heart to all but a selected few is detrimental to true spiritual goodness, which reaches out after a good-will of universal scope. Friendship, likewise, is an aid in overcoming the constraint and the distrust man feels in his intercourse with others, by revealing himself to them without reserve. In this form of association also we must guard against shutting out from our heart all who are not within the charmed circle. Friendship is not of heaven but of the earth; the complete moral perfection of heaven must be universal; but friendship is not universal; it is a peculiar association of specific persons; it is man's refuge in this world from his distrust of his fellows, in which he can reveal his disposition to another and enter into communion with him.

If men complain of the lack of friendship, it is because they themselves have no friendly disposition and no friendly heart. They accuse others of being unfriendly, but it is they themselves who, by demands and importunities, turn their friends from them. We shun those who, under the cloak of friendship, make a convenience of us. But to make a general complaint about the lack of friends is like making a general complaint about the lack of money. The more civilized man becomes, the broader his outlook and the less room there is for special friendships; civilized man seeks universal pleasures and a universal friendship, unrestricted by special ties; the savage picks and chooses according to his taste and disposition, for the more primitive the social culture the more necessary such associations are. But such friendship presupposes weaknesses on both sides; it presupposes that neither party should be open to reproach by the other. If each has something to condone in the other, and neither need reproach himself, then there is equality between them, and neither can assert a superiority.

What then is that adaptation of man to man that constitutes the bond of friendship? Not an identity of thought; on the contrary, difference in thought is a stronger foundation for friendship, for then the one makes up the deficiencies of the other. Yet on one point they must agree. Their intellectual and moral principles must be the same, if there is to be complete understanding between them. Otherwise, there will always be discrepancy in their decisions and they will never agree. Every one seeks to deserve friendship. Uprightness of disposition, sincerity, trustworthiness, conduct devoid of all falsehood and spite, and a sweet, cheerful and happy temper, these are the elements which make up the character of a perfect friend; and once we have made ourselves fit objects of friendship we may be sure that we shall find some one who will take a liking to us and choose us for a friend, and that on closer contact our friendship will grow and become more and more intimate.

But as men are not transparent to each other, it may be that we fail to find what we imputed to our friend and sought in him. So friendships may come to an end. In friendships of taste the relationship loses its basis when with the process of time taste changes and finds new objects, and so a new friend supplants the old. The friendship of disposition is rare because men seldom have principles. Friends drift apart because there was no friendship of disposition between them.

The friendship of disposition calls for the following remarks. The name of friendship should inspire respect; and if by any chance a friend should turn into an enemy, we must still reverence the old friendship and never show that we are capable of hate. To speak ill of our friends is not merely wrong in itself, because it proves that we have no respect for friendship, that we have chosen our friends badly and that we are ungrateful to them; it is also wrong because it is contrary to the rule of prudence; for it leads those who hear us to wonder whether, if ever they became our friends and we subsequently became estranged, they would not be spoken of in the same strain, and so they turn from our friendship. We must so conduct ourselves towards a friend that there is no harm done if he should turn into an enemy. We must give him no handle against us. We ought not, of course, to assume the possibility of his becoming an enemy; any such assumption would destroy confidence between us; but it is very unwise to place ourselves in a friend's hands completely, to tell him all the secrets which might detract from our welfare if he became our enemy and spread them abroad; it is imprudent not only because he might thereby do us an injury if he became an enemy, but also because he might fail to keep our secrets through inadvertence. In particular, we ought to place no weapon in the hands of a hot-headed friend who might be capable of sending us to the gallows in a moment of passion, though he would implore our pardon as soon as he had cooled down.

Is every man a possible friend for us? No. I can be

a friend of mankind in general in the sense that I can bear good-will in my heart towards everyone, but to be the friend of everybody is impossible, for friendship is a particular relationship, and he who is a friend to everyone has no particular friend. And yet there are men of the world whose capacity to form friendships with anyone might well earn them the title of everybody's friends. Such citizens are very rare. They are men of a kindly disposition, who are always prepared to look on the best side of things. The combination of such goodness of heart with taste and understanding characterizes the friend of all men, and in itself constitutes a high degree of perfection. But as a rule, men are inclined to form particular relationships because this is a natural impulse and also because we all start with the particular and then proceed to the general. A man without a friend is isolated. Friendship develops the minor virtues of life.

ENMITY

Enmity is more than lack of friendship. A friendless man is not necessarily a general enemy. He may well have a good heart, but lack the gift of pleasing and attracting ; his dispositions may be upright and honourable, but he may be ignorant of the art of making himself popular by approving the faults of others. Such a man will have no friends, but it does not follow that he is an ill-natured individual. Mutual liking and good-will make friendship ; mutual dislike and ill-will make enmity.

We may dislike a man without bearing him ill-will. We do not like him because we do not find in him the good qualities for which we are looking ; we cannot associate with him ; he cannot be our friend ; but we have no ill-will towards him ; on the contrary, we wish him well, and would even give him something to keep away from us. To bear a man ill-will is definitely to wish him harm, and as enmity postulates both dislike and ill-will, a disposition to be pleased when ill befalls others, we ought to cherish enmity against none. To do so is to have something hateful in oneself, for only the loving man is lovable in his own eyes. But we can have an enemy without ourselves being enemies ; we can avoid him, be angry and hurt, wish him to feel what it means to suffer injustice, without being his enemy and so seeking to bring misfortune upon his head. We may hate a man who has behaved hatefully and has done us an injury by publishing our secrets ; he deserves hatred, but we ought not because of that to be his enemies and do him harm. Enmity is an express disposition to do harm to another.

A man is peaceable if he detests every kind of enmity. There are two ways in which a man can be peace-loving : he may wish for his own peace and he may strive to bring peace to others. The latter is the more noble of the two. But a peace-loving must not be confused with an indolent disposition. An indolent man avoids strife and trouble because they inconvenience him ; he wants peace not from any noble and kindly motives and not because his character is gentle. But a peace-loving disposition grounded in principles makes a man love peace without regard to temperamental gentleness, but solely as a matter of principle.

Misanthropy is hatred of mankind and may arise from either of two sources, shyness or enmity. In the first case, the misanthrope is afraid of men, deeming them all his enemies ; in the second, he is himself the enemy of others. The first is temperamentally timid, thinks himself not good enough for others, underestimates himself and so from very desire for honour flees from men and hides himself. The second shuns other people on principle, considering himself too good for them. Misanthropy is in part due to dislike, and in part to ill-will. If he is moved by dislike, the misanthrope thinks that all men are bad ; he fails to find in them that which he sought ; he does not hate them ; in fact he wishes them well ; but he does not like them ; he is incapable of understanding human nature and is gloomy and melancholy. But the other type of misanthrope, who is moved by ill-will, is a man who desires no one's good but everyone's hurt.

DUTIES DICTATED BY JUSTICE

Rights are determined in law. Now law indicates what actions are necessary from authority or compulsion, while ethics is concerned with actions necessitated by the inner obligation which springs from the rights of others in so far as they are not compulsory.

We must first and foremost consider the underlying principles of our duties. If a man has a right to demand anything from us and we comply with it, our action is not one of kindness or generosity, not an act of love, but the discharge of a debt. We must not call one duty by the name of another. If I deprive a man of anything and when he finds himself in need I do him a kindness, I am not magnanimous ; my act is merely a poor return for that which I have withheld from him. And as our social system is so arranged that we take part in the universal and open give and take of business with peculiar profit to ourselves, our acts of charity to others should not be regarded as acts of generosity, but as small efforts towards restoring the balance which the general social system has disturbed.

Furthermore, all acts and duties which follow from the rights of others are the most important of the duties we have towards others. An act of generosity is permissible only if it does not violate anybody's right ; if it does, it is morally wrong. It is wrong, for instance, to help a man in financial distress and thereby incur heavy debts to others. There is nothing in the world so sacred as the rights of others. Generosity is a superfluity. A man who is never generous but never trespasses on the rights of his fellows is still an honest man, and if everyone were like him there would be no poor in the world. But let a man be kind and generous all his life and commit but one act of injustice to an individual, and all his acts of generosity cannot wipe out that one injustice. At the same time the duties dictated by right or by generosity are inferior to the duties we owe to ourselves.

The duties arising from the rights of others should not

have compulsion as their motive. Only a rogue is just from fear of punishment. Nor does it make any difference if the punishment we fear is the punishment of God.

EQUITY

Equity is a form of right which does not carry with it the authority to enforce it. It is a right without being enforceable. If a man agrees to do some work for me for a stipulated payment and does more than I asked him to do, he can fairly expect to receive payment for his extra work, but he cannot demand it and cannot compel me to pay him any additional sum. If he wants to undo what he has done and I object, he must abstain because he has no right to interfere with what belongs to me. In so far as he went beyond our expressed agreement he has no authority to compel me. He would be entitled to use force against me only if his action was based on an inherent right of his own, a right the imputation of which was backed by a sufficiency of external conditions, that is to say, by adequate external proofs. Thus equity or fairness is an absolute right *coram foro interno*, but not *coram foro externo*, a right in regard to which the grounds for fixing responsibility are valid only before our conscience, but not *coram foro externo*.

INNOCENCE

In law a man is guilty when he has done something against the right of another ; in ethics he is guilty even if he only harboured the thought of doing it. Christ expresses this principle clearly when He says : ' Whosoever looketh on a woman to lust after her hath committed adultery with her already in his heart.' Thus, a man who harbours evil dispositions and does nothing to reform them, is ethically guilty of the offences he might have, but has not, committed ; the intentions are there, but he lacks the opportunity of giving effect to them and it is only circumstances which force him to abstain. We are innocent of moral transgression only if our dispositions are pure. If his dispositions are not pure, man is judged before the court of justice of morality as if he had actually committed the offences. Even the ordinary courts judge a man guilty though he is a victim of circumstances and temptation. Many another man is not held guilty of that particular offence simply because he has not been placed in the same set of circumstances and has not had to withstand the same temptation ; had he been similarly tempted, he also would have fallen. It is a question of circumstances. No virtue is so strong that it can never be tempted, and we have no proper acquaintance with our own dispositions until we have been placed in circumstances where they might have passed into action. For there is no rogue but wants to be good and to think himself such ; yet who can tell whether this man or that has been faced with the temptation to deceive some one and has not succumbed ? We are morally innocent if we prove in practice on every occasion the purity of our dispositions. Often enough we flatter ourselves that we are innocent though we have not withstood temptation. We have every reason to guard against temptation, as Christ tells us in the Lord's Prayer—a prayer which is entirely ethical in its outlook; even the petition for our daily bread looks to frugality rather than care for our physical sustenance—when He tells us to pray that we should not be led into temptation ; for who knows the strength of his moral intentions ? Who has tested them to the full ? Who can say that he is morally innocent ? Heaven knows best the measure of our guilt ; we can be innocent in the *forum externum*, but not before the eyes of Heaven.

INJURY

Little need be said on this topic. It affects the rights of others. If a man has cheated or deceived me, I do not wrong him if I cheat and deceive him in return, neverthe-less I contravene the universal rights of humanity. He cannot complain of my action, but I have none the less acted unjustly. It is not enough to say that we have never wronged a man ; for we may have done wrong in general.

If a man insults me he must indemnify me, or make amends, or, if that cannot be done, apologize. If he shows contrition at having hurt me and is upset about it, but that does not satisfy me, it is to his honour if he apologizes. An apology is not degrading.

VENGEANCE

Vengeance is not synonymous with claiming one's rights. Everyone is bound to assert his rights and to prevent their being trampled upon by others. It is man's privilege that he has rights, and this privilege of mankind should not be given up ; it should be defended as long as possible, for he who surrenders his rights surrenders his manhood. We are all, therefore, intent upon guarding our rights, and when we see a man violating the rights of another we demand that he should be forced to give his victim satis-faction ; we are angered at the sight of injustice and are anxious that the culprit should be made to feel what such conduct implies. Assume that a man refuses to pay us for work done and makes all kinds of excuses ; his excuses are beside the point ; we have a right to be paid, and we ought not to allow anyone to make sport of our right. It is not a question of the few shillings that may be involved, but of our right, which is more valuable than a large fortune. But to insist on one's right beyond what is necessary for its defence is to become revengeful. We become implac-able and think only of the damage and pain which we wish to the man who has harmed us, even though we do not thereby instil in him greater respect for our rights. Such desire for vengeance is vicious.

THE SLANDERER

We can have either an honest or treacherous enemy. The fawning, clandestine, deceitful enemy is far baser than the open one, even though the latter be violent and wicked. We can defend ourselves against the latter, but not against the former. Deceit and cunning destroy all confidence, but open hostility does not. He who openly declares himself an enemy can be relied upon, but the treachery of secret malice, if it became universal, would mean the end of all confidence. This type of wickedness is more detestable than violence ; it is base and inexcusable ; there is not a vestige of good in it. The avowed enemy can be tamed and brought to reason, but for the man in whom there is no seed of good, we can do nothing.

JEALOUSY AND ITS OFFSPRING—ENVY AND GRUDGE

There are two methods by which men arrive at an opinion of their worth : by comparing themselves with the Idea of perfection and by comparing themselves with others. The first of these methods is sound ; the second is not, and it frequently even leads to a result diametrically opposed to the first. The Idea of perfection is a proper standard, and if we measure our worth by it, we find that we fall short of it and feel that we must exert ourselves to come nearer to it ; but if we compare ourselves with others, much depends upon who those others are and how they are constituted, and we can easily believe ourselves to be of great worth if those with whom we set up comparison are rogues. Men love to compare themselves with others, for by that method they can always arrive at a result favourable to themselves. They choose as a rule the worst and not the best of the class with which they set up comparison ; in this way their own excellence shines out. If they choose those of greater worth the result of the comparison is, of course, unfavourable to them.

When I compare myself with another who is better than I, there are but two ways by which I can bridge the gap between us. I can either do my best to attain to his perfections, or else I can seek to depreciate his good qualities. I either increase my own worth, or else I diminish his so that I can always regard myself as superior to him. It is easier to depreciate another than to emulate him, and men prefer the easier course. They adopt it, and this is the origin of jealousy. When a man compares himself with another and finds that the other has many more good points, he becomes jealous of each and every good point he discovers in the other, and tries to depreciate it so that his own good points may stand out. This kind of jealousy may be called grudging. The other species of the genus jealousy, which makes us try to add to our good points so as to compare well with another, may be called emulating jealousy. The jealousy of emulation is, as we have stated, more difficult than the jealousy of grudge and so is much the less frequent of the two.

Parents ought not, therefore, when teaching their children to be good, to urge them to model themselves on other children and try to emulate them, for by so doing they simply make them jealous. If I tell my son, ' Look, how good and industrious John is ', the result will be that my son will bear John a grudge. He will think to himself that, but for John, he himself would be the best, because there would be no comparison. By setting up John as a pattern for imitation I anger my son, make him feel a grudge against this so-called paragon, and I instil jealousy in him. My son might, of course, try to emulate John, but not finding it easy, he will bear John ill-will. Besides, just as I can say to my son, ' Look, how good John is ', so can he reply : ' Yes, he is better than I, but are there not many who are far worse ? Why do you compare me with those who are better ? Why not with those who are worse than I ? ' Goodness must, therefore, be commended to children in and for itself. Whether other children are better or worse has no bearing on the point. If the comparison were in the child's favour, he would lose all ground of impulse to improve his own conduct. To ask our children to model themselves on others is to adopt a faulty method of upbringing, and as time goes on the fault will strike its roots deep. It is jealousy that parents are training and presupposing in their children when they set other children before them as patterns. Otherwise, the children would be quite indifferent to the qualities of others. They will find it easier to belittle the good qualities of their patterns than to emulate them, so they will choose the easier path and learn to show a grudging disposition. It is true that jealousy is natural, but that is no excuse for cultivating it. It is only a motive, a reserve in case of need. While the maxims of reason are still undeveloped in us, the proper course is to use reason to keep it within bounds. For jealousy is only one of the many motives, such as ambition, which are implanted in us because we are designed for a life of activity. But so soon as reason is enthroned, we must cease to seek perfection in emulation of others and must covet it in and for itself. Motives must abdicate and let reason bear rule in their place.

Persons of the same station and occupation in life are particularly prone to be jealous of each other. Many business-men are jealous of each other ; so are many scholars, particularly in the same line of scholarship ; and women are liable to be jealous of each other regarding men.

Grudge is the displeasure we feel when another has an advantage ; his advantage makes us feel unduly small and we grudge it him. But to grudge a man his share of happiness is envy. To be envious is to desire the failure and unhappiness of another not for the purpose of advancing our own success and happiness but because we might then ourselves be perfect and happy as we are. An envious man is not happy unless all around him are unhappy ; his aim is to stand alone in the enjoyment of his happiness. Such is envy, and we shall learn below that it is satanic. Grudge, although it too should not be countenanced, is natural. Even a good-natured person may at times be grudging. Such a one may, for instance, begrudge those around him their jollity when he himself happens to be sorrowful ; for it is hard to bear one's sorrow when all around are joyful. When I see everybody enjoying a good meal and I alone must content myself with inferior fare, it upsets me and I feel a grudge; but if we are all in the same boat I am content. We find the thought of death bearable, because we know that all must die; but if everybody were immortal and I alone had to die, I should feel aggrieved. It is not things themselves that affect us, but things in their relation to ourselves. We are grudging because others are happier than we. But when a good-natured man feels happy and cheerful, he wishes that every one else in the world were as happy as he and shared his joy; he begrudges no one his happiness.

When a man would not grant to another even that for which he himself has no need, he is spiteful. Spite is a maliciousness of spirit which is not the same thing as envy. I may not feel inclined to give to another something which belongs to me, even though I myself have no use for it, but it does not follow that I grudge him his own possessions, that I want to be the only one who has anything and wish him to have nothing at all. There is a deal of grudge in human nature which could develop into envy but which is not itself envy. We feel pleasure in gossiping about the minor misadventures of other people; we are not averse, although we may express no pleasure thereat, to hearing of the fall of some rich man; we may enjoy in stormy weather, when comfortably seated in our warm, cosy parlour, speaking of those at sea, for it heightens our own feeling of comfort and happiness; there is grudge in all this, but it is not envy.

The three vices which are the essence of vileness and wickedness are ingratitude, envy, and malice. When these reach their full degree they are devilish.

Men are shamed by favours. If I receive a favour, I am placed under an obligation to the giver; he has a call upon me because I am indebted to him. We all blush to be obliged. Noble-minded men accordingly refuse to accept favours in order not to put themselves under an obligation. But this attitude predisposes the mind to ingratitude. If the man who adopts it is noble-minded, well and good; but if he be proud and selfish and has perchance received a favour, the feeling that he is beholden to his benefactor hurts his pride and, being selfish, he cannot accommodate himself to the idea that he owes his benefactor anything. He becomes defiant and ungrateful. His ingratitude might even conceivably assume such dimensions that he cannot bear his benefactor and becomes his enemy. Such ingratitude is of the devil; it is out of all keeping with human nature. It is inhuman to hate and persecute one from whom we have reaped a benefit, and if such conduct were the rule it would cause untold harm. Men would then be afraid to do good to anyone lest they should receive evil in return for their good. They would become misanthropic.

The second devilish vice is envy. Envy is in the highest degree detestable. The envious man does not merely want to be happy; he wants to be the only happy person in the world; he is really contented only when he sees nothing but misery around him. Such an intolerable creature would gladly destroy every source of joy and happiness in the world.

Malice is the third kind of viciousness which is of the devil. It consists in taking a direct pleasure in the misfortunes of others. Men prone to this vice will seek, for instance, to make mischief between husband and wife, or between friends, and then enjoy the misery they have produced. In these matters we should make it a rule never to repeat to a person anything that we may have heard to his disadvantage from another, unless our silence would injure him. Otherwise we start an enmity and disturb his peace of mind, which our silence would have avoided, and in addition we break faith with our informant. The defence against such mischief-makers is upright conduct. Not by words but by our lives we should confute them. As Socrates said : We ought so to conduct ourselves that people will not credit anything spoken in disparagement of us.

These three vices—ingratitude (*ingratitudo qualificata*), envy, and malice—are devilish because they imply a direct inclination to evil. There are in man certain indirect tendencies to wickedness which are human and not unnatural. The miser wants everything for himself, but it is no satisfaction to him to see that his neighbour is destitute. The evilness of a vice may thus be either direct or indirect. In these three vices it is direct.

We may ask whether there is in the human mind an immediate inclination to wickedness, an inclination to the devilish vices. Heaven stands for the acme of happiness, hell for all that is bad, and the earth stands midway between these two extremes ; and just as goodness which transcends anything which might be expected of a human being is spoken of as being angelic, so also do we speak of devilish wickedness when the wickedness oversteps the limits of human nature and becomes inhuman. We may take it for granted that the human mind has no immediate inclination to wickedness, but is only indirectly wicked. Man cannot be so ungrateful that he simply must hate his neighbour ; he may be too proud to show his gratitude and so avoid him, but he wishes him well. Again, our pleasure in the misfortune of another is not direct. We may rejoice, for example, in a man's misfortunes, because he was haughty, rich and selfish ; for man loves to preserve equality. We have thus no direct inclination towards evil as evil, but only an indirect one. But how are we to explain the fact that even young children have the spirit of mischief strongly developed ? For a joke, a boy will stick a pin in an unsuspecting playmate, but it is only for fun. He has no thought of the pain the other must feel on all such occasions. In the same spirit he will torture animals ; twisting the cat's tail or the dog's. Such tendencies must be nipped in the bud, for it is easy to see where they will lead. They are, in fact, something animal, something of the beast of prey which is in us all, which we cannot overcome, and the source of which we cannot explain. There certainly are in human nature characteristics for which we can assign no reason. There are animals too who steal anything that comes their way, though it is quite useless to them ; and it seems as if man had retained this animal tendency in his nature.

Ingratitude calls for some further observations here. To help a man in distress is charity ; to help him in less urgent needs is benevolence ; to help him in the amenities of life is courtesy. We may be the recipients of a charity which has not cost the giver much and our gratitude is commensurate with the degree of good-will which moved him to the action. We are grateful not only for what we have received but also for the good intention which prompted it, and the greater the effort it has cost our benefactor, the greater our gratitude.

Gratitude may be either from duty or from inclination. If an act of kindness does not greatly move us, but if we nevertheless feel that it is right and proper that we should show gratitude, our gratitude is merely prompted by a sense of duty. Our heart is not grateful, but we have principles of gratitude. If, however, our heart goes out to our benefactor, we are grateful from inclination. There is a weakness of the understanding which we often have cause to recognize. It consists in taking the conditions of our understanding as conditions of the thing understood. We can estimate force only in terms of the obstacles it overcomes. Similarly, we can only estimate the degree of good-will in terms of the obstacles it has to surmount. In consequence we cannot comprehend the love and good-will of a being for whom there are no obstacles. If God has been good to me, I am liable to think that after all it has cost God no trouble, and that gratitude to God would be mere fawning on my part. Such thoughts are not at all unnatural. It is easy to fear God, but not nearly so easy to love God from inclination because of our consciousness that God is a being whose goodness is unbounded but to whom it is no trouble to shower kindness upon us. This is not to say that such should be our mental attitude ; merely that when we examine our hearts, we find that this is how we actually think. It also explains why to many races God appeared to be a jealous God, seeing that it cost Him nothing to be more bountiful with His goodness ; it explains why many nations thought that their gods were sparing of their benefits and that they required propitiating with prayers and sacrifices. This is the attitude of man's heart ; but when we call reason to our aid we see that God's goodness must be of a high order if He is to be good to a being so unworthy of His goodness. This solves our difficulty. The gratitude we owe to God is not gratitude from inclination, but from duty, for God is not a creature like ourselves, and can be no object of our inclinations.

We ought not to accept favours unless we are either forced to do so by dire necessity or have implicit confidence in our benefactor (for he ceases to be our friend and becomes our benefactor) that he will not regard it as placing us under an obligation to him. To accept favours indiscriminately and to be constantly seeking them is ignoble and the sign of a mean soul which does not mind placing itself under obligations. Unless we are driven by such dire necessity that it compels us to sacrifice our own worth, or unless we are convinced that our benefactor will not account it to us as a debt, we ought rather to suffer deprivation than accept favours, for a favour is a debt which can never be extinguished. For even if I repay my benefactor tenfold, I am still not even with him, because he has done me a kindness which he did not owe. He was the first in the field, and even if I return his gift tenfold I do so only as repayment. He will always be the one who was the first to show kindness and I can never be beforehand with him.

The man who bestows favours can do so either in order to make the recipient indebted to him or as an expression of his duty. If he makes the recipient feel a sense of indebtedness, he wounds his pride and diminishes his sense of gratitude. If he wishes to avoid this he must regard the favours he bestows as the discharge of a duty he owes to mankind, and he must not give the recipient the impression that it is a debt to be repaid. On the other hand, the recipient of the favour must still consider himself under an obligation to his benefactor and must be grateful to him. Under these conditions there can be benefactors and beneficiaries. A right-thinking man will not accept kindnesses, let alone favours. A grateful disposition is a touching thing and brings tears to our eyes on the stage, but a generous disposition is lovelier still. Ingratitude we detest to a surprising degree ; even though we are not ourselves the victims of it, it angers us to such an extent that we feel inclined to intervene. But this is due to the fact that ingratitude decreases generosity.

Envy does not consist in wishing to be more happy than

others—that is grudge—but in wishing to be the only one to be happy. It is this feeling which makes envy so evil. Why should not others be happy along with me ? Envy shows itself also in relation to things which are scarce. Thus the Dutch, who as a nation are rather envious, once valued tulips at several hundreds of florins apiece. A rich merchant, who had one of the finest and rarest specimens, heard that another had a similar specimen. He thereupon bought it from him for 2,000 florins and trampled it underfoot, saying that he had no use for it, as he already possessed a specimen, and that he only wished that no one else should share that distinction with him. So it is also in the matter of happiness.

Malice is different. A malicious man is pleased when others suffer, he can laugh when others weep. An act which wilfully brings unhappiness is cruel ; when it produces physical pain it is bloodthirsty. Inhumanity is all these together, just as humanity consists in sympathy and pity, since these differentiate man from the beasts. It is difficult to explain what gives rise to a cruel disposition. It may arise when a man considers another so evilly-disposed that he hates him. A man who believes himself hated by another, hates him in return, although the former may have good reason to hate him. For if a man is hated because he is selfish and has other vices, and he knows that he is hated for these reasons, he hates those who hate him although these latter do him no injustice. Thus kings who know that they are hated by their subjects become even more cruel. Equally, when a man has done a good deed to another, he knows that the other loves him, and so he loves him in return, knowing that he himself is loved. Just as love is reciprocated, so also is hate. We must for our own sakes guard against being hated by others lest we be affected by that hatred and reciprocate it. The hater is more disturbed by his hatred than is the hated.

ETHICAL DUTIES TOWARDS OTHERS:
TRUTHFULNESS

The exchange of our sentiments is the principal factor in social intercourse, and truth must be the guiding principle herein. Without truth social intercourse and conversation become valueless. We can only know what a man thinks if he tells us his thoughts, and when he undertakes to express them he must really do so, or else there can be no society of men. Fellowship is only the second condition of society, and a liar destroys fellowship. Lying makes it impossible to derive any benefit from conversation. Liars are, therefore, held in general contempt. Man is inclined to be reserved and to pretend. Reserve is *dissimulatio* and pretence *simulatio*. Man is reserved in order to conceal faults and shortcomings which he has; he pretends in order to make others attribute to him merits and virtues which he has not. Our proclivity to reserve and concealment is due to the will of Providence that the defects of which we are full should not be too obvious. Many of our propensities and peculiarities are objectionable to others, and if they became patent we should be foolish and hateful in their eyes. Moreover, the parading of these objectionable characteristics would so familiarize men with them that they would themselves acquire them. Therefore we arrange our conduct either to conceal our faults or to appear other than we are. We possess the art of simulation. In consequence, our inner weakness and error is revealed to the eyes of men only as an appearance of well-being, while we ourselves develop the habit of dispositions which are conducive to good conduct. No man in his true senses, therefore, is candid. Were man candid, were the request of Momus [1] to be complied with that Jupiter should place a mirror in each man's heart so that his disposition might be visible to all, man would have to be better constituted and to possess good principles. If all men were good there would be no need for any of us to be reserved; but since they are not, we have

---

[1] Momus, the god of mockery and censure, demanded that a little door be made in man's breast, that he might see his secret thoughts.

to keep the shutters closed. Every house keeps its dust-bin in a place of its own. We do not press our friends to come into our water-closet, although they know that we have one just like themselves. Familiarity in such things is the ruin of good taste. In the same way we make no exhibition of our defects, but try to conceal them. We try to conceal our mistrust by affecting a courteous demeanour and so accustom ourselves to courtesy that at last it becomes a reality and we set a good example by it. If that were not so, if there were none who were better than we, we should become neglectful. Accordingly, the endeavour to appear good ultimately makes us really good. If all men were good, they could be candid, but as things are they cannot be. To be reserved is to be restrained in expressing one's mind. We can, of course, keep absolute silence. This is the readiest and most absolute method of reserve, but it is unsociable, and a silent man is not only unwanted in social circles but is also suspected ; every one thinks him deep and disparaging, for if when asked for his opinion he remains silent people think that he must be taking the worst view or he would not be averse from expressing it. Silence, in fact, is always a treacherous ally, and therefore it is not even prudent to be completely reserved. Yet there is such a thing as prudent reserve, which requires not silence but careful deliberation ; a man who is wisely reserved weighs his words carefully and speaks his mind about everything excepting only those things in regard to which he deems it wise to be reserved.

We must distinguish between reserve and secretiveness, which is something entirely different. There are matters about which one has no desire to speak and in regard to which reserve is easy. We are, for instance, not naturally tempted to speak about and to betray our own misdemeanours. Every one finds it easy to keep a reserve about some of his private affairs, but there are things about which it requires an effort to be silent. Secrets have a way of coming out, and strength is required to prevent ourselves betraying them. Secrets are always matters deposited with us by other people and they ought not to be placed at the disposal of third parties. But man has a great liking for conversation, and the telling of secrets adds much to the interest of conversation ; a secret told is like a present given ; how then are we to keep secrets ? Men who are not very talkative as a rule keep secrets well, but good conversationalists, who are at the same time clever, keep them better. The former might be induced to betray something, but the latter's gift of repartee invariably enables them to invent on the spur of the moment something non-committal.

The person who is as silent as a mute goes to one extreme ; the person who is loquacious goes to the opposite. Both tendencies are weaknesses. Men are liable to the first, women to the second. Someone has said that women are talkative because the training of infants is their special charge, and their talkativeness soon teaches a child to speak, because they can chatter to it all day long. If men had the care of the children, they would take much longer to learn to talk. However that may be, we dislike anyone who will not speak : he annoys us ; his silence betrays his pride. On the other hand, loquaciousness in men is contemptible and contrary to the strength of the male. All this by the way ; we shall now pass to more weighty matters.

If I announce my intention to tell what is in my mind, ought I knowingly to tell everything, or can I keep any-thing back ? If I indicate that I mean to speak my mind, and instead of doing so make a false declaration, what I say is an untruth, a *falsiloquium*. But there can be *falsiloquium* even when people have no right to assume that we are expressing our thoughts. It is possible to deceive without making any statement whatever. I can make believe, make a demonstration from which others will draw the conclusion I want, though they have no right to expect that my action will express my real mind. In that case I have not lied to them, because I had not undertaken to express my mind. I may, for instance, wish people to think that I am off on a journey, and so I pack my luggage ; people draw the conclusion I want them to draw ; but others have no right to demand a declaration of my will from me. Thus the famous Law [1]

[1] The reference is to John Law (1671–1729) and his Mississippi venture.

went on building so that people might not guess his intention to abscond. Again, I may make a false statement (*falsiloquium*) when my purpose is to hide from another what is in my mind and when the latter can assume that such is my purpose, his own purpose being to make a wrong use of the truth. Thus, for instance, if my enemy takes me by the throat and asks where I keep my money, I need not tell him the truth, because he will abuse it ; and my untruth is not a lie (*mendacium*) because the thief knows full well that I will not, if I can help it, tell him the truth and that he has no right to demand it of me. But let us assume that I really say to the fellow, who is fully aware that he has no right to demand it, because he is a swindler, that I will tell him the truth, and I do not, am I then a liar ? He has deceived me and I deceive him in return ; to him, as an individual, I have done no injustice and he cannot complain ; but I am none the less a liar in that my conduct is an infringement of the rights of humanity. It follows that a *falsiloquium* can be a *mendacium*—a lie—especially when it contravenes the right of an individual. Although I do a man no injustice by lying to him when he has lied to me, yet I act against the right of mankind, since I set myself in opposition to the condition and means through which any human society is possible. If one country breaks the peace this does not justify the other in doing likewise in revenge, for if it did no peace would ever be secure. Even though a statement does not contravene any particular human right it is nevertheless a lie if it is contrary to the general right of mankind. If a man spreads false news, though he does no wrong to anyone in particular, he offends against mankind, because if such a practice were universal man's desire for knowledge would be frustrated. For, apart from speculation, there are only two ways in which I can increase my fund of knowledge, by experience or by what others tell me. My own experience must necessarily be limited, and if what others told me was false, I could not satisfy my craving for knowledge. A lie is thus a *falsiloquium in praejudicium humanitatis,* even though it does not violate any specific *jus quaesitum* of another. In law a *mendacium* is a *falsiloquium in praejudicium alterius ;* and so it must be in law ; but morally it is a *falsiloquium in praejudicium humanitatis*. Not every untruth is a lie ; it is a lie only if I have expressly given the other to understand that I am willing to acquaint him with my thought. Every lie is objectionable and contemptible in that we purposely let people think that we are telling them our thoughts and do not do so. We have broken our pact and violated the right of mankind. But if we were to be at all times punctiliously truthful we might often become victims of the wickedness of others who were ready to abuse our truthfulness. If all men were well-intentioned it would not only be a duty not to lie, but no one would do so because there would be no point in it. But as men are malicious, it cannot be denied that to be punctiliously truthful is often dangerous. This has given rise to the conception of a white lie, the lie enforced upon us by necessity—a difficult point for moral philosophers. For if necessity is urged as an excuse it might be urged to justify stealing, cheating and killing, and the whole basis of morality goes by the board. Then, again, what is a case of necessity ? Everyone will interpret it in his own way. and, as there is then no definite standard to judge by, the application of moral rules becomes uncertain. Consider, for example, the following case. A man who knows that I have money asks me : ' Have you any money on you ? ' If I fail to reply, he will conclude that I have ; if I reply in the affirmative he will take it from me ; if I reply in the negative, I tell a lie. What am I to do ? If force is used to extort a confession from me, if my confession is improperly used against me, and if I cannot save myself by maintaining silence, then my lie is a weapon of defence. The misuse of a declaration extorted by force justifies me in defending myself. For whether it is my money or a confession that is extorted makes no difference. The forcing of a statement from me under conditions which convince me that improper use would be made of it is the only case in which I can be justified in telling a white lie. But if a lie does no harm to anyone and no one's interests are affected by it, is it a lie ? Certainly. I undertake to express my mind, and if I do not really do so, though my statement may not be to the prejudice of the particular individual to whom it is made, it is none the less *in praejudicium humanitatis*. Then, again, there are lies which cheat. To cheat is to make a lying promise, while a breach of faith is a true promise which is not kept. A lying promise is an insult to the person to whom it is made, and even if this is not always so, yet there is always something mean about it. If, for instance, I promise to send some one a bottle of wine, and afterwards make a joke of it, I really swindle him. It is true that he has no right to demand the present of me, but in Idea it is already a part of his own property.

Reservatio mentalis is a form of dissimulation and *aequivocatio* of simulation. If a man tries to extort the truth from us and we cannot tell it him and at the same time do not wish to lie, we are justified in resorting to equivocation in order to reduce him to silence and to put a stop to his questionings. If he is wise, he will leave it at that. But if we let it be understood that we are expressing our sentiments and we proceed to equivocate we are in a different case ; for our listeners might then draw wrong conclusions from our statements and we should have deceived them. Lies of this nature, if intended to lead to good, were called by the Jesuits *peccata philosophica* or *peccatilla*. Hence the modern terms ' peccadillo ' and ' bagatelle '. But a lie is a lie, and is in itself intrinsically base whether it be told with good or bad intent. For formally a lie is always evil ; though if it is evil materially as well, it is a much meaner thing. There are no lies which may not be the source of evil. A liar is a coward ; he is a man who has recourse to lying because he is unable to help himself and gain his ends by any other means. But a stouthearted man will love truth and will not recognize a *casus necessitatis*. All expedients which take us off our guard are thoroughly mean. Such are lying, assassination, and poisoning. To attack a man on the highway is less vile than to attempt to poison him. In the former case he can at least defend himself, but, as he must eat, he is defenceless against the poisoner. A flatterer is not always a liar ; he is merely lacking in self-esteem ; he has no scruple in reducing his own worth and raising that of another in order to gain something by it. But there exists a form of flattery which springs from kindness of heart. Some kind souls flatter people whom they hold in high esteem. There are thus two kinds of flattery, kindly and treacherous; the first is weak, while the second is mean. People who are not given to flattery are apt to be fault-finders.

If a man is often the subject of conversation, he becomes a subject of criticism. If he is our friend, we ought not invariably to speak well of him or else we arouse jealousy and grudge against him; for people, knowing that he is only human, will not believe that he has only good qualities. We must, therefore, concede a little to the adverse criticism of our listeners and point out some of our friend's faults; if we allow him faults which are common and unessential, while extolling his merits, our friend cannot take it in ill part. Toadies are people who praise others in company in the hope of gain. Men are meant to form opinions regarding their fellows and to judge them. Nature has made us judges of our neigh-bours so that things which are false but are outside the scope of the established legal authority should be arraigned before the court of social opinion. Thus, if a man dis-honours some one, the authorities do not punish him, but his fellows judge and punish him, though only so far as it is within their right to punish him and without doing violence to him. People shun him, and that is punishment enough. If that were not so, conduct not punished by the authorities would go altogether unpunished. What then is meant by the enjoinder that we ought not to judge others? As we are ignorant of their dispositions we can-not tell whether they are punishable before God or not, and we cannot, therefore, pass an adequate moral judg-ment upon them. The moral dispositions of others are for God to judge, but we are competent judges of our own. We cannot judge the inner core of morality: no man can do that; but we are competent to judge its outer mani-festations. In matters of morality we are not judges of our fellows, but nature has given us the right to form judgments about others and she also has ordained that we should judge ourselves in accordance with judgments that others form about us. The man who turns a deaf ear to other people's opinion of him is base and reprehensible. There is nothing that happens in this world about which we ought not to form an opinion, and we show considerable subtlety in judging conduct. Those who judge our conduct with exactness are our best friends. Only friends can be quite candid and open with each other. But in judging a man a further question arises. In what terms are we to judge him? Must we pronounce him either good or evil? We must proceed from the assumption that humanity is lovable, and, particularly in regard to wickedness, we ought never to pronounce a verdict either of condemnation or of acquittal. We pronounce such a verdict whenever we judge from his conduct that a man deserves to be condemned or acquitted. But though we are entitled to form opinions about our fellows, we have no right to spy upon them. Everyone has a right to prevent others from watching and scrutinizing his actions. The spy arrogates to himself the right to watch the doings of strangers; no one ought to presume to do such a thing. If I see two people whispering to each other so as not to be heard, my inclination ought to be to get farther away so that no sound may reach my ears. Or if I am left alone in a room and I see a letter lying open on the table, it would be contemptible to try to read it; a right-thinking man would not do so; in fact, in order to avoid suspicion and distrust he will endeavour not to be left alone in a room where money is left lying about, and he will be averse from learning other people's secrets in order to avoid the risk of the suspicion that he has betrayed them; other people's secrets trouble him, for even between the most intimate of friends suspicion might arise. A man who will let his inclination or appetite drive him to deprive his friend of anything, of his fiancée, for instance, is contemptible beyond a doubt. If he can cherish a passion for my sweetheart, he can equally well cherish a passion for my purse. It is very mean to lie in wait and spy upon a friend, or on anyone else, and to elicit information about him from menials by lowering ourselves to the level of our inferiors, who will thereafter not forget to regard themselves as our equals. Whatever militates against frankness lowers the dignity of man.

Insidious, underhand conduct uses means which strike at the roots of society because they make frankness impossible ; it is far viler than violence ; for against violence we can defend ourselves, and a violent man who spurns meanness can be tamed to goodness, but the mean rogue, who has not the courage to come out into the open with his roguery, is devoid of every vestige of nobility of character. For that reason a wife who attempts to poison her husband in England is burnt at the stake, for if such conduct spread, no man would be safe from his wife.[1]

As I am not entitled to spy upon my neighbour, I am equally not entitled to point out his faults to him ; and even if he should ask me to do so he would feel hurt if I complied. He knows his faults better than I, he knows that he has them, but he likes to believe that I have not noticed them, and if I tell him of them he realizes that I have. To say, therefore, that friends ought to point out each other's faults, is not sound advice. My friend may know better than I whether my gait or deportment is proper or not, but if I will only examine myself, who can know me better than I can know myself ? To point out his faults to a friend is sheer impertinence ; and once fault-finding begins between friends their friendship will not last long. We must turn a blind eye to the faults of others, lest they conclude that they have lost our respect and we lose theirs. Only if placed in positions of authority over others should we point out to them their defects. Thus a husband is entitled to teach and correct his wife, but his corrections must be well-intentioned and kindly and must be dominated by respect, for if they be prompted only by displeasure they result in mere blame and bitterness. If we must blame, we must temper the blame with a sweetening of love, good-will, and respect. Nothing else will avail to bring about improvement.

One of our general duties towards mankind is humanity (*humanitas*). Humanity is a habit of harmony with all other men. Its practical form is sociability, which can be either

[1] The last woman burnt in England suffered in 1789, the punishment being abolished in 1790. In point of fact, burning of women was considered more ' decent ' than hanging and exposure on a gibbet.

negative or positive. It is negative if it is merely compliant and complaisant; it is positive if it takes the form of zeal to serve. This positive humanity must be distinguished from courtesy. An act of courtesy can relate only to the amenities of life and it imposes no obligation upon the recipient. If a man sends one of his servants to show me the way, it is an act of courtesy; but if he gives me a meal he has done me a service, for it entailed some sacrifice for him. The negative form of sociability is of smaller value than the positive; there is less value in compliance than in service. There are persons who become intoxicated for the sake of sociability; they are invited to drink and have not sufficient strength of character to refuse; they would be only too glad to be rid of their company, but, being in it, they are sociable. To lack the courage and strength of will to act according to the dictates of one's own mind betrays weakness of character and is unmanly. Such men have no principles of character and conduct. They find their counterpart in the self-willed. These latter have one principle : never to accommodate themselves to the opinions of others; the former will never place themselves in opposition to other people's opinions, and so must rank below the self-willed; for the latter at least have principles, while they have none. It is better, therefore, to be a little self-willed than to be too accommodating. The determination of conduct by principles is not self-will, unless the principle of determination is drawn from private inclination and not from sources of universal satisfaction. Then it is self-will, and self-will is the mark of a fool.

The man who abhors dissension and discord and is ready to accommodate himself to the sentiments of others, so long as no moral issue is involved, is conciliatory and one need fear no quarrel with him. He is more than conciliatory, he is tolerant, if in the desire to avoid dissension, he will put up with opinions which go against his grain and does not hate others for their mistakes. The man who cannot contemplate the imperfections of others without hatred is intolerant. We often meet men who are intolerant of the views of others from personal dislike; their intolerance makes them intolerable and they get themselves disliked in turn. Tolerance is therefore a universal human duty. Men have many defects, real and apparent, but we must endure them. In matters of religion we show our tolerance by contemplating without hatred religious views which we dislike and which we regard as defective or mistaken. Why should I hate a man because he holds to be true something which according to my own religion is untrue? That does not make him an object of hatred. I ought to hate no one who does not deliberately initiate wickedness. Even a man who seeks to do good through evil and error is not an object of hate. There is a type of hatred to which priests are prone, called *odium theologicum*. It arises in this way. The theologian ranks some vanity of his own among the things of God, and conceives a hatred which is rooted in pride. He thinks that because he is a minister of God he can claim to be God's plenipotentiary, sent by God as His deputy, invested with authority to rule men in His name. *Odium religiosum* is a religious ban pronounced against a man whose errors are believed to be high treason against God, and are declared to be *crimina laesae majestatis divinae*. His views are misrepresented and all manner of false constructions are put upon them in order to prove that they are *crimina laesae majestatis divinae* and to subject him to the *odium religiosum*. A man who proceeds on these lines is called a *consequentiarius*, because he ascribes to his victim ideas which he never dreamt of and attaches to him some opprobrious label to bring him into general contempt. He may, for instance, call him an atheist. His hearers open their eyes wide and say to themselves: 'What! an atheist? Now I shall discover what an atheist looks like!' So the appellation makes him intolerable and hateful to others.

There is no such thing as a *crimen laesae majestatis divinae*; no one can be guilty of such an offence; the very idea of it is absurd. The orthodox assert that their own conception of religion must necessarily be right and ought to be universal; but what is orthodoxy? If we were all to appear before the gates of heaven and the question were put to us, 'Which of you is orthodox?' the Jew, the Turk, and the Christian would shout in unison, 'I am.' Orthodoxy should use force against no one.

We call a man a dissenter if, while not differing from us in matters of practical importance, he takes a different view on some speculative points in religion. We may consider that he is wrong, but that is no reason why we should hate him, and we are lovers of peace only if we avoid hostility towards dissenters.

Syncretism is a form of sociability. It consists in agreeing with everyone for the sake of avoiding discord. It is very harmful. For he who agrees with everyone has no views at all. Let men err rather; for so long as they can distinguish one view from another, they can also be freed of their errors.

The spirit of persecution, when it is secret and works behind a man's back, discussing him and calling him an atheist, is a spirit of meanness. But it may be refined, so that it does not persecute with hatred those who are not of its opinion, but merely abhors them. The spirit of persecution for the honour of God will stick at nothing, but will pursue alike friend and benefactor, mother and father. The persecutor will consider it meritorious to burn his victim at the stake for the honour of God. But religious truth does not require force for its support; it should rely on reasoned argument. Truth can defend itself, and to use force against error is to prolong its life. Freedom of investigation is the best means to consolidate the truth.

POVERTY AND CHARITY

Acts which have in view the welfare of another and are prompted by and proportioned to his wants are acts of kindness. They may be magnanimous, if they entail the sacrifice of an advantage; they are acts of benevolence if they alleviate real needs; and if they alleviate the extreme necessities of life they are acts of charity. Men believe, or assume to believe, that they satisfy their duty to love mankind if they first provide fully for their own material wants and then pay their tribute to the universal provider by giving a little to the poor. But if men were scrupulously just there would be no poor to whom we could give alms and think that we had realized the merit of benevolence. Better than charity, better than giving of our surplus is conscientious and scrupulously fair conduct and a helping hand in need. The giving of alms flatters the giver's pride, requires no trouble and no consideration whether the recipient is worthy or unworthy. Alms degrades men. It would be better to see whether the poor man could not be helped in some other way which would not entail his being degraded by accepting alms. There are moralists who seek to soften our hearts and to commend acts of kindness done from tenderheartedness; but true generosity springs from a brave and honest mind, and to be virtuous a man must be brave and honest. Charity to one's fellows should be commende 1 rather as a debt of honour than as an exhibition of kindness and generosity. In fact it is a debt, and all our kindnesses are only trifles in repayment of our indebtedness.

SOCIAL VIRTUES

Baumgarten discusses accessibility, affability, politeness, refinement, propriety, courtesy, and ingratiating and captivating behaviour. It may be remarked generally that some of these qualities call for no large measure of moral determination and cannot, therefore, be reckoned as virtues. They demand no self-control and sacrifice, do not conduce to the happiness of another and have no bearing upon his wants, but merely upon his pleasures. They relate to the pleasure and charm of social intercourse and to nothing more. But even though they are no virtues, they are a means of developing virtue. Courtesy and politeness make men gentle and refined and so lead to the practice of goodness in the small details of life. There is many an occasion which does not call for the manifestation of virtue, but only of good social qualities, and social charm in another often pleases us to such an extent that we overlook his vices. Courtesy and modest behaviour are qualities much more frequently called for in social intercourse than honesty and generosity. We may ask here whether books are of any value which serve no purpose beyond amusement, which entertain our imagination, and which may even treat of certain passions, such as love, at a degree of intensity which passes the recognized bounds of ordinary conduct. They are. Even although they may overdo the charms and passions of which they treat, yet they refine our sentiments, by turning the object of animal inclination into an object of refined inclination. They awaken a capacity to be moved by kindly impulses, and render the indirect service of making us more civilized, through the training of inclination. The more we refine the crude elements in our nature, the more we improve our humanity and the more capable it grows of feeling the driving force of virtuous principles.

Baumgarten next examines the spirit of contradiction, the love of paradox and of eccentricity in judgment. Paradox has its uses; it should not be used to clinch a special point, but only to put a new face upon a particular view; it is the unexpected in thought which often puts the mind upon a new track. The spirit of contradiction manifests itself in a dogmatic attitude; but the man who is always in the right has no place in social conversation, the purpose of which is entertainment and the promotion of culture. Important subjects, which are apt to produce dogmatic controversy, should not be discussed in social intercourse. When they arise, one should either state one's conviction or else make light of them by some entertaining story.

HAUGHTINESS

Baumgarten calls it *superbia*. We must distinguish between haughtiness and arrogance. *Arrogantia* is the pride which pretends to an importance which it does not possess ; haughtiness feels itself superior to others and undervalues them. The proud man does not underrate his fellows, but he insists upon his own merits ; he will not bow and scrape before them ; he considers that he has a definite worth and will yield to none in that respect. Such pride is right and proper, provided it is kept within bounds ; but in common parlance we call a man proud when he advertises his worth and his pride becomes a fault by passing the limits of what is proper. Haughtiness does not consist in claiming to be worth as much and to be as important as others, but in claiming an extraordinary worth and an especial importance for oneself while under-estimating others ; it is detestable and ridiculous, for its self-estimation is subjective. If I want to be held in honour, it is useless to set about it by demanding honour and depreciating others ; that will not arouse respect, but only ridicule for my presumption. All haughty people are fools ; their sole preoccupation is their own superiority and this makes them contemptible.

Fastus, or snobbery, shows itself when a man gives himself airs and claims precedence, not on account of any intellectual or intrinsic merit, but on the ground of external appearances. The snob is vain in matters of social pre-cedence, attaches importance to things which are of little account, and on any and every occasion, no matter how trifling, he claims the limelight. He would deprive himself of food rather than of his fine clothes and his carriage and pair. He aims at titles and position, and the appearance of gentility. A man of true merit is neither haughty nor a snob ; he is humble, because he cherishes an Idea of true worth so lofty that he can never rise high enough to satisfy its demands. Therefore he is humble, in the consciousness of his own shortcoming. Snobbery is particularly rampant amongst the lower, and especially the middle, classes ; it is amongst these classes that one finds the social climbers, and snobbery is just the scramble for social position.

SCOFFING

The scoffer may be either scornful (*médisant*) or mocking (*moquant*). Scorn is malicious, mockery frivolous. The mocker seeks to make fun at the expense of other people's faults ; the slanderer is full of malice. The latter is frequently a person lacking in conviviality who dwells upon and magnifies the defects of others so that his own may appear small by comparison ; his self-love prompts him to malice. But we fear calumny less than we fear raillery. The slanderer works surreptitiously : he speaks behind our backs ; he must choose his company and we cannot overhear him ; but the mocker is no respecter of company or occasion. Raillery lowers our self-esteem more than malice, for it makes us a laughing-stock for others, strips us of our worth and holds us up to ridicule. We need not always grudge the mocker his pleasure, because often it means nothing either to us or to him and we lose nothing by it. But an habitual scoffer betrays his lack of respect for others and his inability to judge things at their true value.

DUTIES TOWARDS ANIMALS AND SPIRITS

Baumgarten speaks of duties towards beings which are beneath us and beings which are above us. But so far as animals are concerned, we have no direct duties. Animals are not self-conscious and are there merely as a means to an end. That end is man. We can ask, ' Why do animals exist ? ' But to ask, ' Why does man exist ? ' is a meaningless question. Our duties towards animals are merely indirect duties towards humanity. Animal nature has analogies to human nature, and by doing our duties to animals in respect of manifestations which correspond to manifestations of human nature, we indirectly do our duty towards humanity. Thus, if a dog has served his master long and faithfully, his service, on the analogy of human service, deserves reward, and when the dog has grown too old to serve, his master ought to keep him until he dies.   Such action helps to support us in our duties towards human beings, where they are bounden duties.   If then any acts of animals are analogous to human acts and spring from the same principles, we have duties towards the animals because thus we cultivate the corresponding duties towards human beings.   If a man shoots his dog because the animal is no longer capable of service, he does not fail in his duty to the dog, for the dog cannot judge, but his act is inhuman and damages in himself that humanity which it is his duty to show towards mankind.   If he is not to stifle his human feelings, he must practise kindness towards animals, for he who is cruel to animals becomes hard also in his dealings with men.   We can judge the heart of a man by his treatment of animals.   Hogarth [1] depicts this in his engravings.   He shows how cruelty grows and develops.   He shows the child's cruelty to animals, pinching the tail of a dog or a cat ; he then depicts the grown man in his cart running over a child ; and lastly, the culmination of cruelty in murder.   He thus brings home to us in a terrible fashion the rewards of cruelty, and this should be an impressive lesson to children.   The more we come in contact with animals and observe their behaviour, the more we love them, for we see how great is their care for their young.   It is then difficult for us to be cruel in thought even to a wolf.   Leibnitz used a tiny worm for purposes of observation, and then carefully replaced it with its leaf on the tree so that it should not come to harm through any act of his.   He would have been sorry—a natural feeling for a humane man—to destroy such a creature for no reason.   Tender feelings towards dumb animals develop humane feelings towards mankind.   In England butchers and doctors do not sit on a jury because they are accustomed to the sight of death and hardened.   Vivisectionists, who use living animals for their experiments, certainly act cruelly, although their aim is praiseworthy, and they can justify their cruelty, since animals must be regarded as man's instruments ; but any such cruelty for sport cannot be

[1] Hogarth's four engravings, ' The Stages of Cruelty ', 1751.

justified. A master who turns out his ass or his dog because the animal can no longer earn its keep manifests a small mind. The Greeks' ideas in this respect were high-minded, as can be seen from the fable of the ass and the bell of ingratitude.[1] Our duties towards animals, then, are indirect duties towards mankind.

Our duties towards immaterial beings are purely nega-tive. Any course of conduct which involves dealings with spirits is wrong. Conduct of this kind makes men vision-aries and fanatics, renders them superstitious, and is not in keeping with the dignity of mankind ; for human dignity cannot subsist without a healthy use of reason, which is impossible for those who have commerce with spirits. Spirits may exist or they may not ; all that is said of them may be true ; but we know them not and can have no intercourse with them. This applies to good and to evil spirits alike. Our Ideas of good and evil are co-ordinate, and as we refer all evil to hell so we refer all good to heaven. If we personify the perfection of evil, we have the Idea of the devil. If we believe that evil spirits can have an influence upon us, can appear and haunt us at night, we become a prey to phantoms and incapable of using our powers in a reasonable way. Our duties towards such beings must, therefore, be negative.

DUTIES TOWARDS INANIMATE OBJECTS

Baumgarten speaks of duties towards inanimate objects. These duties are also indirectly duties towards mankind. Destructiveness is immoral ; we ought not to destroy things which can still be put to some use. No man ought to mar the beauty of nature ; for what he has no use for may still be of use to some one else. He need, of course, pay no heed to the thing itself, but he ought to consider his neighbour. Thus we see that all duties towards animals, towards immaterial beings and towards inanimate objects are aimed indirectly at our duties towards man-kind.

[1] Philipp Camerarius *Operae horarum subcisivarum centuria prima*, 1644, cap. XXI.

DUTIES TOWARDS PARTICULAR CLASSES OF HUMAN BEINGS

Baumgarten examines the particular duties we have towards different classes of human beings according to age, sex and rank, but all such duties are merely derivative from the general duties which we have already discussed. Amongst the various classes which fall to be considered there is one whose intrinsic worth would appear to differentiate it from the rest. It consists of men of learning. The differences between other classes rest on externals, but scholarship seems to make an intrinsic difference. Other professions and occupations concern themselves with physical things, which are merely means to human life, but the scholar's main preoccupation is the acquisition of knowledge. This would seem to constitute an intrinsic difference, a real difference of value. The learned are seemingly the only class to observe the beauty which God has placed in the world and to use the world for the purpose for which God made it. For why should God have made nature and its works beautiful unless it was for our contemplation? And, as none but men of learning completely fulfil the purpose of creation they might, it seems, claim for themselves intrinsic worth not possessed by others. They acquire knowledge, and God created the world for knowledge; they alone develop the gifts and talents of mankind. Can they not, therefore, claim superiority over their fellows? Have they not a higher intrinsic worth? But listen to Rousseau; he turns the argument round and says: 'Man was not made for erudition, and scholars by their learning pervert the end of humanity.' What, then, are we to say? Does the scholar by studying the world's beauty and by cultivating his talents fulfil the purpose of creation, and is the world his and his alone? No individual scholar sets himself specifically to contemplate nature's beauty, to cultivate nature's gifts and to realize the complete perfection of the world; like men in other occupations he seeks honour, the honour which accrues to him from communicating his knowledge to his fellows; he cannot, therefore, as an individual, claim to be superior to other citizens; scholars as a class, and taken as a whole, promote the end of humanity, but no single member of the class can presume so far, and, after all, an artisan adds his quota to the world's welfare just as much as the scholar. Honour, the universal source of human activities, thus creates a harmony in the purposes of the world. But, if that is so, is Rousseau right in denying that man was intended for learning? Ought every one of us to aim at being a scholar? Man is certainly not intended for learning only, and all of us cannot be scholars. Life is too short for that, and just as some are soldiers and some sailors, it is only some of us who ought to devote and dedicate ourselves to scholarship. Life is even too short for any one of us to make full use of the knowledge he acquires. Had God wished us to penetrate deep into the recesses of learning he would have given us longer life. Newton must die at the moment when he could use his knowledge to the full. His successor must begin again at the A, B, C, and pass from stage to stage until he too at length reaches the heights of learning. But just when he would turn his knowledge to proper account, he too grows feeble and dies. Individually, therefore, we are not predestined to learning, but learning as a whole advances the end of humanity. Scholars as a class are a means to that end and contribute their quota towards human worth, but they do not thereby themselves acquire superior worth. Why should a scholar be held of greater account than any citizen who is industrious, provides for his family, and leads a clean and honest life? The universality of the scholar's business carries with it his rank and destiny. Rousseau is, therefore, right up to a point, but when he goes on to talk of the damage that science does, he is badly at fault. No true scholar could speak so proudly; the speech of true reason is humble. All men are equal, and only he who has superior morality has superior intrinsic worth. The sciences are principles for the betterment of morality. In order to apprehend the concepts of morality, discernment and the elucidation of concepts are necessary. Wide learning ennobles man, and the love of study stifles many a base inclination within us.

Hume says that no man can be a scholar unless he be at least an honest man. On the other hand, morality serves the development of science. A man who is righteous and respects the rights of other people and of his own person, greatly promotes his own capacity for understanding. An upright man writes his faults in large letters and does not conceal from himself the weak points of his character. Morality of character thus has a great influence upon science. The man who is deficient in this respect hawks the products of his mind like the merchant who hawks his wares by concealing the weak spots and deceiving the public. Such are the duties to be observed in relation to learning.

DUTIES OF THE VIRTUOUS AND THE VICIOUS

Virtue is an Idea. No man can be truly virtuous. A virtuous man, like a wise man, is a practical impossibility. We all strive to attain as near as possible to virtue, as we do to wisdom, but none of us can reach the acme either of the one or of the other. Between the two extremes of virtue and vice we can conceive a middle state, the absence of both. Virtue and vice are positive in their nature. Virtue implies ability and readiness to overcome our inclination to evil on moral principles. It implies that in the contest with immoral inclinations, our moral dispositions show themselves possessed of such strength that they always come out triumphant. Thus holy beings are not virtuous, for the reason that they have no evil inclinations to overcome; their will is of itself sufficient for compliance with the law. The man who is not virtuous is not necessarily vicious: he merely lacks virtue. Vice is positive; lack of virtue is negative. To have no respect for the moral law constitutes lack of virtue, but vice means an active contempt for the law. The man who lacks virtue simply fails to comply with the moral law, but the vicious man acts in opposition to it. The former is positive, the latter negative. Vice therefore has a content of its own, and a large one.

A kind heart does not necessarily imply a virtuous character. Virtue is good conduct not from instinct but on
principle, while a kind heart is in instinctive harmony
with the moral law. We may be born with a kind heart,
but virtue is not so easy to achieve. We can only become
virtuous by practice ; we must suppress our evil inclinations by bringing moral principles to bear upon them so
that our conduct comes into line with the moral law.
That being so, can a vicious man become virtuous ? There
exists a temperamental wickedness which is incorrigible
and cannot be altered, but a bad character can always be
converted into a good one. Since character works by
principle, the evils in character can be gradually eradicated
by good principles, until no natural disposition to wickedness has control over it. It is said that Socrates had by
nature a wicked heart, but overcame that inborn wickedness by the soundness of his principles. We sometimes
meet men whose faces show them to be incorrigible rogues,
destined, almost, for the gallows ; for such men it is very
difficult to become virtuous. On the other hand, an honest
and upright man cannot become vicious ; he may now and
again give way to vice, but he will return to the path of
virtue because sound principles are deeply ingrained in
him. We must distinguish between betterment and conversion. We can become better merely by altering our
mode of life ; but we become converted only by acquiring
firm principles and a sound basis for living only in virtue.
Fear of death frequently works an improvement in us, but
we are at a loss to say whether we are improved or converted. Would the improvement have taken place if
death were not in sight and we had hopes of longer life ?
We have been converted if, no matter how long we may
live, we firmly determine to live in virtue. Penitence is
an ill-conceived term ; the word implies penance and
chastisement ; it implies self-punishment for sins ; recognizing that we have deserved punishment we punish ourselves, hoping that then God will not punish us. So we
become penitents. But such remorse is vain and useless.
The only remorse which is of use is that inner remorse over
our sins which results in a firm determination to live a
better life : that is true repentance.

There are two by-paths of vice : the path of baseness or brutality, and that of devilish malice. The first of these leads by way of violation of the duties we owe to our person to a level below that of the beasts ; the second is the way of the man who makes it his business to turn his mind to evil, until no good inclination survives in his soul. While he retains a single good disposition, a single wish to be good, he remains human, but if he is wholly given over to wickedness, he becomes a devil. Vice is slavery to the power of inclination ; the more virtuous a man, the more free he is. The hardened sinner is the man with no desire for betterment. The fellowship of virtue is the kingdom of light ; the fellowship of vice is the kingdom of darkness. Be a man ever so virtuous, there are in him promptings of evil, and he must constantly contend with these. Every man must guard against moral self-conceit, against believing himself morally good and having a favourable opinion of himself. This feeling of moral self-sufficiency is self-deception ; it is an incurable hallucination. It arises from working over and over the moral law until it has been made to fit our inclinations and convenience. Virtue is the moral perfection of man. It combines power, strength and force, and is the conquest of inclination. Inclination in itself is unregulated ; the moral state is the subjugation of inclination. Angels in heaven can be holy ; man can at most be virtuous. Because the basis of virtue is principle and not instinct, to practise virtue is to act on principles, providing them with driving force so that they become dominant, and not allowing anything to divert us from them. To be virtuous we must have character. Strength of character is strength of virtue ; indeed, it is virtue itself. In practising virtue we cannot but meet with obstacles ; these must be overcome by religion and by rules of prudence. To this end we must have a contented mind and a soul at peace and free of reproach, true honour, respect for oneself and for others ; we must be steadfast in the face of evil of which we are guiltless and meet it with calm unconcern. These requisites are not sources of virtue, but aids to it ; they are the duties of the virtuous.

As for the vicious, it seems vain to speak of duties in

connexion with them.   None the less, every vicious man has
a concept of virtue in himself, he has the understanding to
recognize what is evil, and is not dead to moral feeling.
No one is such an unmitigated blackguard that he might
not at least wish to be good.   It is upon the basis of this
moral feeling that we can build a system of virtue.   But
the moral feeling is not the primary factor in the judgment of virtue ; the primary factor is the pure concept of
morality which must be linked up with the moral feeling.
If a man's concept of morality is pure, he can build up
virtue upon it ; he can stir up his moral feeling and take
the first steps towards morality.   Truly there is a wide
field for his first negative efforts, for he must first purge
himself of his guilt by complete abstinence from everything that discourages his inclination to goodness.   The
way to achieve this is to keep himself occupied with one
thing or another ; and though the positive achievement
of morality is difficult, this negative task is well within
his reach.

DUTIES ARISING FROM DIFFERENCES OF AGE

Baumgarten's treatment of this subject is somewhat
muddled.   He should have divided these duties into three
classes ; those arising from difference of sex, from difference of condition, from difference of age.   Difference of sex
is more far-reaching than is usually believed.   Men act
from motives which are very different from those which
actuate women, but on this subject we must refer to the
text-books of anthropology, from which we can infer the
duties that arise.   When we come to consider difference
of age, we are reminded of the fact that we have duties
towards others not as human beings merely, but as fellow-
citizens.   This raises the question of the duties of citizen-
ship.   But the field of ethics is inexhaustible.   Baumgarten discusses duties towards the sick and the healthy,
but if we took this line, we might as well draw a distinction between duties towards the handsome and the ugly,
towards the tall and the short.   These are not particular

duties, but merely particular situations in which we have
to observe our general duties to mankind. Childhood,
youth and manhood are the three classes into which we
must divide mankind in point of age. The child cannot
maintain itself ; the youth can maintain himself and can
propagate his species, but cannot maintain his children ;
the man can maintain himself, can propagate his species
and can maintain his progeny. There is a difference in
this respect between the savage and the civilized man.
The savage reaches manhood as soon as he is capable of
propagating his species, but not so civilized man ; civilized
man must not only be able to propagate his species, but
to maintain himself and his children. But because in this
respect the savage state is more in keeping with nature,
whereas civilization conflicts with nature, Rousseau maintains that civilization does not comply with nature's end.
In fact, it does. The age of early youth is intended by
nature for the propagation of the human race. If our
bodies did not become mature until we reached our thirtieth
year, this would conform to the age of our maturity as
citizens, but in that case uncivilized man would not multiply
at the requisite rate. There are many causes which reduce
the rate at which uncivilized man multiplies, and therefore
an early maturity is essential ; in civilization these causes
cease to operate and their place is taken by the raising
of the age at which we can make use of our sexual instinct.
The period in between, however, gives rise to a multiplicity of vices. How then is civilized man to be trained
both for nature and for civil society ? For the education
of man in respect of his natural and of his civil condition
are the two ends of nature. The rule of education is the
chief end, the forming of the mind for the civil state. Two
aspects must here be distinguished, the development of
the natural disposition, and the imparting of practical
capacity. The former is the cultivation of the mind, the
other is teaching or instruction. In terms of this difference we might distinguish a ' tutor ' (*gouverneur*) from a
' teacher '.

The cultivation of the mind should be merely negative ;
its aim should be simply the restraint of whatever is
unnatural. Practical instruction, however, can be both

negative and positive. In its negative aspect it should secure that no faults creep in; on the positive side it should impart knowledge. The negative aspect both of instruction and of culture is discipline; the positive aspect of instruction is doctrine. Discipline must precede doctrine. Discipline cultivates heart and temperament, while character is rather cultivated by doctrine. Discipline is correction. But correction does not teach the child anything new; it merely restricts its unlimited freedom. Man must be disciplined, because he is by nature raw and wild. He can be brought to proper behaviour only by training. Animal nature develops of its own accord; human nature must be trained. If we allow nature unfettered sway, the result is savagery. Discipline implies compulsion; but as compulsion is opposed to freedom and freedom constitutes man's worth, the compulsion of discipline must be so applied to the young that their freedom is maintained. Compulsion there must be, but not slavish compulsion. All education must be free, so far as the pupil does not interfere with the freedom of others. The main ground of discipline on which freedom depends is that the child should recognize its position as a child and that its duties should all be derived from the consciousness of its childhood, age and limited capacities. The child ought not to exercise greater powers than are in keeping with its years. It is a child and weak; it must not, therefore, attain its ends by ordering and commanding, but by beseeching. If it tries to obtain something by force and one gives in in order to quieten it, it will repeat the procedure, and more strongly; it will forget its weakness as a child. A child ought not, therefore, to be brought up to be domineering; it must not get its way by wilfulness, but only through the courtesy of others, and it will win their courtesy by showing itself courteous. If it obtains nothing by force, it will form the habit of compliance and of asking for what it wants. A child accustomed to command in the home grows up dictatorial, meets in life with all kinds of resistance to which it is unaccustomed, and finds itself unfitted for society. The trees in the forest discipline each other; they cannot obtain air for growth in the spaces between them, but only up above, and so they grow tall and straight ; but a tree in the open is not restricted and so grows crooked, and it is then too late to train it. So it is with man. Trained early, he grows up straight along with his fellows ; but if he is never pruned, he becomes a crooked tree. The first discipline consists in obedience, and there are many uses to which it can be put. It is applicable to the body and to the temperament. Thus if the child is passionate, it must be severely opposed ; if it be lazy, it ought not to meet with compliance. It applies to the disposition, which always requires opposition, especially where there are indications of tendencies to malice, destructiveness and joy in inflicting or witnessing pain. It applies to character, upon which nothing has such an injurious effect as any tendency to lying and deceit. Lying and falseness are defects of character which characterize the coward, and any sign of them ought to be severely suppressed by the educator. Naughtiness is in a way a sign of strength and only requires discipline ; but any secret, deceitful viciousness contains no seed of good.

Having dealt with discipline and correction we now pass to the subject of instruction or doctrine. Man is taught in three ways : by nature and experience, by exposition, and by argument and disputation. The basis of all teaching is experience. A child should not be taught more than it can confirm for itself by experience and observation. It must be taught the habit of observing, for through observation those concepts develop which are derived from experience. Teaching by exposition presupposes concepts and judgment, and argument must be adapted to the age of the child. In the early stages instruction ought to be empirical and should not rely on a priori grounds ; it must be based on results in experience. If a child tells a lie, for example, it should be treated as unworthy to take part in conversation. The mode of upbringing depends to a very large extent on the age of the child and must be varied accordingly.

There are three stages of education from the standpoint of age, viz. the education for childhood, youth, and manhood respectively. In each case the training must precede the stage in question. In training the child for youth, the child must be given reasons ; in the training of the infant for childhood this cannot be done. Young children ought merely to have things shown to them as they are, or they get puzzled and ask question after question. But as we approach the age of youth reason appears. At what age ought the education for youth to begin ? Roughly, at the age of ten years, when by nature the child enters the stage of youth and begins to reflect. A child can only be told that such and such a thing is improper and must take it for granted ; it can have no idea of propriety, but the youth already has. The youth ought to have an inkling of social duties and so obtain a conception of propriety and of love of mankind. He is capable of having principles ; his religious and moral ideas can be cultivated, and he is able to attend to his own refinement. A child must be trained by obedience, but a youth can be disciplined by appeal to his sense of honour. At the third stage the youth must be fitted for entry into manhood, when at last he will be able not only to maintain himself, but also to propagate children and maintain them. He is at the brink of manhood when he reaches the age of sixteen years. He ought then no longer to require training and discipline ; he ought to become gradually more and more conscious of his destiny and learn to know the world. As he enters upon manhood he must be taught his real duties, the dignity of humanity in his own person and respect for humanity in others. His character must be developed by doctrine.

The greatest care should be exercised that the passions, of which the sexual passion is the strongest, are not abused. Rousseau asserts that it is a father's duty to give his son at this age a complete conception of sex and make no secret of it, clearing his mind on the subject and explaining the purpose of the desire and the harm that comes from the abuse of it. He must represent to him on moral grounds the heinousness of the abuse of sex, and show him the degradation of the worth of humanity in his own person which it entails. This is the last and most delicate point in education. It will be a long time before schools recognize this, and in the meantime vice will continue to be prevalent.

THE ULTIMATE DESTINY OF THE HUMAN RACE

The ultimate destiny of the human race is the greatest moral perfection, provided that it is achieved through human freedom, whereby alone man is capable of the greatest happiness. God might have made men perfect and given to each his portion of happiness. But happiness would not then have been derived from the inner principle of the world, for the inner principle of the world is freedom. The end, therefore, for which man is destined is to achieve his fullest perfection through his own freedom. God's will is not merely that we should be happy, but that we should make ourselves happy, and this is the true morality. The universal end of mankind is the highest moral perfection. If we all so ordered our conduct that it should be in harmony with the universal end of mankind, the highest perfection would be attained. We must each of us, therefore, endeavour to guide our conduct to this end ; each of us must make such a contribution of his own that if all contributed similarly the result would be perfection. How far has the human race progressed on the road to perfection ? If we look at the most enlightened portion of the world, we see the various States armed to the teeth, sharpening their weapons in time of peace the one against the other. The consequences of this are such that they block our approach to the universal end of perfection. The Abbot of St. Pierre has proposed that a senate of the nations should be formed. If this proposal were carried out it would be a great step forward, for the time now occupied by each nation in providing for its own security could then be employed for the advancement of mankind. But the Idea of right has less authority with princes than the Idea of independence and individual sovereignty, or the lust for despotic power, and therefore nothing is to be hoped for from this direction. How then is perfection to be sought ? Wherein lies our hope ? In education, and in nothing else. Education must be adapted to all the ends of nature, both civil and domestic. Our present education, both in the home and at school, is still very faulty, in respect of discipline, doctrine and the cultivation of talent as much as in respect of the building of character in accordance with moral principles. We care more for skill than for the disposition to use it well. How then can it be hoped that persons improperly educated should rule a State to better advantage ? Let education be conceived on right lines, let natural gifts be developed as they should, let character be formed on moral principles, and in time the effects of this will reach even to the seat of government, when princes themselves are educated by teachers fitted for the task. But so far no prince has contributed one iota to the perfection of mankind, to inner happiness, to the worth of humanity ; all of them look ever and only to the prosperity of their own countries, making that their chief concern. A proper education would teach them so to frame their minds that conciliation would be promoted. Once planted, the seed would grow ; once propagated, conciliation would maintain itself by public opinion. But the ruler cannot do it alone ; men of all ranks in the State would have to be similarly trained ; then would the State be built on a firm foundation. Can we hope for this ? The Basedow institutions give us hope, warm even though small. The realization of the full destiny, the highest possible perfection of human nature—this is the kingdom of God on earth. Justice and equity, the authority, not of governments, but of conscience within us, will then rule the world. This is the destined final end, the highest moral perfection to which the human race can attain ; but the hope of it is still distant ; it will be many centuries before it can be realized.